The Chrysanthemum and the Rose

By Russell Watson

Contents

Much of this book was originally written around 2002 – 2005. Some parts have been updated while other sections have been more or less left intact. They present a snapshot of the situation at that time and as such I felt they needed no further elaboration. All images used are my own or are in the public domain as far as I have been able to ascertain.

Foreword

Both Buddhists and Hindus share a core belief in reincarnation. The soul undergoes many cycles of birth and death in order to perfect itself on its journey toward a higher level of existence. The earliest incarnation of this book was "Britain and Japan – Comparison and Contrast"; my graduation thesis written in early 1999 to complete my Bachelor of Arts Degree in Asian Studies. It has been through numerous rewrites and rebirths since that time.

Dr. Alexander Al. Jamie of the Distance Learning Center, Tokyo suggested I expand my original thesis into a full blown book. Plenty of thesis papers end up that way he cheerfully pointed out to me as I submitted my work and hoped for the best.

The sections on Literature, Marriage, National Character and Stereotypes are largely unchanged aside from minor additions and being edited down from the rather ponderous style I tended towards during those days.   The other chapters have been periodically updated and reworked over the past fifteen years until I was finally satisfied that it was ready for publication. I have already authored five other works prior to this, but "The Chrysanthemum and the Rose" as it finally came to be known is the book that launched me on my literary journey.

I sincerely hope my readers exact even a fraction of the pleasure I got from writing it.

This book is dedicated to the irrepressibly upbeat and erudite Professor Alexander Al-Jamie for his help and encouragement.

Also by the author on Amazon

- The Twain Shall Meet – An Outline History of Foreign Interaction with Japan
- Meeting the Twain – An Outline History of Japanese Interaction with the West
- Another Rat on the Wheel
- Sting in the Tale – Short Stories - with Craig Muirhead
- The Day the Earth Moved
- Duck Before it Hits the Fan

INTRODUCTION

Take a look at even an average map of the world and you'll see two medium-sized islands on opposite edges of the Eurasian continent. Both have approximately the same land mass. One is within swimming distance of France. The other is separated from the Korean Peninsula by a somewhat wider expanse of sea. These are two small island nations that have both greatly impacted on the history of the world. This is more than their relatively modest land masses or populations might have otherwise suggested.

From Britain came the English language. It is unquestionably the medium that most of the world's business people use or attempt to use when engaged in commerce and international communication. Estimates around the turn of the 21st century reckoned that approximately 86% of the Internet consisted of English language websites and home pages.

Japan went from being crushed at the end of the Second World War, to hosting the Olympics 19 years later. Thereafter it became an international economic superpower, the envy of the world. It was one that momentarily challenged the United States for economic domination at the turn of the 1980s.

Britain and Japan, the former the country of my birth and the latter my home for half of my life, have much in common. This book also explores the differences and suggests some possible reasons. It also highlights and in many cases refutes the myths and stereotypes that surround both countries. Some are the result of clinging to impressions that were formed by 19th century observers. Their understanding of what they were seeing was rudimentary at best, or distorted by their own preconceptions and prejudices.

Many aspects of Japanese and British history are similar. This is especially true in the manner that both absorbed successive waves of ideas and influences from the mainland. They then adapted these to suit their respective cultures. This is erroneously regarded by some as being unique to Japan.

One of the main topics focuses on the family, particularly on how it has fared in both Japan and Britain as a result of the changes of the past century. That Britain has one of the highest divorce rates in Europe is common knowledge. Perhaps less well known is that between 1970 and 2010, the percentage of failed marriages in Japan rose from well under one in ten to 35%. This is still lower than the rate found in many Western countries.

The Japanese are neither unique nor virtually impossible to comprehend.

Taking ideas from other cultures and refining them to suit native tastes and conditions is not unique to Japan. A similar process took place throughout history in most cultures.

Both in the case of the Romans and the Chinese, their ways were respected even by those who invaded and conquered them. Rome was defeated by Germanic invaders, but these self-same people adopted their customs. Similarly, in the Middle Ages British Crusaders in the "Holy Land" returned home with innovations ranging from shampoo to advances in astronomy. The adoption, then adaptation of an idea, religion, or technological innovation is accompanied by changes not only to that which is adopted, but in those who adopt it.

Psychologists often classify societies as being either collectivist or individualist. The United States is individualist, as is Europe and countries such as Australia and New Zealand where most of the inhabitants are descended from European colonists. African and Asian cultures are generally collectivist in nature. [1]

Broadly speaking, in a collectivist culture, the needs of the group, being the extended family, company, or the wider community take priority over the wishes and wants of the individual. "Star Trek's" Mr. Spock and his famous line "The needs of the many outweigh the needs of the one." In some collectivist societies, the whole concept of what makes an individual can be quite different. For example, when asked to describe people in his community, an Indian man made such statements as "She gets on well with everyone." or "He is a good son." Simply to say such things as "She is outgoing," or "He has a strong sense of duty," didn't occur to him, for he could not imagine that person without directly taking account of those around him or her. While the meaning is the same, it suggests a markedly different reality construct.

In an individualist culture, to varying degrees, the opposite is true. The individual is (in theory at least) equally as important as the group or groups he or she is belongs to and has a stronger sense of self. The United States is arguably as individualistic as a society can be and still remain cohesive. The widespread use of lawsuits to settle even the most trifling of issues is one result of a culture where the individual will always stand up for what he or she regards as "rights." The emergence in the early 1990s of militias and survivalist groups who often opposed what in their estimation was government oppression was another. They were hostile to any level of central government and hint at what could conceivably happen if society's members became too self-centred to live together. "Like trying to herd cats" is how one American militia leader described instilling order among his members. Since the election of President Obama, the "Tea Party" movement on the libertarian far right is another example of this rejection of central authority and government control.

Japan was right at the other end of the scale. Arguably about as collectivist as a culture can be and still retain at least a semblance of being a democracy in the Western sense of the word.

One version of an individualistic scale

USA.............................Britain/Europe...Japan
(High-level)   (Mid to high level)   (Low-level)

In Japan, however, some might suggest that the whole notion of individualist versus collectivist cultures has largely become irrelevant in recent years given how Westernized the Japanese lifestyle has been for several decades now. By the 1970s, British diplomats had already concluded that most city-dwelling Japanese were leading essentially Western lifestyles.

Individualistic cultures are also classified as having a low-context communication style. This means that communication is precise, direct and specific. Unlike in high-context communication, reading between the lines is not necessary in low-context communication. This explicit communication is used to reduce the chance of misunderstanding between cultures. The ability to articulate thoughts and opinions as well as to express them eloquently is encouraged. This is persuasive speaking. Low-context communication focuses on content not context. [4]

Some might argue that Britain could be set at a mid-level but once again this is largely academic. Sometimes Britain can be seen to lean towards one side of the scale or the other. Some is clearly down to geographical similarities between Britain and Japan. Both countries and especially Japan are far more crowded than the USA. Early American settlers could simply move on, claiming huge tracts of land for themselves. This lack of space and finite resources, coupled with the sense of being isolated is a feature of the "island culture" common to both Japan and Britain. To some extent perhaps this might also apply to countries such as Finland and New Zealand. This was true of the first people to arrive in Japan and until a later date, in Britain as well, but by the Middle-Ages, many city dwellers were living in cramped conditions, with little personal space.

Nearly half of Britain is farmland and eighty percent of the population is crammed into about twelve percent of the total land area.

Britain is separated from the rest of Europe by the English Channel and the North Sea. Japan is also cut off by the sea from the rest of Asia. This is significant. Both island countries sustain an ambivalent relationship with the mainland from whence the bulk of their culture originated. Each has used this common geographical factor to quite literally keep a distance from its neighbours. Japanese people seldom describe themselves as "Asian." Likewise, more than four decades after becoming a member country of the EU, relatively few Britons regard themselves as "European." Mainland Asians and Europeans alike appear to have no trouble with their dual identities.

I've tried to remain impartial. Comparison is not criticism after all. On occasion, it is impossible to remain merely a passive observer. Having lived in Japan for a quarter century in total, I inevitably came to some conclusions of my own about the society and customs of my host country. I see some things that work better than in Britain (or for that matter anywhere else as far as I can tell.) This is obvious.

One simple example: the Japanese remove their footwear in the hallway of their homes, called the "genkan." This is generally lower than the floor of the house or apartment and clearly marked out. In the West, most people walk into the house, shoes on, after giving them a desultory wipe on the mat. Just by leaving them by the door, we could eliminate a lot of the drudge of keeping our floors clean. Why such simple logic never occurred to people in the West is one of life's oddities. It may originate from how the Japanese in common with other Asian cultures maintain a stronger sense of "inside" and "outside." This is reflected in the raised floor.

In the West, in earlier ages, chickens and other farm animals ran in and out of the kitchen, whose floor was nothing more than bare earth. There was no clear distinction between inner and outer life and no need to remove shoes or keep the floor especially clean. On the other hand, why double-glazing has never caught on in Japan is similarly a mystery to this writer.

This only goes to show how different cultures have much they can learn from a frank exchange of ideas. A society that closes itself off from the outside world will, over time, begin to stagnate and decay. This happened to Japan during the Edo period (1603-1868). The "Sakoku" edicts issued during the 1630s were policies that effectively closed the country to the outside world while maintaining limited trade. Some of Japan's rigidity and social conformity can be traced back to this time.

There were voices raised in Britain in the early 1970s in support of a kind of economic "Sakoku" from Europe. People with a vision of Britain as a member of the European community won the day. Many on the left at the time saw the EU as a "capitalist's club," while some on the right still longed for what was even by then an anachronistic "Britain ruled the waves" kind of Kipling-inspired wet dream.

This same attitude resurfaced early in the new century and increasingly so during the second decade. This time it regards the Euro and the possibility of Britain joining Europe's single currency. The increasingly dictatorial attitude of the EU and the steady erosion of sovereignty are driving ever increasing numbers of people both in the UK and other European nations to question the wisdom of remaining a member of this bureaucratic monstrosity.

History demonstrates that neither Britain nor Japan was unique in showing isolationist tendencies. The United States chose to remain outside the League of Nations upon its foundation just after the Great War ended. America stayed out of the Second World War until the Japanese bombed Pearl Harbor in 1941. Korea was for many years known as "The Hermit Kingdom" until Japanese and American pressure prized it open in the 1870s.

Another similarity between the situation in Japan and Britain was in the pressing need to acquire sufficient food for its peoples. This was one factor behind both British "soft colonization" in various parts of the world and Japan forcing Korea to begin trade. Both countries built up powerful navies. According to W. Scott Morton in "Japan, its History and Culture," this was "Doubtless from reservoirs of skill gained in fishing and trading. Finally, both (countries) in modern times have had to make strenuous efforts in manufacture and export trade in order to feed their island populations." [2]

Another attempt at comparison of two cultures and in particular the character of the people is through the medium of literature. It demonstrates similarities between the Japanese and British, although arguably quite a few of these are universal. This only reinforces the simple notion that people are much the same wherever we go.

The popular 1960s television show "Star Trek" was widely interpreted as being a parable of the world geopolitical situation at the time. The United States and its European allies were "The Federation", The Soviet Union was the evil

Klingon Empire and the coldly logical Vulcans were, presumably, the Japanese. It's this "Mr. Spock" image that many people associate with Asians and Japanese in particular. Interestingly, in the late 1980s "Star Trek- the Next Generation," the Vulcans were less prominent and the ruthless, capitalistic Ferengi were among new opponents for the Federation to face off against. There was another nemesis, this being the robotic Borg and their society which resembled a colony of ants. Perhaps once again, each in their way represented the fear that some people in the West experienced as Japan's economic might threatened to overwhelm them.

One misconception is the image that many people in the West have of the robotic, seemingly almost emotionless worker bee Japanese. In the same vein, the old stereotype of the "stiff upper lip" Englishman is equally false. Japanese people can and do show their feelings, although sometimes less directly than Westerners. The British too and it is surprising how these false impressions endure.

The section on the Japanese family, in particular the relationship between husband and wife and mother and son gives both my own feelings and other commentators' theories. Many wonder why many Japanese men and in particular the laughably dubbed "elite salarymen" are almost pathetically incapable when at home trying to relate to their own wives and children. However, they demonstrate such obvious business acumen and deal adroitly with their clients and issues of global significance when outside.

On the other hand, the Japanese might retort that the West has nothing to brag about. They would conclude that communication alone does not ensure a successful marriage. Divorce in the United States hovers around the 50% mark, while in Britain, it had risen to about 47% by 2009. In both Japan and the West, family life has suffered for a number of reasons. Even experts in Japan assert that "The Japanese family is basically dysfunctional," as reported recently in a Daily Yomiuri newspaper article.

I have drawn on both anecdotal evidence, as well as reports from the media to express my own impressions and of how the Japanese themselves are aware of the myriad problems they face. They are far from the self-satisfied and contented people many had once assumed them to be, very far from it. During the mid 1990s and for some while afterwards, they seemed preoccupied with questioning almost every aspect of their culture, society and lives.

This is partly due to the lingering recession that was threatening for a while to slide into depression. To some extent, it is also the realization that the once so successful "Japanese model" is badly in need of reinvention. Economically and certainly from a geopolitical viewpoint, the world underwent considerable change in the 1990s. No longer can social systems that ably served Japan before be relied upon to do so in future. Japan faced such a challenge before, rising out of the rubble of the Second World War. It seems only logical to assume it will be able to do so successfully again, although what effect this will have on the makeup of society as a whole is harder to imagine. By early 2002 Japan had no choice but to accept levels of unemployment over 5%. This was something that might have caused a national outcry a decade or so previously.

Britain went through the kind of changes in the 1980s that Japan is now contemplating. Just shedding the surplus workers alone would result in over 10% unemployment, something that Britain once suffered. Britain has already changed remarkably since the end of Conservative rule, Scotland and Wales now have their own assemblies for the first time in living memory and Northern Ireland seems to be slowly, painfully inching its way in the direction of a real and lasting peace.

While the "Irish question" is just conceivably on its way to a solution, there seems no end in sight for the stand-off between Japan and Russia over how to resolve the problem of the four "Northern Isles" that both countries claim. Nor do the two Koreas seem likely to end their mutual hostility and suspicion.

SOURCES

(1)   Collectivist/individualistic society see "Basic Psychology" by Henry Gleitman pages 555-58 (Pub. Norton)

(2)   W. Scott Morton "Japan- Its History and Culture." (Pub. McGraw-Hill)

(3)   Daily Yomuri Newspaper articles
        Throughout this book, stories from which I have quoted were chiefly collected between July 1998 and August 2002

(4)   Drawn from J. Dan Rothwell's "In the Company of Others, an Introduction to Communication" Pub Oxford University Press   pp. 65 - 84

HISTORY

About 12,000 years ago, as the Ice Age was beginning to melt away, people migrated to Britain from the mainland on land bridges that eventually disappeared as the seas rose. One claim was made that primitive man arrived in Japan as early as 500,000 years ago, also by making use of natural bridges that later vanished. Investigators revealed that much of the archaeological evidence appears to have been planted by a Japanese university professor, thus casting serious doubt on his credibility. It's safe to say that humans first reached Japan somewhere between twenty and thirty thousand years ago. On both islands, the newcomers found thickly wooded lands, plentiful in rainfall, which were easily able to support their simple hunter-gatherer lifestyles.

Although similar in size, Britain and Japan differ geographically on a number of fronts. Firstly, nearly 85% of Japan is mountainous, whereas much of England is fairly flat with the only mountains of any significance in the Highlands of Scotland and in Wales. Japan also has earthquakes, sometimes unleashing tremendous destructive power. Britain is on the northern edge of the earthquake zone in Europe. Perhaps every dozen years or so, a sizable tremor occurs, but there are rarely more than minor quakes that are hardly noticed outside of a meteorologist's station. Apart from coal, Japan is resource poor, whereas Britain had large deposits of a variety of raw materials. Japan also has thousands of hot springs bubbling up all across the nation; Britain has only a handful, several are in the aptly named town of Bath. The southernmost parts of the UK are further to the north than the tip of Hokkaido, Japan's most northern island.

In Japan, the "Stone Age" began somewhere before 10,000 and ended around 300 BC. It is known as the Jomon Period. It was similar to life in Britain at the beginning of the Bronze Age around 3,500 BC. Unlike Britain, Japan never went through distinct developmental stages of first working with bronze then later iron. The reason was that the technology for working in both metals was imported from the mainland more or less simultaneously. In both countries, more aggressive newcomers displaced weaker tribes.

Descendents of the Ainu people are now confined to Hokkaido in the north, but once occupied northern regions of the main island of Honshu as well. They were hunter-gatherers who lived in tent villages and have been compared to Native American tribes who in many ways they resemble.

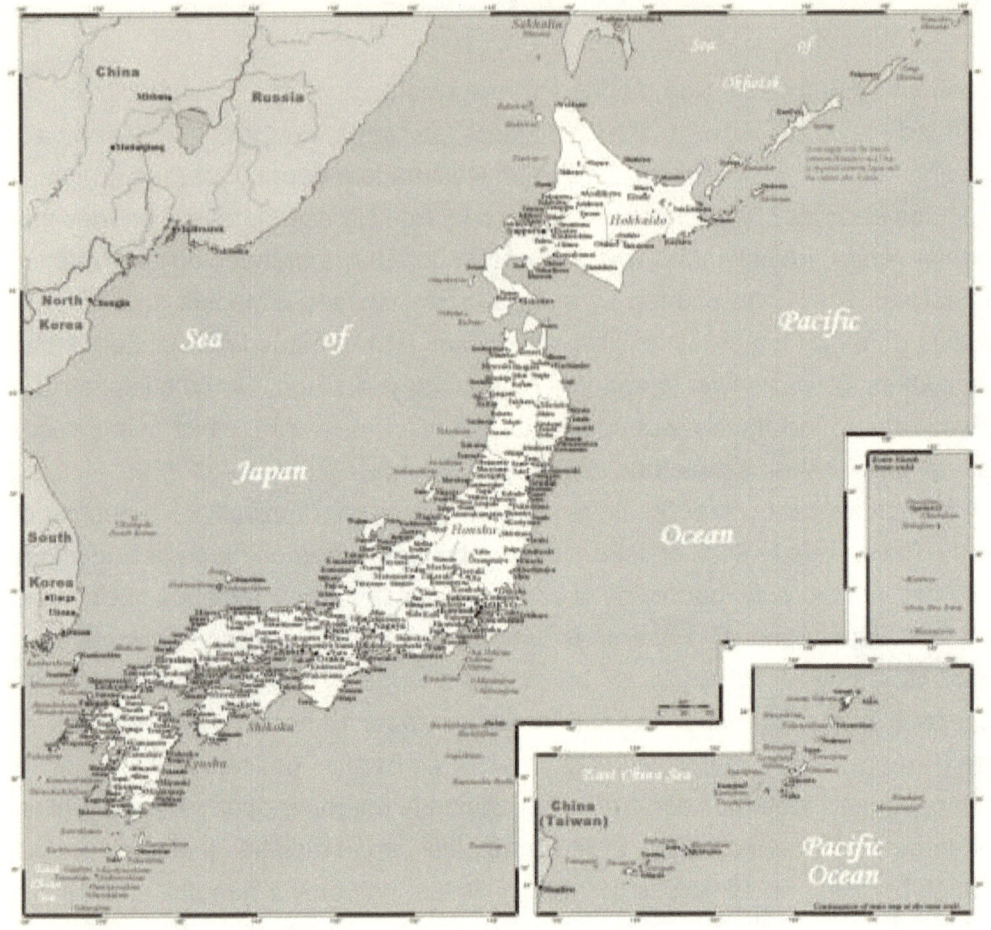

Ainu features are more Caucasian than Japanese and they are generally more hirsute. Moreover, the Ainu language is quite dissimilar to Japanese. They have made strenuous efforts to maintain their cultural identity. Archeological and anthropological research suggests that the Ainu people might have originated in the North Ural Mountains and then spread from Finland to Northeast Siberia, finally arriving in Hokkaido between 700 BC and 700 AD. Interestingly, Finnish and Japanese share some similarities in their grammar. There is also cultural congruence such as removing shoes at the door, cleaning the house thoroughly on New Year's Eve and similarly stoic national characters.

In Britain and elsewhere in Europe, we have many tales of "the little people" who could be defeated by iron. These may be folk memories of how the superior iron weapons of the invaders easily dispatched the physically smaller spear-wielding locals. The Cornish language in the South West of Britain is

14

wholly unrelated to English, as too is Welsh and these were areas where remnants of the original inhabitants were driven to.

Although Japan's land area is 30% greater than Britain's, the available area of flat land in Japan is barely 17% of the total, the rest being mountainous. England has fewer mountainous areas and even those are not particularly high when compared to Japan. This had a direct effect on the distribution of population and in the greater consumption of fish in Japan. All the earliest Japanese village and urban centres were near the sea. Even so, more than 80% of the inhabitants are crammed into less than 20% of the land, with the South having the greatest density of population. There are hundreds, perhaps thousands of hot springs bubbling across the whole of Japan but under a dozen in Britain. This ultimately led to the bathing culture of Japan, which was largely absent from Britain, apart from the appropriately named city of Bath, home of the main natural hot spring spas in the country and a few other areas where visiting mineral spas became popular during Georgian times.

Around 300 BC, Pythagoras sailed around Britain, then known as Albion, from which is derived the word albino. Presumably this was due to the famed White Cliffs of Dover being the first view of Britain for most early visitors. Pythagoras mapped the British Isles, accurately describing them as being very roughly triangular. The most detailed early account of Britain and its people appears in the memoirs of Julius Caesar. He first made landfall in 55 BC along with some eighty ships carrying two legions of loyal soldiers, coming ashore near present-day Dover. The native Britons greeted the Roman troops on horseback and in chariots, launching volley after volley of javelins at them.

The Han Chinese made the earliest known reference to Japan by a foreign nation in 57 AD. This describes the visit of a Japanese envoy to the court. Around 292 we have the first real information about the Japanese in the records of the Wei Dynasty of China. "The 'Wa' people ("Wa" being the old name for Japan) are said to have lived in one hundred countries or tribes. They had respect for the law and were careful to observe social differences. Also, they were said to practice agriculture, spinning, weaving and fishing."

Likewise, in his memoirs, Caesar describes a country of numerous tribes. He told of how one result of the Roman invasion was to put a stop to the almost continual fighting that went on between them. The Britons appointed one of their own to the position of supreme commander. There was already some trade between the mainland and Britain. Caesar was able to glean valuable information from the Gauls regarding the nature of the people across the channel. Indeed part of the reason for Caesar's invasion was lingering anger at the help that some Briton tribes had given the Gauls when Rome's armies first encroached on their lands.

On a humorous note, the Wei described how the Japanese were exceedingly fond of liquor, while Julius Caesar wrote "There followed (in Britain) several days of continuous bad weather, which kept our men in camp and also prevented the enemy from attacking." [1] It is oddly satisfying to see that some things haven't changed much in the past couple of thousand years!

Both the British and Japanese tribes at this time were farmers, with rice cultivation having been introduced into Japan by settlers about 300 BC. These newcomers probably originated in the Upper Yellow Valley in China. There is evidence that the idea of growing rice in wet fields may have arrived even sooner in some parts, but historians agree that with the arrival of rice, the Jomon Period was over and the Yayoi Period, (300 BC to 300 AD.) where most people became farmers rather than hunters, had begun.

During the Jomon period, the pottery figurines known as dogu appeared. They may have been fetishes, but their purpose is uncertain. They were unearthed in both graves and settlements. Many seem to be wearing goggles or helmets and are highly stylized. UFO fans might recall how Erik Von Dankein in his "Chariots of the Gods" cited them as evidence that extra-terrestrials had visited the Earth at some time in prehistory. The dogu are unique to Japan once again helping to refute the often-repeated lie that the Japanese are somehow incapable of creating anything original.

The writer Graham Hancock believed that he might have discovered twelve thousand-year-old ruins off the coast of Okinawa, southeastern Japan. He postulated that these could have been part of the civilization often referred to as "Mu" that some believe existed prior to the flooding that occurred at the end of the Ice Age. This is a controversial issue, as his critics believe that all he uncovered were natural structures.

Caesar wrote, "Most of the tribes in the interior do not grow corn but live on milk and meat. All the Britons dye their bodies with woad, which produces a blue colour and shave the whole of their bodies except the head and upper lip. Wives are shared between groups of ten or twelve men, especially between brothers and between fathers and sons...For money they use either bronze or gold coins...husbands have power of life and death over their wives as well as their children...the common people are treated almost as slaves, never venture to act on their own initiative...most of them bind themselves to serve men of rank, who exercise over them all the rights that masters have over slaves." [1]

A fairly similar social order existed in Japan during the Kofun period from around 250 to 538 AD. People were organized into clan like structures known as "Uji." There were also the "Be" and "Tomo." which were groups of workers, allied with, but unrelated to the clans. They provided various services, such as weaving, making weapons and such. In return, they were under the protection of the Uji they served.

By the end of the Kofun period, Japan already had a distinctly centralized society. Some writers have suggested this was a direct result of the close cooperation that was necessary when most people were involved in rice growing and other farming. Most collectivist societies are primarily agricultural. They had no alternative but to work together, sharing the rice paddies and agreeing when and where to plant and harvest.   Any other way would have resulted in chaos. In Britain too, for much of the time, the majority of people were tenant farmers, working on small strips of land. There was doubtlessly some degree of cooperation there as well.

The Kofun Period is so named for the "kofun" or tomb mounds that even today can still be seen. They are similar to the megalithic gravesites that exist in Britain and Europe. Building stone monuments was common across Europe. In Ireland, the Newgrange tomb resembles a kofun in Nara Prefecture. Both have tunnels and chambers with a mound and chamber constructed from huge stones. One major difference is that European mounds were built well over fifteen hundred years earlier than those in Japan. They were also used primarily for the interment of cremated remains, while those in Kofun Period Japan were reserved solely for interment of important individuals. In Ancient Egypt, numerous objects were buried with the deceased for his or her use in the afterlife. This was also true of European mounds where swords and other objects have been recovered.

Keyhole-shaped kofun near Nara   Male and female haniwa figures

In Japan, from the kofun, small clay figures known as haniwa have been excavated, along with swords, ornamental mirrors and such. The presumed purpose of these figures was to accompany the dead on their journey, as with the Ancient Egyptians.

In Britain, prior to the coming of the Romans, cultural advances came chiefly from the mainland Gauls and Celts. Likewise, Japan saw many innovations introduced from China, or to be more precise, from China via Korea.

The early Shinto faith of Japan and the Druidic religion practiced in Britain and Gaul were both concerned chiefly with nature worship. One important difference was that Druids carried out human sacrifice and they apparently believed in reincarnation. Neither committed their teachings to writing. The Druids because their religion forbade it and in Japan, because prior to the introduction of Chinese characters, ideographs known as kanji, there was no native written language. Actually it is not known precisely what the Druids beliefs were. The modern day

Druidic Society in Britain has created a sort of "New Age" nature worshipping ecologically friendly faith, which claims somewhere between 30,000 and 50,000 members across the country. Some of them attempt to circumvent hastily erected police barricades around Stonehenge, the ancient circle of massive stone blocks in southern England during the Solstice.

Written English first appeared in the sixth century, derived from Latin, with the addition of three symbols from the old runic alphabet of the Anglo-Saxons to represent sounds not found in Latin. This was about the same time as Japanese first began using Chinese characters. They faced a considerably bigger challenge in adapting a foreign born script to be used for writing their language than the Anglo-Saxons did.

After 410 AD, with their empire in serious trouble, the Romans abandoned Britain, thus ending more than 350 years of occupation. This resulted almost immediately in waves of settlers from the continent arriving in force. It was less of an organized invasion, more in the nature of mass immigration, with the Angles, Saxons, Jutes and others taking land wherever they liked. From them, of course, come the terms "English," and "Anglo-Saxon."

Naturally there was some resistance, but the Celts had been softened up by generations of Roman living; hot baths, piped water and roads as straight as a die. For the most part, they were quite unprepared for battle. Many moved north to Scotland, or into Wales and Cornwall, some left for Northern France and a few fought.

One of these could possibly have been the semi-legendary King Arthur, often assumed to have been a Celtic Briton, a local chieftain whose tribe battled against the newcomers encroaching on his lands in the South West. If he existed, Arthur doubtlessly bore scant resemblance to the Hollywood version, drawn from the Arthurian stories of Mallory that were written in the Middle Ages. Guinevere, the Holy Grail, even Excalibur were all fictional additions. However, the magician Merlin does seem to have been based on a historical person, perhaps a Druid, or a holy man of some description. In any case, he flourished some 70 years earlier than Arthur and in Scotland. That they never even heard of each other, let alone met is all but certain.

Japan had its own semi-legendary ruler, Queen Himiko, who was said to be a great and powerful leader. She is mentioned in the extensive chronicle of ancient Japan, the "Nihonshoki," which was completed around 720. Other accounts describe her more in the nature of a shamanic priestess. As with the Arthur legends, it is often a challenge to separate historical facts from the embellishments of writers eager to impress their readers.

From about the fifth century, the Japanese had control of the southern half of their country and the Kanto Plain, which also included the site of present-day Tokyo. The Ainu people were still present in the north, but were being driven steadily out. The Japanese animated movie, Princess Mononoke is a fantasy story but it suggests how invaders from the South steadily encroached on land occupied by the original inhabitants. This brings to mind the story of Queen Boudicca, of the Iceni tribe who fought fiercely against the Romans and swallowed a lethal dose of poison rather than be taken prisoner when defeat was certain.

Up until this point the cultural development and the structure of society was congruous in both countries. One important difference was that the Japanese were already a distinct race by the fifth century. Their origins are the stuff of conjecture, but it appears they came from not only Mongolia and Korea, but also China and in all probability, the Polynesian Islands as well. The last of these is controversial, but there is some evidence to suggest links.

The first is the similarity of some construction styles in both Polynesia and Japan. Buildings were traditionally raised off the ground and the Ise Shrine, to the Japanese what Canterbury Cathedral was once to pilgrims in England, is a good example. It also has crossed beams forming its roof, another feature of Polynesian architecture. Linguistic similarities between Japanese and Polynesian languages are also apparent.

It is not known exactly when Christianity first reached England's shores. There is evidence of Christian communities from the late 2nd Century. The first martyr in England was St. Alban around 300 AD. By 410 AD when the Romans had left, Christianity had made inroads in many areas. For a time, with the arrival of large numbers of pagan Anglo Saxons in southern regions, Christianity was very much a minority faith. It was strongest in the east and especially in Wales. This time of separation from Rome gave rise to significant differences in Church structure as with Buddhists in Japan who had little regular contact with Mainland Asia.

The Japanese made over 25 separate attacks on the Korean kingdom of Silla between 100 and 500 AD. (Korea was divided into three kingdoms at this time.) Around 400 AD, in gratitude for military assistance, the ruler of Paikche, another of the Korean kingdoms sent peace offerings, including scholars learned in the Chinese classics and the teachings of Confucius. In 552, that same kingdom

dispatched missionary monks with images of Buddha and scriptures to Japan.

Meanwhile, in Britain, in 597, Augustine of Canterbury (the first Archbishop until his death in 604) arrived on the shores of Kent in South West England accompanied by about 40 missionaries, on orders from Pope Gregory in Rome. He promptly converted the King of Kent. Augustine (shown here in an 8th Century portrait) and his party met with such success that by 700, Britain had been largely Christianized. It appears, however, that pockets of paganism were able to survive for some time. The Church was unable to stamp out the old beliefs entirely. There were just too many isolated villages. Even in 1935, the construction of a new road into Cheddar Gorge (from where we get the cheese) in the Southwest of England revealed the existence of a village so remote that the inhabitants had not even seen a priest for decades. The villagers had hardly any idea of what was going on the outside world.

Buddhism's arrival in Japan sparked off religious wars over whether or not it should be introduced at all. The Soga family supported Buddhism, while their opponents, the Mononobe and Nakatomi vehemently opposed the foreign religion. The Soga won and the teachings of Buddha quickly became the religion of the aristocracy. Unlike in Britain, where conversion to Christianity was uniform, it was some time before the common people adopted the new religion.

The regent, Prince Shotoku Taishi (572-622) was a prominent figure.

Sometimes called the Constantine of Japan, Shotoku Taishi (left) was a devout Buddhist, deeply influenced by the Confucian teachings brought to him by Korean monks. He was directly responsible for reforming the government of Japan along Chinese lines and for the long lasting Confucian influence on society. Thus the Japanese tendency to form groups and their strictly hierarchic social order, were both reinforced. The deference to seniority, yet another trait of Japanese society had its origins in Confucianism; the system of social order that first appeared in China around 400 BC. Japan also began eagerly importing techniques of Chinese art and architecture.

Around the same time in Britain, Christianity had quickly replaced the pagan beliefs of the English as the national religion. In Japan, the old religion of Shinto and Buddhism were able to exist side by side since they complimented rather than competed with each other. In England, Continental techniques of art and particularly manuscripts, written chiefly in Latin, were copied laboriously by monks in chilly monasteries across the nation. Christianity and the old religion continued to co-exist as well, although perhaps less overtly than with Buddhism and Shinto in Japan.

Christianity had already undergone adaptations in the Vatican's relentless drive to convert pagans. Biblical historians tend to agree that the historical Jesus Christ was likely as not born in September. His birthday was moved to December 25th in order to displace Saturnalia, a major pagan festival primarily concerned with feasting, gift-giving and generally having a good time. Churches were built on the sites of pagan worship. Halloween replaced Samhein, an existing pagan festival and ultimately became a harmless fancy dress party for the kids. Pan, a god of the old religion became the image of the Devil in the new. Lucifer, another name for the Devil was a deity of the Romans associated with Venus and known as the Bringer of Light. The image of Mary and baby Jesus predates Christianity. Egyptian statues of Isis and baby Horus being prime examples. They are almost identical. The mother and baby motif is universal. Indeed, there are those who argue that much of Christianity is a hodgepodge of Manichean thought and Mithraic [3] beliefs all woven together with even older legends.

In Britain, many of the festivals are clearly pre-Christian in origin. The Maypole dance possibly has roots in fertility rituals. Dancers weave and dodge their way around the Maypole clutching ribbons. There are also parades of floats where people dress up in animal costumes. In Cornwall, southwest England, there was a custom where during one pageant a couple wearing an outfit that vaguely resembles a kind of crocodile wove in and out of every house in the village. British farmers in the Southwest used to call down the corn in a ceremony reminiscent of Shinto harvest festivals. Santa Claus replaced Odin in Norse legends. Odin was an old man with a white beard riding a flying horse bringing presents for the good children. Families left carrots outside for his horse and something stronger for Odin to enjoy. This is not much of a stretch to flying reindeer and a sleigh.

Rather than try to stamp out every aspect of the old religion, the early Church found it simpler to permit many pagan practices to endure as harmless festivals, their original meanings soon forgotten. In spirit, these festivals are similar to the "Matsuri" of Japan. Many are unmistakably drawn from fertility rites, such as the "Nebuta Matsuri" in the north of Japan. There huge wooden effigies of erect penises are paraded around. Or in Nagoya, to the east of Kyoto where young women go to shrines to pray to similarly shaped objects of worship. Even today, men and women sometimes only partly dressed carry the portable shrines down streets swarming with onlookers. They rejoice in an alcohol-soaked celebration of pure silliness, much like carnivals around the world.

Belief in astrology has continued into the Christian era, despite the Church's official position on fortune telling which condemned it as sorcery. Former President Reagan was rumored to have regularly consulted an astrologer, in spite of his public image as a born-again Christian.

In Britain, many folk-remedies, some ludicrous, others, proven effective beyond question were still used well into recent times. In some isolated rural areas, these were surely remnants of the old lore passed on verbally from one generation to the next. Some writers suggest that the witch trials in Medieval Europe show that pagan worship endured in some regions for several hundred years after most assumed it had been exterminated. Indeed, parts of Europe were not converted to Christianity until the end of the 13th century. Other opinions are that this may be only part of the truth, along with the misogyny and contempt for the "weaker" sex that permeates most organized religion, particularly Islam and Christianity. Priests in Europe and elsewhere found it only too convenient to brand women witches then condemn them to burn at the stake.

Buddhism and Shinto in Japan were able to co-exist because they each addressed different concerns. The night shift and the day shift, so to speak! The teachings of Buddha as introduced into Japan concentrate chiefly on the afterlife and the cycle of rebirth. Shinto, by contrast, is a simple religion of the here-and-now and has nothing specific to say about what might or might not happen to its believers after death.

This may be true, but even so, there were clearly tensions for some people in trying to follow both creeds. The writer of "The Tale of Genji," Murasaki Shikibu detailed the dilemma faced by Princess Senshi, who was the high priestess of the Shinto shrine of Kamo. From her poetry, we can see that she was "constantly torn between the demands of ritual purity, which forced her to avoid all forms of pollution, including Buddhism and her deeply felt need to find salvation." [4]

During the Heian Period, (794-1158) Japan continued to develop as a nation, with Kyoto the glittering capital and the regions run by governors. By 1000, Kyoto was the 5th most populous city in the world with about 175,000 people living within its walls. During this time in the British Isles, Edgar, the first King of all England ruled from 959-75 and unified several kingdoms into one. Scotland and Wales were still separate entities with their own local rulers. Somewhat in the same manner as in Japan, the country outside of the capital was in the hands of earldoms, which eventually challenged the rule of the central monarchy, just as the regional governors and Buddhist monasteries became increasingly powerful, ultimately overwhelming the effete courtiers of Kyoto.

One major difference between the situation facing Britain and Japan was in the nature of its neighbours. Japan had little to fear from most of the countries of East Asia. China showed no inclination to invade; Korea was divided into three warring states and in fact, was sometimes the victim of Japanese aggression in antiquity. The only people to attack Japan were the Mongols in 1274 and again in 1281 and a united front of samurai fighters saw them off, with a little help from the convenient appearance of a typhoon. This was the origin of the term "kamikaze" or "divine wind" since the grateful Japanese presumed the Shinto gods had sent the storm to aid them in the battle against the invaders.

Britain not only saw the Romans, Angles, Saxons and Jutes invading, but later, the Vikings, the Danish and Norwegians and of course the Normans. Britain was somewhat closer to the mainland and regularly faced aggressive, expansionist foes. It is easy to imagine just how the history of either island would have been different if the Koreans and Chinese had been hell-bent on conquest, while the Europeans had been content to stay home and mind the farm.

Japan was engulfed in civil wars from the end of the Heian Period (1185) on and off until the final unification of the country in 1603. Britain also went through something similar for much of the same time-period, with numerous battles, wars of succession and the Hundred Years War with France, which began in 1339 and was actually 114 years in duration.

Every British schoolchild knows 1066, the most famous date in his or her history. In this year, William "The Conqueror," and his Norman army defeated King Harold and his forces, which had just returned from fighting off yet another invasion from Scandinavia. We could compare this to the battle of Sekigahara in 1600. In both cases, the victory of one army led to profound changes in the makeup of the country, a turning point in history.

Sekigahara was the battle in which Ieyasu Tokugawa emerged victorious, establishing the Shogunate that was to rule Japan until 1868. In Britain, William established the royal dynasty whose family tree wound its way right up to the Windsor's of contemporary Britain. Incidentally, both The Battles of Hastings and Sekigahara took place in the month of October.

The impact of these victories cannot be overstated. However, each had the opposite effect. As a result of the Norman Conquest, a period began of linguistic, cultural and architectural innovations, all of which changed Britain forever.

In direct contrast, Japan was progressively sealed off from the outside world from the third decade of the sixteenth century until 1853 and the arrival of Commodore Perry. This policy was known as "sakoku." Christianity, which had made inroads in the southwest was banned and nearly exterminated. The whole country became a police state, in which everyone's lives were strictly regulated. Ieyasu Tokugawa was concerned above all else with the unity and prosperity of Japan. He had initially been tolerant of Christianity, but ultimately came to view it as a threat, assuming that Christians would divide their loyalty between the Pope in Rome and the Shogunate.

The first Europeans had arrived in Japan in 1543. They were Portuguese, from a land in the grip of almost fanatical religious fervour. The Church wasted no time in dispatching missionaries soon after, including St. Francis Xavier, who visited Japan in 1549. The first Englishman to reach Japan was William Adams, a sailor who was shipwrecked in 1600. He spent the remaining twenty years of his life in the country. Adams was an advisor to Tokugawa Ieyasu and is the inspiration for the fictional John Blackthorne of James Clavell's novel "Shogun." He appears to have died from a fever aged 55 years old.

The first record of Japanese who spent time in the UK concerns two sailors. They were known only by their Christian names. The older, around 20 years old, was called Christopher (originally perhaps Cristóbal). The younger was Cosmas (probably Cosme), aged about 16. Little is known about their origins. Both were said to be very capable and reliable. They were picked up in 1587 by the English explorer Thomas Cavendish (1560-92). Cavendish captured the Spanish galleon Santa Ana off Mexico. He claimed its rich cargo as bounty and burned the ship on the beach. Cavendish took with him a few of its crew including the two Japanese. "He took out of this great ship two young lads born in Japan, which could both write and read their own language."[12] They spent about three years in England, presumably in the employ of Cavendish since they once again sailed with him in late 1591. Cavendish, his ship and crew were all lost in the South Atlantic a few months later.

The next Japanese to reach England were likely the trio of Iwakichi, Kyukichi and Otokichi in 1835; three sailors who had drifted across the Pacific in 1834 after being blown off course. They had been sent to England in an unsuccessful attempt to establish trade links with Japan. Thirty years later there were the Choshu Five. They were five samurai from the Choshu clan who were smuggled out of Japan by anti-shogun forces and who spent eighteen months learning all about the West, mainly in Scotland. They included future prime ministers Inoue Kaoru and Ito Hirobumi. They were astounded by the advanced technology and the brazen display of meat in the butchers' shop windows. A story goes that one of them, when subjected to a racial slur, swung his pocket watch on its chain and smacked his heckler soundly around the head.

The arrival of firearms in Japan probably hastened the process of Japan's unification, but only by a few decades at most. The country had been fighting on and off since the end of the Heian Period in 1185 and was thoroughly war-weary.

Following their victory in Britain, the Normans settled in, adopting the customs of their hosts and struggling to learn English. William the Conqueror tried, but never managed to master the language. Over ten thousand words found their way into English from the Normans, three quarters of which we still use, including "jury, justice, petty, marriage and govern" to name but a few. It is often said that the point at which the gulf between the aristocracy and the common people opened up was in the fact that the Normans spoke a dialect of French and the rest of the people used Anglo Saxon. Harold had been what might be called a "peoples king" who fought alongside his men. The sense of separateness that the aristocracy carried with them for centuries afterward can be traced back to the time of the Normans.

At fairly similar times, two heroes appeared in the literature and histories of both countries, characters that remained in the hearts and minds of the people for generations. In Britain, this is Robin Hood, while in Japan, Minamoto no Yoshitsune (1159-89). One was almost entirely fictional, while the other is to a far greater extent based on a historical samurai figure. It is interesting how closely the stories resemble each other.

Of the historical figure Robin of Locksley, historians are divided. Some believe he was a real person while others are convinced that little or nothing is true. In the earliest stories he is merely a wily thief. Even his name, "Robinhood" was possibly a 13th century alias used by poachers or petty criminals. Another theory is that he was based on a Saxon freedom fighter who battled against the Norman invaders. In the first decade of the 13th century, noblemen were struggling to gain more influence. Ultimately, their success resulted in the Magna Carta (Great Charter) of 1215. This was the beginning of the shift in power from the king to the barons and lords and ultimately in the coming centuries, to the common people. The fictional Robin became associated with the battle against tyranny.

Everybody knows the stories of how he fought against the evil Sheriff of

Nottingham hiding out in the forests dressed in medieval camouflage green. His nobler motives: "Robbing from the rich to give to the poor" these were added on in later versions of the story. By the 15th century, the tales had been embellished with additional characters such as Maid Marian and his loyal followers, Friar Tuck and Little John. The latter was ironically named since he was said to be a giant. There is even a grave in Nottingham claiming to be that of the real Little John. Reportedly, an excavation some years ago unearthed a large thighbone that indicated its former owner would have been over six feet tall. That's not so remarkable by today's standards, but he would have towered head and shoulders above most of his contemporaries, who averaged only about five feet in height. The statue of Robin Hood shown here can be seen in Nottingham.

Yoshitsune was just a baby when a rival samurai family murdered his father. He grew to manhood vowing revenge. Like Robin, he was a fugitive on the run for some of the time. Ultimately, he achieved victory over his enemies, but in the end, was betrayed and forced to commit ritual suicide at the age of thirty. He was said to be able to catch flies buzzing around his head with just a pair of hand held chopsticks. Robin Hood won a battle of wits with Friar Tuck who then tossed him in the river but thereafter became his loyal follower. Yoshitsune met his "Friar Tuck," Benkei on a bridge. Similar to the Robin Hood story, the warrior monk refused to give way and was bested in a fight, after which he became totally loyal. Benkei died on his feet, pierced by hundreds of arrows, held up for a time by his armour. Where Robin had Maid Marian, Yoshitsune had his loyal mistress, Shizuka. Robin Hood dies like Yoshitsune, betrayed by those he thought were his friends. In Robin Hood's case, he is stabbed to death while weak from having too much blood drained from him (a medieval medical treatment.)

The parallels between Robin Hood and Yoshitsune might seem surprising but each is an example of tales that recall either real or invented characters. Both contain essential elements such as the dashing hero, his true love and some

kind of bittersweet ending. Over time, just like in the Greek Myths, the tale grows with each telling and in the end it matters little how much of it is true, it fills a universal desire for heroic figures.

16th Century woodblock print showing Benkei and Yoshitsune viewing cherry blossoms

No two languages could be much less alike than English and Japanese yet both developed in quite a similar fashion. Japanese is older than English. It is related to Mongolian and Korean with which it shares grammatical similarities and is a member of the Altaic group of languages. There is also the likelihood of some Polynesian influence. Japanese and Polynesian both share a love of double onomatopoeic descriptive words such as "pika-pika" meaning "shiny" or "goro-goro" the rumble of thunder. In Polynesian, for example, two bird names are "koto-koto" and "riro-riro". To the best of my knowledge, this is not found in any other languages apart from Korean with such frequency. Immigrants arrived and over time, their language became mingled with that of the indigenous people.

We can see this in English as well. About twenty words survive from Celtic in English and even fewer from Roman times. These are chiefly place-names. A lot of vocabulary is drawn from Anglo-Saxon although it comprises only about 1% of the total number of words in the English language. However, these are among the most commonly used, so that in any typical sample of modern English writing about half of it will consist of original Anglo-Saxon words such as "man, wife, eat, drink, love and fight."

A lot of Norman French was eventually adopted into usage in English. Initially, only the aristocracy spoke a northern French dialect while the peasants continued to speak English. Over time, isolation from France, intermarriage with native English speakers and a growing sense of being English rather than Norman helped English not only to reassert itself, but ultimately absorb the Norman dialect altogether. In doing so, a new language was created. This process took some three hundred years, during which time, most literature was written in either French or Latin.

In Japan the idiomatic Chinese-character system known as "kanji" was introduced around the same time as Buddhism. It was wholly unsuitable as a medium for Japanese. In China, the several languages and regional dialects are mutually incomprehensible. Use of kanji unified the country by allowing everyone to be able read the same text, as each character represented a word, but was read in whichever language was spoken in that area of China. Chinese can still read Confucius in his original words 2,400 years later! Kanji are vaguely like the Ancient Egyptian system of hieroglyphics; many being stylized images of the object, idea, or whatever it is they represent.

Bill Bryson explained how writing can be read across languages. When we write "1, 2, 3" in English we read it as "one, two, three." A Spaniard reads it as "uno, duos, tres," in Dutch it is "eins, zwei, drei" and so forth. The Japanese title of this book, "Kiku to Bara" means "Chrysanthemum and Rose" these being flowers associated with Japan and Britain respectively. Kiku is 菊, while bara is 薔薇. One symbol can often be read in different ways.

Japanese borrowed some vocabulary from the older languages of Northern China. One example is the word "ai" meaning "love" in both Chinese and Japanese. The word for "water," "mizu" is the same in Japanese and Hungarian. There are ancient linguistic links between the two countries. Morton believed the Hungarian-Magyar Language, Finnish and Japanese all have a common Central Asian source.

Several generations of Japanese wrote everything in Chinese symbols, a laborious process where they took the sound (not the meaning) of a character and matched it with the sound of a Japanese word or syllable. When we think that all the Anglo-Saxons had to do was add a few characters to the Latin alphabet from their own script, it represents quite an achievement.

By the mid-ninth century, kana, a phonetic system had been derived from Chinese characters. For ease of usage, it is vastly superior to Kanji and consists of two alphabets each with 46 characters. One of these, hiragana is used to write native Japanese and the other, katakana is for foreign names and words, or sometimes to highlight something. Returning to this book's title once more, "Kiku" is written きく, while "bara" comes out as ばら. In katakana they are written キク and バラ. Both systems are quite straightforward to learn. Some students master them in a matter of weeks.

At this point, some might wonder why the Japanese simply didn't dispense with using kanji altogether and save themselves a lot of trouble. That is like asking why the Catholic Church didn't abandon Latin. China was to the Japanese what ancient Greece was to the Romans, or what Latin and French were to the educated classes in Britain. Nobody would have even considered the idea, although in recent years, the number of Kanji taught in schools has been reduced to an official 1,975 or so. Reading a newspaper requires the mastery of between two and three thousand. Just as written English didn't assert itself for at least three hundred years after the Norman Conquest; it took a similar length of time for Japan's native prose to begin to break away from Chinese.

Thus some would say that written Japanese is needlessly, almost fiendishly complex due to the retention of Chinese characters. Chinese is entirely different from Japanese. Its grammar resembles English in word order. It is a tonal language, in contrast to Japanese, which is spoken with very little intonation and all vowel and syllable sounds are evenly stressed.

A Japanese student of English would be equally justified in bemoaning the incredibly complex and confusing grammar of the English language. As in the case of kanji and Japanese, this is the fault of what could be called linguistic mismatch. English grammar is based on Latin and again here are two languages with not a whole lot in common. The English were just as much slaves to the classics of Greek and Latin, as the Japanese were to Chinese. Latin was assumed to be superior, so English had to conform to Latin rules.

Bill Bryson, the American writer in his book "Mother Tongue" describes basing English grammar on Latin as "like asking people to play baseball using the rules of football. It is a patent absurdity. But once this insane notion became established, grammarians found themselves having to draw up even more complicated and circular arguments."

At least the grammar of Japanese is relatively straightforward. For example, it has only two irregular verbs, "to come" and "to do," all the rest follow one of two patterns and can be conjugated without too much trouble. There are over 250 irregular verbs in English!

During the Middle ages in both Britain and Japan "a parallel feudal system existed in which land was granted in return for military service to an overlord who granted protection to all in his domain. The circumstances were genuinely parallel in that a strong lord-vassal relationship was a necessity in both Japan and Europe as the only available barrier to the anarchy and chaos that threatened society after the breakdown of an earlier, stable order."

In Britain, this came earlier, with the withdrawal of the Romans, while in Japan it arose after the end of the Heian Period in 1185. The system that the Japanese had adopted from T'ang Period Japan some five hundred years earlier fell apart when the samurai soldiers and the regional governors became too powerful.

The samurai and the knights have a number of points in common. They showed loyalty to their lords, (mostly). They had deep religious convictions and led Spartan lifestyles. Both were skilled in the arts of warfare and especially in their dexterity with the sword. They lived by a strict code of behaviour, which to break was to bring dishonour on their heads. (In the case of the samurai this meant committing ritual suicide known as "hara-kiri" or "seppuku.") The knights had their own crests of arms, while the samurai could be identified by different coloured breastplates and also family crests just like in Britain and Europe. Even today we can sometimes see the "kamon" or family crest on the entrance to older houses, just like clan badges in Scotland and elsewhere.

One way that the samurai were starkly different from their knightly European counterparts was the absence of chivalry from their code of conduct. The European knight traditionally showed compassion for weaker folk and a near deification of women. To the samurai such notions would have been almost incomprehensible.

During the Edo period (1603-1868) a rigid class system was imposed. The samurai were at the top (naturally enough, they were the ones who created it in the first place.) The farmers, artisans and lastly the merchants followed the samurai in descending social order. Ironically, as time went by, the merchants grew to be the wealthiest and most powerful, while some samurai were increasingly impoverished. They went from being warriors to little more than sword-wielding bureaucrats. Inflation ate into the value of their fixed incomes. Over time, some of them resorted to marrying into merchant families, managing to overcome their distaste for commerce. This ensured the future prosperity of their family, as their sons would inherit the rank of samurai and have money into the bargain.

In many ways, the class system in Britain was equally as rigid. Nobody ordained that you must remain a farmer, or an artisan, although in practice, hardly anyone could escape the grinding poverty and back breaking labour. For all but a very lucky few, there was effectively no way of climbing the social ladder. Henry Fielding wrote in "Tom Jones" how "Nothing can be more reasonable than that slaves and flatterers should exact the same taxes on all below them, which they themselves pay to all above them." Then, as now, wealth was concentrated in the hands of a few.

At the turn of the 20th century, about 80% of Britons were what would be considered working class. One hundred years later, this represented no more than 30% of the population. Even so, over 50% of British people still regarded themselves as working class. Paul McCartney said once that he was still the same blue-collar Liverpool lad he had been when the Beatles first played together. In Britain, the class system endures even today. In contrast, about 85% of the Japanese considered themselves to be middle class by the late 1990s.

Britain was the first nation to undergo what was eventually dubbed "the Industrial Revolution." Japan was the first country in Asia to achieve the same. In both cases this resulted in a tremendous shift of population from the country to the cities. In Japan, this had already begun during the Edo Period and accelerated from the late 19th century onwards. By the 1990s, almost 80% of the population was urban. Many villages and small towns have become seriously depopulated and are often little more than communities of retired people.

Britain's industrialization began in the 1790s with the first manufacturing machines powered by engines appearing. Displaced farm workers, rendered redundant by the enclosure of small strips of farmed land into larger fields and others looking for work moved to the cities in droves. By the 1990s, some 90% of British people lived in towns and cities. As in Japan, the same problem has been experienced in small villages and a handful of areas of Britain that have been hit by depopulation.

By the late 19th century, many of the landed aristocracy were in much the same position that the samurai had found themselves in during Edo times. They were broke, staring poverty in the face, sitting in their huge stately homes with no money to buy coal for the fire. They too married into members of industrial families, which brought in much needed income. This also resulted in a shift from the Liberals to the Conservatives as the "natural party of government."

Britain and Japan both carved out empires. Britain's was far more enduring than Japan's of course and covered almost a quarter of the globe at one time, ranging from parts of Africa and the Indian sub-continent to America, Australia and Hong Kong. The days of Japan's empire really began with taking control of Taiwan in 1895 and later, the annexation of Korea in 1910. During the Great War, Japan also gained the protectorate over South Manchuria from Germany [1] and the island of Sakhalin from Russia.

During the industrial revolution, Britain's population rose rapidly from 16 million in 1820 to 27 million by 1840. Japan went from 26 million people in 1867 to 52 million by 1913. In both countries, there were too many mouths to feed and this was a major factor impelling each to colonize. This was also true of other European countries that, Britain included, were busy carving up Africa.

The British divided Ireland in 1921, more or less along religious lines. Likewise, the Korean peninsula has been split into two since the early 1950s indirectly as a result of Japan having occupied it in the first place.

Ireland was divided into several kingdoms in 1169 when the English landed on the eastern coast of Country Wexford. The king of Leinster had invited them. It was the wish of Rome that England take control of Ireland to reorganize it and integrate the Irish Church into the Roman Church system. They later lived area called Pale and from this was derived the expression "beyond the pale." There were no religious issues at that time since both countries were Roman Catholic.

After the Reformation, England tried to suppress Catholicism in Ireland, especially during the rule of Oliver Cromwell in the Irish campaign of 1549-50. This was not a success. Only in Ulster, where many were descended from those original English settlers did the Anglican Church prosper. Thus the stage was set for the enduring tragedy that has been Northern Ireland's story for so long.

The Japanese invaded Korea in ancient times. Then it was as an ally of one of the three warring Korean kingdoms. In the 1590s, the Japanese fleet once again sailed to Korea, although the real goal was to invade China.   Finally in 1910, when reacting to the murder of Ito Hirobumi, a Japanese ex-Prime Minister and the Resident-General of Korea by an assassin the previous year, they annexed the country. The British had tried to stamp out Catholicism in Ireland in Cromwell's time and in Korea, people were forced to take Japanese names. The schools conducted lessons in Japanese, banning the native Hangul script. In 1945, when the Allies arrived in the Southern part of the country, the Japanese were forced out. The Northern part of Korea was occupied by Russian soldiers, which eventually led to the Korean war of 1950-53 and the partition of the country into the Communist North and pro-Western South.

Christians were present in the British Isles long before Augustine began preaching in Anglo Saxon Kent in 497. Buddhism came to Japan about 45 years before that. In many ways, the manner in which religion developed, then declined is quite similar in both countries The imported religion changed slowly over time to suit the temperament of the native population. Buddhism took on Japanese traits over the centuries and in Britain a similar thing happened to Christianity. The relative isolation of Britain meant that the Vatican must have seemed a remote, almost mythical place to many medieval Britons. Likewise, Japanese Buddhists had very irregular contact with Korea at best, as exchanges between the two countries had declined considerably by the beginning of the Heian Period in 794.

In Britain, as early as 1164, the king decreed that appeals to Rome in cases of ecclesiastical crimes would be limited. Before his death in 1384, John Wycliffe translated the Bible into English and asserted that it alone should be the source of Christian dogma and ritual. The authorities persecuted Wycliffe's followers, who were known as Lollards and the movement was eventually stamped out. Here we can already see what seemed like the seeds of English Protestantism, predating that fomented by Luther and Zwingli on the continent by over a hundred years.

Around the same time that Wycliffe was challenging the authority of the Church the radical Priest John Ball was active. He was one of those who inspired the Peasant's Revolt of 1381 preached a sermon including the words "When Adam delve (dug) and Eve span (spun) who was then the gentleman?" as a direct attack on the aristocracy. The revolt was crushed when the leaders were killed and the crowd of protesters dispersed.

King Henry VIII was initially unsympathetic to the ideas expressed by Luther. Nonetheless, he declared the Church of England to be independent from Rome, with himself at its head largely over the question of his right to divorce. Three years later, Parliament confirmed this in the 1534 Act of Supremacy. Initially, the makeup and doctrines of the Church of England remained essentially Catholic, but over time, Protestant trends began to enter the country and eventually, it took on a very English feel. Easygoing, for the most part and generally tolerant, some people complain it is too tolerant.

In 805 and 806, two scholar-monks returned from China after studying Buddhism. One of them, Saicho, founded the Tendai Sect, which became the closest thing Japan had to state Buddhism. The other monk, Kukai founded the Shingon Sect. Its teachings are obscured by the fact they are kept secret from outsiders, imparted by a master to his most outstanding and promising pupils.

During the thirteenth century, the Pure Land Sects appeared. These were aimed far more at the common people than the Tendai and Shingon, which appealed exclusively to the aristocracy. They could be compared to the developments in Europe during the reformation, or even the Methodist Church, which the Wesley brothers promoted in the 1770s. Theirs was a simpler creed emphasizing salvation by faith in divine grace. Methodism and the Pure Land Sects both stressed the need to take the message to the masses and they both had great success. The Methodists found many converts among the mill owners and capitalists of the 18th and 19th centuries.

The Pure Land sect known as Shinshu is today the largest Buddhist group in Japan. Another similarity between Protestantism, the Church of England and Japanese Buddhism was its tolerance of married priests, something not found in either Catholicism or the older forms of Buddhism in Mainland Asia.

Another sect is the Sokka Gakkai. They claim over ten million members in Japan and another three million around the world. Many Japanese regard them as a secretive and even sinister organization, cult-like with their supposedly authoritarian practices and dabbling in politics.

The history of Religion in both Britain and Japan has been one of steady decline. Churches in Britain have closed. Congregations continue to dwindle, whatever gimmicks the Church of England tries. In Japan, many keep up the rituals, such as burning incense on the family alters in their homes for certain ceremonies, but a visit to a temple is more like a day out to a museum for many Japanese. They go through the motions, just as British people show up occasionally to Church for a wedding, funeral or some special day on the Christian Calendar. Indeed, Methodism has also seen its influence in Britain decline and there was talk some years back of a possible union with the Church of England. In America, the Methodist Church maintains its strength. Former

First Lady Hilary Clinton is among its congregation.

There are many reasons cited for this falling away of religious belief. One that might go at least some of the way to explain it is the rapid urbanization that cut people off from their roots. The ancestral family grave is sometimes at a shrine on the other side of the country, a remote place indeed for which many must feel less affinity for with each successive generation. In Britain, the Church has long been seen as an irrelevance and people too have lost touch with their rural and farming origins.

In Japan, a strong belief in being a unique people, called "Nihonism," was sometimes described as a kind of ersatz creed. Literature espousing this idea is for the most part ludicrous, self-absorbed nonsense. In one book, the author even seemed to be trying to suggest that the Japanese were one of the lost tribes of Israel! Plenty of writers try to convince anyone who will listen that in one way or another, the Japanese are unlike everyone else on the planet, ranging from the theory that they use different parts of their brains when speaking or thinking in Japanese to speakers of every other language, to doctors asserting that the Japanese have longer intestines than anyone else. Such writers seem almost desperate in their desire to prove a non-existent point. In Britain, some people have suggested, on a somewhat humorous note, that football has become the national religion for many people.

Whatever the reasons, it has been concluded that Japan is one of the most secular countries in the world. Even in Communist China various religions are growing, not stagnant or declining as in Japan. Likewise, in Britain today, around one in ten of the population regularly attends church services. Only 16% regard religion as being very important in their lives as against nearly 60% in the US. Britain has become a multi-faith country with almost 5% of the population following Islam. Up to a third of them apparently believe in extreme and intolerant interpretation of what many regard as already being an extreme and intolerant belief system. About 1.5% of the UK is Hindu and various cult groups also exist. Crackpot evangelical sects have seen their membership rise. Even so, the majority of Britons are only nominally religious. The 2011 census in the UK showed that almost a third of respondents declared themselves as atheist or agnostic. ("No religion" 25% or "none stated "7%). Some polls show even higher figures for the non-religious. This is often true of Continental Europeans as well.

The ban imposed on Christianity was lifted in 1873 two decades after Japan had reopened to the West once more. An initial flurry of interest died out well before the end of the 19th century. There was a similar spike in the post-war years under American occupation, but the best efforts of every kind of missionary have yet to raise the number of Japanese Christians to even 2% of the population.

America, in contrast remains a country where polls suggest that between 40 and 50 percent of the population regularly attends church services. Many of these Churches, especially in southern and rural areas are intensely puritanical and intolerant of minority lifestyles. Their followers effectively control parts of the Republican Party. They have an enormous influence. Fundamentalists in the state of Kansas succeeded for a time in getting evolution removed from a list of compulsory units to be studied in biology courses in state schools. It is hard to imagine something like this even being debated in either Britain or Japan, much less passing into law.

The horrifying incident in 1995 where the Aum Shinrykyo sect attacked passengers on a Tokyo subway with the deadly nerve gas Sarin seems to have left many Japanese not just disinterested, but actively hostile to religion, according to polls taken around that time. The Unification Church, which originated in Korea and arguably isn't even Christian, has also attracted mostly negative publicity with a famous actress who alleged she was subjected to brainwashing when she briefly joined the cult. This is an accusation that is frequently directed at the "Moonies" in Europe and America.

Japan's isolation from the rest of the world ended in 1853, when Commodore Perry sailed from America almost within sight of Tokyo, forcing the country to open up to trade by threatening to turn his cannons on the capital. This came at a time when the Shogunate had become far weaker than before and not long after, the military regime was toppled in a coup that ushered in a spell of modernization and dizzying change during the Meiji Period.

The Industrial Revolution began in the UK in the 1790s. Britain was the first European country to begin the transition from a largely agricultural to an industrialized economy. Once Japan emerged from over 230 years of semi-isolation, it became the first Asian nation to industrialize, at a dizzying pace. This began in the mid-1860s with the "oyatoi gaikokujin" initiative where foreign specialists were hired to do everything from building lighthouses and railways to training up students in the skills they needed. Approximately 3,500 individuals were hired across the country. The programme was terminated in 1899 when it was no longer needed. Japan already had a mercantile economy in place and caught up to the West within a few decades. By the 1890s, its navy was able to defeat the Russian fleet in battle.

At some point, individualism began to appear in the West. Originally, Britain and Japan had much the same social structures with the descriptions of Britain made by Julius Caesar being in essence similar to those made by the Chinese regarding Japan. There were numerous tribes, many of them warlike and the common people were allied to clans who offered them protection, but in return expected both loyalty and service; two collectivist societies.

Some historians point to the Protestant reformation, which placed each individual in a direct relationship with God. The teachings of Christ came not from the bureaucracy of Rome, but directly from the Bible. In the Abrahamic religions, the individual is more important. Buddhism teaches that every life is just one in a long cycle of death and rebirth. Each incarnation is only a step on the journey, whereas in the Judeo-Christian tradition, there is only one life followed by some kind of frozen eternity in either Heaven or Hell. There, we are to presume, the deceased carries on being that self same individual for all time. Hindus also believe in the wheel of reincarnation and that we might be rich and famous in one life, then perhaps a blind pauper in the next.

There are still more clues in art. In early Western art and the paintings of China and Japan as well, there is usually little depiction of character or individuality. Everyone looks almost the same, be it in the Bayeaux Tapestry that depicts the Battle of Hastings, or in the 13th century scrolls showing scenes from "The Tale of Genji." The only difference is in the portrayal of leaders, kings or saints. Even these tend to be stylized and share similar features.

Up until the middle Ages, most art was anonymous. "John Sabini argued that our Western individualism has much in common with the value we place on artistic creativity...the unique self is regarded as a thing of value in itself."

Alex Kerr in his book "Lost Japan" agrees that the rice farmers developed a close cooperative society out of necessity. He feels that the mountain dwellers of Iya, where he lived for many years are far more individualistic and "the hunters and foresters of Iya, whose rocky slopes hardly supported a single rice paddy were independent, free and easy people."

America, with the presence of the frontier in the 18th and 19th centuries and the pioneer spirit brought into being an even stronger individual-oriented society than that which existed in the countries of Europe. Recently, even American writers have observed that their country is becoming increasingly individualist.

Similar sentiments are often aired in both Britain and Japan. At this point the histories of both countries are increasingly intertwined with the politics of the day. The next chapter continues the story.

SOURCES

(1)   Julius Caesar- The Conquest of Gaul   page 103

(2)   Morton – History of Japan pages 5-6, also Bill Bryson – Mother Tongue

(3)   Mithra. Probably mythical figure whose life and death closely resembles that of the Biblical Jesus Christ.

(4)   From the Diary of Murasaki Shikibu

(5)   Bryson – P.128

(6)   Morton – P. 63

(7)   Japan – The living Tradition (on the Uji)

(8)   Introduction to Modern Psychology – P. 558

(9)   Daily Yomuri Newspaper (Article on kofun)

(10)   Alex Kerr-Lost Japan

(11)   Japan was allied with Britain during WW1 and used this as a pretext to seize German occupied areas in China at this time.

(12)   Quoted from "Voyages of Thomas Cavendish" by Richard Hakluyt (p.287)

POLITICS AND DEMOCRACY

On May 1st 1997 the Conservative Party, lead by John Major was duly evicted from the corridors of power. It was the biggest shift from a governing party to the opposition in the entire 20th century. Altogether the Conservatives lost 178 of their notional 343 members of parliament. The Labour Party snatched seats from the Conservatives in every region of the country, even rock solid "true blue" for generations seats fell. The "Tories" were wiped off the map in Scotland, Wales and in the lower half of the South West of England. Tony Blair, who had never held government office before became at nearly 44 the youngest Prime Minister since William Pitt the elder in 1812.

After eighteen partisan years of doctrinaire rule marked by an ever-deepening cesspit of corruption and incompetence, the Tories were shattered. Major duly resigned as leader, to be replaced by 37 year-old William Hague. Even by mid term, at the end of 1999, the governing Labour Party still enjoyed poll ratings of about 54% to a paltry 28% for the Tories. By the age of 40 William Hague was widely seen as the most ineffective Conservative leader in living memory. His off the cuff claim to have regularly drunk fourteen pints of beer as a teenager was widely ridiculed in the media. A mere 19% of the electorate regarded Hague as a good leader of the opposition.

The election of June 2001 came and few observers seriously expected the Conservatives to recover significantly. They made the grand total of one net gain. Hague resigned and another balding hard line demagogue, Ian Duncan Smith, became his replacement. The Tory Party was torn between regaining the middle ground or of lurching off into the giddy extremes of hard right dogma. Indeed, a few critics virtually wrote the political obituary of the Conservatives as serious contenders for power by themselves ever again. They have fewer than 10,000 activists under 30 and the average age of the membership is over 60. Regardless of electoral success or otherwise, demographically their future seems uncertain.

By the election of 2010, with the worn-out Labour government entering its thirteenth year in office, The Conservatives became the largest party in Parliament and went into coalition government with the Liberal Democrats. Voters in many parts of the globe including Britain and Japan have become increasingly volatile and have little real loyalty to any one party any more. Given the venal nature of most politicians and parties is this really very surprising?

In the late 1990s, a trend became apparent across Europe quite some time after it had begun, as is often the case. Following a decade or more in the wilderness, resurgent left-of-centre opposition parties defeated long entrenched conservative governments, often decisively. In most cases, the ousted party or parties struggled thereafter to find their feet in the somewhat unfamiliar role of official opposition. By 2010 this had begun to reverse itself with populist and far-right parties capitalizing on widespread fear of immigration to increase their support but as yet, seldom taking power by themselves.

Britain was generally seen to have followed America in swings to the political left and right since the Second World War. From Truman and Atlee in the late 1940s, Kennedy and Wilson in the 60s, up to Carter and Callaghan in the 70s; Thatcher and Reagan in the 80s; and so on. This no longer has any meaning. The Labour Party now occupies similar political territory that was claimed by moderate conservatives thirty years ago.   Former Prime Minister Tony Blair came to be loathed by many of his erstwhile supporters who regarded him as a pawn of the US government. To the left in the UK, he was no more than a warmongering conservative wolf in social democratic sheep's clothing.

Japan saw the same party, the Jiminto or Liberal Democratic Party (LDP) continue to dominate the political landscape virtually from the time of its inception in 1955 well into the 1990s. Even in 2005, it was still the leading member of the coalition government, only a few seats shy of an absolute majority. Following the election that year, it won a landslide.

In 1993, for the first time, the LDP lost power to a new party led by Morihiro Hosokawa.   His short-lived administration attempted some reforms. There then followed the extraordinary spectacle of the LDP/JSDP- Japan Social Democratic (formerly Socialist) Party coalition with the grandfatherly Mr. Murayama, leader of the JSP becoming Prime Minister. In Britain, barring a national crisis, such a thing would be an unthinkable marriage of convenience. The LDP won the subsequent election.

However, in 1998, in the Upper House election, the LDP got a mere 25% of the vote and lost 17 seats. This was hardly an earthquake when compared to the Tories' slaughter in the UK the previous year, but the Japanese media called it one. The LDP clung to just 105 seats out of a total of 252, while the merely two year-old Democratic Party of Japan managed to take 54.

Some pundits suggested that what had happened in Britain and elsewhere was beginning in Japan. In the wake of the election, LDP support fell to just 21%, although it recovered to over 30% a year later. For a while, it was only marginally ahead of the Democratic Party in the polls, which had won about 21% in the July 1998 poll. The Communist Party of Japan saw its vote rise to around 15% in that year, its best result for decades. Prime Minister, Ryutaro Hashimoto duly resigned. He was branded "Hoover Hashimoto" by the scathing media for his resemblance to the hapless former US president Herbert Hoover, in the White Office at the time of the 1929 Wall Street crash.

In Asia, as in Europe, a similar housecleaning took place in the late 1990s in several countries. In Indonesia, the once mighty Golkar party was flung from office. It had regularly won 70% or more of the votes cast in successive elections since the coup that brought it to power in 1965. However, in a free and fair poll in 1999, it managed barely to register 19%, a very poor second to the winning grouping. In Korea, former dissident Kim Dae Jung become the first opposition leader to be elected president, followed by a reformist successor in 2004.

Initially, it seemed that Prime Minister Obuchi, Hashimoto's bland replacement would fare no better than the eleven or so men who had preceded him in the previous sixteen years. His support rate slumped to just 23%, not far above the point where most Prime Ministers feel the tap on the shoulder from concerned LDP power brokers who sense it is time to "change the head on the suit". Obuchi was nicknamed "cold pizza" for his boring public image.

Obuchi confounded his critics, partly because the public had almost zero expectations of him. In January 2000, he registered a healthy 45% approval rating and seemed likely to survive until the elections that would be held by the end of the year. Obuchi died in April 2000 following a massive stroke.

The Japanese are intrinsically conservative when it comes to politics. Yet again they fell in line behind the LDP in the June 25th election in sufficient numbers to sustain the three-party coalition government, albeit with a far smaller majority. The opposition parties in Japan had a long history of splitting into factions. They were incapable of winning much support and resembled a token presence rather than genuine parties of government-in-waiting.

Around the turn of the 21st Century, it finally seemed remotely possible that the Democratic Party of Japan would wrest power from the LDP with its charismatic leader Naoto Kan. He was ousted in a party vote following a minor scandal, where it appeared he had spent the night in a hotel with one of his female employees. He denied any wrongdoing, but it didn't save him. Although the Democrats gained 32 seats for a new total of 127, they fell a long way short of removing the LDP from office. In the election of 2004, they rose to 177 seats. Under their new leader, Okada, they firmly established themselves as the main opposition. The dawn of two-party politics in Japan had seemingly arrived.

A wild card on the Japanese political scene was the Communist Party. By distancing themselves from hard line Communist movements elsewhere in the world and pursuing a determinedly independent line, they were able to stave off the collapse in support that Communist parties in other countries suffered following the end of the Cold War. The Communists once boasted nearly half a million paid up members. Although membership had fallen to about 320,000 by 2014, it was reported to be growing once again. They had a reputation for honesty and integrity, a scarce commodity among Japanese politicians. They tried to soften their image and move a little to the political centre. They focus on grass roots issues such as welfare, care of the elderly and retention of a pacifist constitution. In many ways, they come across more like radical liberals or social democrats in their tone than that of hard line followers of Marx and Lenin. The Communists slipped back to only 20 seats in June 2000 down from 26. Then in 2004, they were reduced to a rump of just 9. In 2014 they recovered to take 21 seats.

In Britain, between 1951 and 1997, the Conservative Party held power for 35 out of the 46 years, a full 76% of the time. Not quite as impressive as the LDP's almost unbroken run in power between 1955 and 1993, but not far off. The LDP was sometimes compelled to seek coalition partners during those years, something the Conservatives never needed to do.

The LDP is called a "conservative" party and in some ways this is true. It is anti-Communist, pro-America and supportive of big business. However, its economic policies were closer to those of social democratic or socialist parties in the West. It invested directly in industry and protected its markets from competition by erecting trade barriers and enough red tape to keep most imports out. The LDP also spent vast sums when in power building up the infrastructure of the country with railways, bridges and investment in nuclear power and technology. They also support maintaining a welfare state based pretty much on the British model.

Formerly, the UK Conservative Party resembled the LDP in that it was for a long time ideologically quite vague. It could therefore appeal to a broader segment of the population, including a fair chunk of the working classes. Most of the party was made up of "one nation Tories" who stressed consensus and grudgingly accepted some parts of the Welfare State such as the Health Service.

The election of Margaret Thatcher in May 1979 ended that quite abruptly. Surely no commentary on British politics would be complete without some mention of the woman who destroyed forever the comfortable post-war consensus. Some people still regard her as having rescued the British economy, dragging the dinosaur into the modern age. Others remember her with bitterness as deeply divisive, power-mad and extreme, with a heart of stone. Her grating voice could inspire apoplexy among the 55% of the electorate who never voted for her. She ruined the lives of countless working people consigned to the scrap heap in the name of her ruthless economic experiments.

Thatcher remained in power for so long for a number of reasons besides her own abilities. One was the pitiful state of the UK opposition at that time. The Labour Party had seen 26 right wing members break away to form the Social Democratic Party. It had elected the veteran peace campaigner Michael Foot as its new leader.   With his flowing white hair, pop-bottle glasses and shambling style he instantly became a national joke. Much of the press, both the tabloids and more serious papers were Thatcher- sycophants. Even so, by early 1982, she was looking like ending up as a one-term leader.

Then the Falklands War came, which Thatcher turned to her advantage. A negotiated settlement to the Argentine invasion of the disputed South Atlantic islands was in sight, but Thatcher ordered the sinking of the Belgrano, an Argentine troop ship full of conscripts heading toward a port in Argentina. Some charged that she had deliberately sent over 900 young men to a watery grave to ensure her re-election. Even so, she won a landslide in 1983 and again in 1987, with a slightly reduced majority.

The Britain that she helped to create has the most secretive and centralized power structures in Europe. While it may be true that some of the economic reforms were inevitable, Thatcher closed down many coalmines that were still viable. This was due to her hatred of the miners, whose industrial action had brought down the previous Conservative government. In 1986, Britain became the only country in Europe without an elected local government in its capital city. Thatcher abolished the Greater London Council out of spite when London voters had continued to back the Labour-led administration of the populist Ken Livingstone.

Wales had no Conservative controlled local councils thus a non-elected board was charged with running the region. These were handpicked for the most part to carry out Thatcher's orders. Local Government was effectively emasculated, once again because most of it was in the hands of the Liberal Democrats or Labour. A litany of Thatcher's relentless attack on democracy could go on almost indefinitely.

The Poll Tax eventually finished her. Under this system, introduced in the late 1980s, every adult under the same roof paid a flat rate local tax, regardless of income. Thus the blatantly unfair situation arose where a single millionaire living in a country mansion would have paid half as much as a married couple on the poverty line in an inner city slum. Both Thatcher's personal ratings and those of the Conservative Party slumped. Fearing electoral meltdown, Thatcher's lapdog party swiftly concluded that she was increasingly listening only to the voices in her own head. They grew a pair and unceremoniously ousted her as leader.

When Thatcher died in 2013, many let their feelings be known. Former London Mayor Ken Livingstone said: "She created today's housing crisis, she produced the banking crisis and she created the benefits crisis. It was her government that started putting people on incapacity benefits rather than register them as unemployed because the Britain she inherited was broadly at full employment.

She decided when she wrote off our manufacturing industry that she could live with two or three million unemployed and the legacy of that, the benefits bill that we are still struggling with today. In actual fact, every real problem we face today is the legacy of the fact she was fundamentally wrong. He added "that it was to Tony Blair's shame that he broadly carried on most of her policies."

In Japan Reagan and Thatcher's contemporary was Prime Minister Yasuhiro Nakasone He was approximately the ideological equivalent of Thatcher, with the charisma of Ronald Reagan. Also like Thatcher, he came from a relatively modest upbringing which was highly atypical in the LDP. Popular at home, he was regarded in most of East Asia as a tactless war-mongering reactionary. Part of this was a result of his regular pronouncements on a variety of topics. These ranged from xenophobic remarks or attempts to downplay Japan's aggression during the war, to comments that were just plain stupid.

Nakasone's visit to Yasukuni Shrine where war criminals are interred caused much anger among Japan's neighbours. His decision to raise Japan's defense spending above 1% of the budget was seen as provocative and caused protests both in Japan and Asia. In the 1960s, as a cabinet minister, Nakasone allowed the nationalist writer Yukio Mishima and his crackpot friends to play soldiers on self-defense forces land.

Politically as well as socially, Britain and Japan have similar attitudes to mainland Asia and Europe respectively. Japan wants to trade with the rest of Asia. Indeed it has no choice and yet doesn't appear to regard itself as being culturally a part of Asia. Likewise, Britain has long maintained a sense of being on the outside edges of Europe, culturally as well as geographically. The lack of a land bridge to the mainland has helped sustain this mindset.

Britain joined the EU (Then called the EEC) in 1973 after a referendum in which 67% of voters backed the idea of entry. What the polls didn't show was the reluctance most people felt when saying yes to membership of the European Community. Most Britons were hostile to the idea of metrication. Even in 2010, it is astounding that many people over forty still cannot understand the metric system properly. Far younger people habitually use imperial measures in conversation. The BBC still frequently refers to "stones" when describing a person's weight. Apart from older Australians and New Zealanders, pretty well nobody outside of Britain has the faintest idea that a stone is fourteen pounds. A poll carried out in 2014 showed that among Britons, enthusiasm for the EU is the lowest of all the member countries. This is perfectly understandable. Many are sick to the back teeth of the EU and its arrogant, dictatorial attitude. Up to a half of the UK would vote to withdraw if given the chance.   Around 40% express support for continued membership although many of those are far from enthusiastic.   Prime Minister Cameron has promised a referendum on continued EU membership.   Most observers suggest the vote will be quite close.

Unlike Germany, Japan took a considerable time in coming to terms with its past misdeeds. The Emperor did more around the turn of the century to make amends than most Japanese politicians had managed in the previous ten or twenty years combined.

On a trip to Britain early in 1998, there was quite a tide of anti-Japanese sentiment expressed in the media. War veterans planned major protests. The Emperor was able to turn much of this around with a heartfelt apology to the people of Britain for what his people did during World War Two. Many observers were convinced that he really meant it. It's hard to imagine many Japanese politicians pulling that off (or even attempting to.)

In October 1998, the Emperor made a similar apology to the President of South Korea, Kim Dae Jung, while the latter was on a state visit to Japan.

Incredibly, some senior LDP members opposed plans by the government to try and atone for its rule over the Korean peninsula from 1910 to 1945. A few years later, it is hoped these reactionary voices are increasingly in an aging minority. Around the time of the Emperor's visit to the UK, one British newspaper "The Independent" commented that "As the Japanese move out into the wider world, they drag their politics like a ball and chain behind them."

Japan is probably the most democratic country in Asia, but to be brutally honest, that is not saying much. Britain, on the other hand, is often regarded as being one of the least open and democratic nations in Europe. On the one hand, Britain was one of the few European countries not to go fascist between the wars, or to be invaded by Nazi Germany. However, Britain came close to civil war just prior to the First World War. Debatably, it was only the outbreak of hostilities that prevented this.

From a historical perspective, it is clear that neither Japan nor Britain was initially particularly warm to the ideas of liberty and democracy. This tendency has endured into the present day. There are several incidents in both Britain and Japan that lend credence to this opinion.

In Britain the authoritarian mindset of the Thatcher years still endures. Many don't consider it to have changed significantly under Tony Blair. He personally saw to it that the Welsh Assembly was forced to pick his choice of First Minister, resulting in a surge for the leftish Plaid Cymru Party that denied Labour its expected majority in the newly established body.

The same thing happened in the May 2000 election for the London Mayor, disastrously for Labour and Blair. Ken Livingstone, the former GLC leader was denied the chance to run for Mayor, with the result that he stood as an independent and won anyway, easily seeing off the Tory Party and Labour which limped in a distant third. He won a second term in 2004, but lost to the eccentric Tory Boris Johnson in 2008. Blair did himself a good deal of harm with his perceived image as a "control freak." Laws to limit the movements of known football hooligans, while welcomed by some were also seen as being anti-democratic. Likewise, the draconian smoking ban, while welcomed by many was decried by smokers as simply picking on a soft target.

At the same time, Tokyo had an independent at the head of its Metropolitan government. Shintaro Ishihara, a far right-wing author who, similar to Livingstone, sees himself as a man of the people and quit the ruling party to stand as an independent candidate for Tokyo Governor in 1999. Like Livingstone, he ran rings round his opponents, one of whom was a former UN career diplomat, General Akashi, who was persuaded to accept LDP backing, but really hadn't a clue how to fight a political campaign.

Unlike Livingstone, who moved to a more moderate inclusive position, Ishihara evidenced much that suggested he wasn't remotely interested in democracy, most peoples' definition of it at least. He seemed more akin to the 19th century politicians of the Meiji Restoration who saw it more as a means to an end than as a desirable goal in itself. In his case, that end appears to be little more than self - promotion and power for the sake of it. One report commented: "The governor said he himself, the bureau chief responsible and two special secretaries studied the feasibility of the new taxation formula in secret (this being a proposed local city bank tax.) Ishihara said, 'When one plans something, it should be done secretly.'"   In 2006, "it was revealed that his 40-year-old son was closely involved with projects undertaken by Tokyo Wonder Site--a group of facilities established to promote cultural activities run by the metropolitan government. This prompted public criticism that the relationship had blurred the line between public and private matters. At one point Ishihara commented, "It [happened] because he's the only person suitable for the job," but he later backtracked saying, 'My words were insufficient.'" (From the Yomuri Daily)

Japanese intellectuals and foreign residents alike despised him, but he had plenty of support in Tokyo for his blunt outspoken manner.   He won re-election in 2007 with just over half of the votes cast.   Tokyo was finally rid of Ishihara in 2012 when he stepped down to concentrate on his role as co-leader of the new far-right "Japan Renaissance Party".

Former PM Obuchi was no better. The local residents of Tokushima, on the southern island of Shikoku voted 94% to oppose the construction of a dam that would cause great damage to the local environment. The Prime Minister simply brushed aside their concerns with a remark something to the effect that he would seek their understanding, but the construction must go ahead whatever.

Edo Period Japan was effectively a police state, run by a military clique with a figurehead emperor. Nobody had a vote, the Shogunate was the government. The Shogunate was more like a monarchy than anything else since the Shogun was always a member of the Tokugawa family. Britain at the same time was governed by a small number of landowning gentry. Many of these were elected in what were known as "rotten boroughs." These often had only a handful of voters, sometimes little more than merely the immediate family members of the

Member of Parliament in question. Old Sarum in Wiltshire, for example had only three houses and seven voters who sent two MPs to Parliament. (One of these was the 18th Century Prime Minister William Pitt the Elder. By the late 18th century, out of 405 elected members, 293 were chosen by fewer than 500 voters each. The agricultural labourers, miners and factory workers were for the most part illiterate and denied the right to vote. By today's standards, they had only the most basic human rights.

At almost the same time, Britain and Japan underwent great changes. In 1867, the Meiji Restoration saw the downfall of the Shogunate. Less than two years of civil war had ousted the military rulers. Keiki, the last Shogun resigned and lived quietly until his death in 1912.

The restoration was initially a coup rather than a move toward greater participation in the democratic process by the masses. Historians have debated this point, but it seems likely that few if any of its original leaders had intended to establish Western-style democracy. Indeed, many of them preferred the idea of a ruling council of elder statesmen, the "Genro" continuing to run the country. They saw no need for political parties. They were more interested in modernization of the economy. They wanted to retain the essential character of Japan and were keen to build railways and a modern army, but were less than enthusiastic about the wholesale importation of Western ways.

John Reddie Black (1826-1880) was a long-term Tokyo resident from the UK who started an English language newspaper in the 1870s. The Meiji government was initially supportive until he started writing editorials calling for voting rights. They effectively silenced Black by hiring him as a consultant on condition that he relinquish control of his newspaper then promptly firing him from his new post. Laws were enacted to bar foreign residents from publishing newspapers.

British reforms were also in part a reaction to the French Revolution of 1789-92. In the 1820s, the British government took harsh repressive measures to quell the dissent caused by the Corn Laws. Trade Unions were legalized in 1824, but even after that, individuals who tried to form them were sometimes imprisoned or transported to penal colonies in Australia. In 1832, the "Rotten Boroughs" were abolished and all men paying over a certain amount of rent per year were enfranchised. This enlarged the electorate by about half, but still did nothing to grant voting rights to the working classes.

In 1867, in the same year that the Shogun was forced to resign in Japan, the

49

vote was finally extended all British working men. Once again, this had been in reaction to pressure rather than any genuine desire for wider democracy among the ruling classes. Later, the Labour Party was formed and a few years after that, the first working class MPs were elected to Parliament.

Women aged 30 or more were only granted the vote in 1918 in Britain as a result of nearly two decades or more of campaigning by members of the suffragette movement. It was only in 1928 that this was lowered to 21 years old, the same as for men. In Japan, universal suffrage only came at the end of the Second World War.

Japan's parliamentary system developed, although based on German models, it is basically quite similar to Britain's. The Upper House was made up of "Blood, wealth and unusual talent." The Lower House consisted of "Commoners, men paying a direct national tax of at least 15 yen." This was much like the situation in Britain until 1867. Most men, to say nothing of women were effectively denied the right to vote. It also ensured that those who did were more likely to support the status quo.

The samurai were abolished as a class in 1877. The events that followed were used as the basis for the movie "The Last Samurai" starring Tom Cruise. The bearing of swords and the wearing of the topknot were banned and many samurai moved into other professions such as farming, politics, or industry. A few of them committed suicide while others chose to fight their quixotic last stand against the inevitable. The Meiji Restoration was less a move to democracy than a coup by other samurai clans. It served their interests, once they had taken power, to abolish the class that they originated from.

In the late 19th Century, politics developed in Japan as the various factions and some of the "genro" leaders formed political parties. This had been resisted by some of the genro. They mistrusted the whole idea of political parties, regarding them as being little more than "private cabals." Looking at the history of the LDP it is easy to conclude that they weren't far wrong. The Japanese parties saw wider democracy as a means to an end rather than a desirable goal in itself. "It was easier to appeal to men's interests than to change their values." They sought to build up a power base. In 1889 the Meiji Constitution was unveiled, an ambiguous document that allowed for either democratic or authoritarian rule. Under the new constitution, the Emperor was given direct political power, for the first time since the close of the Heian Period (795-1185). The politician Ito Hirobumi had spent eighteen months in Europe in the early 1880s, studying the various political systems from which to model Japan's new constitution upon. He felt that the Prussians offered the most suitable for Japan to emulate. Other members of the Cabinet concurred and support for French and British political institutions was increasingly sidelined in favour of the Prussian system of governance.

One of those who had the ear of Ito was Lorenz Von Stein (1815-90). Stein supported a kind of top-down democracy with any reforms emanating from the monarchy rather than having any input from the common people. He had no sympathies with the ideas of universal suffrage or party politics. Von Stein's political beliefs in a nutshell were to advocate a kind of benign dictatorship.

Even over one hundred years later, the LDP was seen as less of a political party in the Western sense of the word and more of a coalition of half a dozen or so support groups each centred on its leader. Whichever of these leaders became the Prime Minister was then obliged to placate the other groups by handing out ministerial positions as evenly as possible. The differences between the factions were usually personal rather than political. Seniority took precedence over genuine ability as the new prime minister was obliged to include many from the upper echelons of his and other's factions. Thus the average age of the cabinet was always over sixty.

After Koizumi took the helm, the factions declined in power and continued to exist as "little more than groups of colleagues that meet to discuss insider information, what's going on and where," in the words of one former faction leader. The factions may have been undesirable in many ways, but their emasculation robbed the LDP of much of its vitality. This was another reason the LDP was basically running on fumes for the last decade of its rule.

Both Britain and Japan saw social unrest as the 20th Century progressed. In 1918, the Rice Riots took place, where hordes of protestors demonstrated against the rising price of rice, reminiscent of the opposition to the Corn Laws in Britain almost a century earlier. The army killed over a hundred protestors. In Britain during the General Strike of 1926, the country was brought to a standstill and the army was called in to restore order. It ended after nine days and resulted in the freedom of the unions being restricted by an act of Parliament the following year.

In Japan, a number of factors contributed to the effective takeover by the military in the late 1930s. The public was largely apathetic towards politics. Many feared the spread of Communism in Japan, which had found many sympathizers.

In 1925, the same year that Japan first achieved universal male suffrage; the "Peace Preservation Law" was passed which permitted crackdowns on dissenters. The military came to regard themselves as having a mission to "Purify Japan of deteriorating economic and social conditions, most of which they blamed on foreign influences." The military became increasingly dominant. Finally, in 1940, all the Japanese parties were merged into one, "The Society for Assisting the Imperial Rule," and the military took virtual control for the next five years. (The Communist Party had been banned several years previously.)

One way in which the Japanese political system differs from that of Britain is in the incredible power of the bureaucracy. These faceless, nameless men are seen by many as the real government. They draft legislation, formerly wrote most speeches for the politicians to read out and sometimes they even spoke on behalf of them in parliamentary debates. In July of 1999, the government scrapped the system called "seifu-iin" where bureaucrats took the lead in parliamentary discussions. The politicians suddenly find themselves having to debate in the same manner as in Britain or America where fierce exchanges ensue across the chambers.

Norihiko Koike, a professor of political science said "The basic role of a Japanese politician was to divide the pie in his constituency's favour during the days of high economic growth. However the focus has shifted to how the nation should be run at a time when the pie has become smaller." This is one factor behind the LDPs long domination of Japanese politics. While the economy was booming, they got the bridges built, or the new train link and became popular in their constituency. People would criticize the sleaze and corruption of the LDP, but keep voting for their man knowing he would deliver.

Nowhere was this more apparent than in the June 2000 General Election. Prime Minister Mori, a lumbering dimwitted buffoon who appeared to be one of the least capable leaders in recent memory, made a series of what the Japanese press euphemistically dubbed "controversial remarks." One of these was that Japan was a divine country with the Emperor at its centre. Another was that those people who didn't support him should stay in bed on Election Day. He used archaic terms associated with Japan's militaristic past in one of his speeches. In almost any other country, someone like that would have been slaughtered at the polls. His personal rating fell to 18% and yet the LDP and its two partners were able to cling to power albeit with a considerably reduced majority.

In Britain, it was once estimated that an incumbent Member of Parliament could count on around 1,700 extra votes at election time, especially if he or she had become well respected in the local community. This "personal vote" in a close race could make all the difference between victory and defeat. Clearly this effect was magnified many times over in a Japanese election. No matter how contemptuous of the LDP voters became, enough people stuck with their local member.   They were seen in a far more favourable light than the party as a whole. Thus the seemingly endless round of (typically financial) scandals entrapping LDP politicians had relatively little impact on the subsequent general election results.

With less money to throw around, this came to an end. "To LDP politicians elected from single-seat constituencies, for example, a lack of popular support for their party's policies means that they may be defeated in elections, a scenario that could eventually oust the LDP." Prophetic words indeed.

Another major difference between Japanese and British politics is in the large number of Diet (Parliament) members who are effectively "inheriting" their seats from either fathers or other family members. Nearly a third of LDP candidates and about 12% of all members of the current Lower House sit there mainly because their father was also a politician. Many Japanese are less than happy with this situation.

In Britain, this was formerly the norm, with the Lords made up mostly of men who had inherited their title. The House of Commons was packed with a ruling clique many passing down their seat to a family member or relative. Nowadays having a famous politician in the family is debatably anything but helpful to someone aspiring to enter politics. In the 1990s, when Labour MP Dr. John Golding decided to step down from Parliament, his wife Lynn was selected to take his place. The by-election campaign was dominated by accusations of nepotism and Mrs. Golding held the seat by barely 700 votes, in what had previously been a stronghold for Labour. When the highly respected London M.P. Bernie Grant died, the local party rejected his wife as a replacement candidate, despite her being a popular activist with a lifetime's commitment to the party. There are a few relatives of famous former Members of Parliament in the House of Commons. One of these was the late Winston Churchill, grandson of the Wartime Prime Minister of the same name. His constituency in the midlands was in a different region from the one once held by his illustrious ancestor.

In his entertaining and informative book, "The Straightjacket Society," the late Misao Miyamoto described the thankless lives of Japan's so-called elite bureaucrats. Miyamoto, himself a former bureaucrat told of men who worked so long, that in their offices, couches are provided for them to make use of when they have missed the last train (generally between midnight and 1 a.m.) and have already given up hope of returning home that night. The bureaucrats seem to have the most miserable existence imaginable, one bordering on the masochistic. It seems strange indeed that to enter the ranks of the bureaucracy was for long one of the most sought after prizes of university graduates. Miyamoto's feeling was that they wanted everyone to suffer the same gruelling workload that they struggled on with.

Attempts to reform the bureaucracy have been stiffly resisted. Indeed, for a while, it seemed that such plans had been put indefinitely on the back burner. Fixing the economy was of course the overriding priority. By the spring of 2001 the number of ministries was reduced from 22 to about 13. This was a start, but only a very small one.

It could be argued that until these self-serving people are cut down to size, they will work hard to block anything that threatens the status quo and their dominant position. Certainly Japan's bureaucrats must sense the rising tide of contempt, if not hostility the public feels towards these once-highly-respected men. During the late 90s, hardly a week seemed to go by without yet another scandal involving one ministry official or another. It was almost as if they were trying to commit a bureaucratic hara kiri. By mid- 2002, one poll showed that under a quarter of Japanese people had a favourable view of the bureaucrats and about 70% regarded them with varying degrees of contempt.

In Britain, the bureaucracy is known as the Civil Service. While certainly strong, it was never as directly controlling of the government as its Japanese counterpart. During the 1980s Thatcher stripped the Civil Service of much of its power, even removing the rights of defense workers to strike, in a case that won them much sympathy. They were finally given back that right by the incoming Blair government in 1997.

Perhaps it is surprising that Japan even retains the level of democracy that it does. The widespread use of loudspeakers is, to many observers, evidence of a lingering authoritarian mindset. A relic of Japan's militaristic past between the two World Wars. No Western democracy makes such widespread use of them. Local Government broadcasts remind citizens to pay their taxes, to vote and there is even one for children where they play Dvořák's "New World Symphony" while telling them it is time to go home. It is as unpleasant and condescending as it is unnecessary.

Moreover, rightists are permitted to howl out their deafening, objectionable nonsense from the top of so-called sound trucks: armoured vans daubed with slogans flying the rising sun flag. Many wonder why the government tolerates such horrible noise pollution. One theory is that it prevents the rightists from turning to more violent means to get their brain-dead messages across to the masses. They certainly seem to have very limited direct support. Some argue they have their sympathizers in the LDP and the ear of reactionaries such as Ishihara, the former governor of Tokyo.

At election times, loudspeakers are also the main method that candidates employ during election campaigns. Basically, the vans ride around town, blaring out something to the effect that "My name is Sato of the XYZ Party, please vote for me." It takes the place of door-to-door canvassing by election workers, which rather oddly is banned. Surely it would not be any greater an annoyance than having all that yelling into microphones to have a couple of canvassers on the doorstep who you could simply tell to go away.

One way in which Japanese and British politics are similar is that in America issues such as school prayer and abortion rights regularly overshadow other concerns, while in Britain and Japan, they do not. At the time of writing, there are thankfully few signs that they will either for the foreseeable future. Even when former Tory leader William Hague made some remarks regarding limiting the term for a legal abortion, few saw it as anything other than a cynical move to shore up the small religious vote and buttress his hard-right credentials.

Neither Britain nor Japan has anything comparable to the American "religious right." School prayer is virtually a non-issue and a clear majority of British and Japanese are pro-choice regarding the question of abortion as a personal, not a political concern. In the 1997 election in Britain, an anti-abortion party emerged that won just a handful of votes. None of the major political parties in Britain or Japan has any intention of making an issue out of abortion. In Britain, any party that made outlawing the procedure part of its manifesto would surely lose far more votes than it gained, in Japan too, in all probability. In this light, Hague's comments did more to question his political savvy than anything else. During the 2005 election, there was again some mention of reducing the 24-week period in which a woman can legally have a termination. The resulting outcry led all three main party leaders to back off from any suggestion that they were seeking to limit abortion, much less even to make a political issue of it.

In many parts of America the religious right or the Tea Party movement effectively controls the Republican Party and has forced it to adopt much of its intolerant, extremist agenda. In Japan, one of the parties in the governing coalition, New Komeito is backed by the Buddhist Soka Gakkai. Its policies though are pretty much middle of the road. There are some in Japan though who fear that Komeito may have a "hidden agenda" of eating into the LDP's core vote and becoming increasingly powerful. Perhaps the fact that they lost several seats at the last election and currently hold only about thirty suggests that their plan isn't working out very well at the moment! Komeito became a vote-gathering machine for the LDP. Following the ouster of the LDP from power in 2009, Komeito distanced itself somewhat from its erstwhile ally for a time.

In Britain and Japan, parties do make vague noises about moral issues from time to time. John Major tried this approach and watched it fail miserably. He dubbed it his "Back to Basics" campaign, but it was overshadowed by scandal after scandal involving Members of Parliament from his ruling Conservative Party. It made a mockery of his attempts to raise standards in public life, when his own people were seen to be wallowing in sleazy deals, taking bribes, having extramarital affairs and the rest. (Ironic indeed, that after he had left office, it was revealed that he had been having an affair with Edwina Currie, a married female member of his cabinet.)

In Britain, many religious voters tend to vote Conservative but a fair number support Labour or the Liberal Democrats. One poll of Church of England Vicars in the 1980s showed that half of them were Liberals and only about a quarter preferred the Conservatives. Indeed, former UK Prime Minister, Tony Blair regarded himself as a born-again Christian and was quite open about his deeply held religious convictions. This is a rarity in British political life, not to mention Japan.

In Japan, some teachers in the last decade of the 20th century waged a campaign against the singing of the national anthem and raising the "Hinomaru" (rising sun or circle of the sun) flag at school ceremonies. They regard it as being too closely associated with Japan's militaristic past. For the most part, though, the Japanese come across as almost wholly apolitical. They have some sense that things are not quite right, but like a layperson with a broken leg, have little idea of what needs doing in order to fix it. The same applied to many of the corrupt, self-serving and aimless politicians of the Liberal Democratic Party of Japan.

The same situation existed in the UK in 2005. Blair was widely disliked and distrusted for the perception that he lied in order to take Britain into the Iraq War. He won again and again due to the utterly ineffectual opposition. Britain and Japan alike have a large apathetic population that holds the government in contempt. They increasingly refuse to participate in the democratic process. It is sometimes said that the public is more concerned with the outcome of a vote on a reality TV programme such as "Big Brother" or "Survivor " than as to who will be running the government for the next five years. The writer William Connolly was describing Western democracy when he argues that "Any set of norms or standards that become endowed with authority and legitimacy represents an ambiguous achievement, since it will establish its hegemony by excluding and denigrating forms of otherness which do not fit into its confines. Modernity prefers the discipline of social harmony and the ideal of a self-inclusive community." Cultural comparison is often no more than a question of identifying to what degree something is focused upon and to what degree it is enforced. This applies to a far greater extent within Japanese society.

The Los Angeles Times of late summer 1998, regarding the sorry state of politics in Japan: "Much touted electoral reform has failed to deliver one-man-one-vote, enabling rural interests (the farm vote) to dominate party debates. The old guard of the LDP clings to power." This refers to the disparity between city and country where it sometimes takes as many as two and-a-half times more votes to elect a politician from an urban as from a rural seat.

In August 2000 there were rumblings of discontent coming from many younger LDP members. They were increasingly frustrated with both Prime Minister Mori's bumbling performance and the "business as usual" attitude of the old guard. Moreover, recent polls showed that the LDP was regarded as being "old fashioned" and even irrelevant by many people, including some of its supporters. Two years on the initially massively popular Junichiro Koizumi was seen as a busted flush, not far off being a stopgap prime minister until someone else could fill the suit. He began to revive strongly in the autumn of 2002 with the self-destructive tendencies of the Japanese opposition helping him along.

Periodically, there was talk of the odious Ishihara forming a new political party and surging to power on a populist wave. However, by 2005 Ishihara was said by some pundits to be losing interest in politics, rarely attending meetings of the Tokyo Government and concentrating on writing a novel. Regardless of Ishihara, the mainstream of politics in Japan has moved towards a more nationalistic stance. Using the Self Defense forces as peacekeepers in foreign lands is no longer regarded as an extreme position and many Japanese political opinion leaders are urging more aggressive foreign policy from the LDP.

The stage was set for further realignments in Japanese politics, one that some suggested could conceivably see the breakup of the LDP and the beginning of genuine political change.

In June of 2006, Koizumi was on the point of retiring after his five-year tenure. The LDP was "in tatters" according to the Yomiuri report.   Tamisuke Watanuki, leader of a minor political grouping, the People's New Party complained:"Koizumi has turned Japan from a democracy to a dictatorship where everyone must do whatever he tells them to."   He had been a thirty-year veteran member of the LDP until Koizumi unilaterally dissolved the Lower House over the question of postal privatization.   Abe, who succeeded Koizumi, was seen to be a hard-liner in his image.   The LDP no longer has the "iron triangle" of Government, bureaucrats and big business that virtually assured its continued dominance.

One year on and the LDP was demolished in elections to the less powerful Upper House, winning just 87 seats to the 110 gathered by the Democrats. For the first time ever, the opposition had a clear majority, although it would not prevent the LDP remaining in power, it was seen as a foretaste of things to come. Talk was of the sun finally setting on the LDP's long hold on power.

In the UK, in complete contrast, Gordon Brown was steadily sinking in his bumbling performance as prime minister and it finally seemed conceivable that the Conservatives would return to power after the General Election expected by the spring of 2010 at the latest.

After an inconclusive election, the Conservatives failed to secure an outright majority and were compelled to go into coalition with the Liberal Democrats. Even with the supine attitude of their junior partners, who saw their principles along with their electoral support melt away under the glare of government, the Tories were not entirely able to enact every aspect of their hard right agenda. Nevertheless, UK politics tacked strongly to the right from that moment on.

The seemingly inexorable rise of the anti-EU United Kingdom Independence Party suggested the distinct possibility it would make significant gains in the 2015 UK general election, conceivably even hold the balance of power. This is another sign that UK politics may be trending towards right wing populism. The same has happened across much of Europe.   In the event, UKIP won around

13% of the vote but only one seat. Since then, it seems to have stalled in the polls leaving Britain firmly in the grip of the Conservatives with an ineffectual and divided opposition. This is similar to the situation in Japan.

Finally in August 2009, the LDP faced its electoral Armageddon. It won just 25% of the vote and about as many Lower House seats. The Democratic Party of Japan swept to power in a landslide. A few months later, the LDP was languishing with just 20% support and seemingly on the brink of breaking up. However, the ongoing financial scandals swirling around Democratic Party bigwig Ozawa and others suggest that simply "changing the head on the suit" has yet to usher in the kind of sweeping reforms and the clean-up that many in Japan so enthusiastically endorsed back in the sweltering summer when they thought they might be making a difference.

Three years later the LDP returned to power in a landslide and the opposition was reduced to a scattered collection of minor parties. Welcome back to business as usual.

SOURCES

(1)   Daily Yomuiri

(2)   The Pacific Century page 207

(3)   Quote taken from "The Intellectuals and the Masses" by John Carey
         (Faber & Faber)

(4)   Ken Livingstone quote from Huffington Post April 8th, 2013

NATIONAL CHARACTER AND SUCH

"Ugly Americans, Ugly Japanese" proclaims the title of a book by Min-Byoung-Chul and Nevitt Reagan. This undemanding, somewhat lighthearted comparison of what Japanese and Americans find strange, incomprehensible, or just plain offensive about each others' customs and habits afforded me an amusing afternoon's reading and a useful way to introduce this chapter. This chapter serves, in a somewhat less that totally serious manner, to highlight a few of the character traits and distinctive features of the Japanese and the British. Once more, this seems to demonstrate the tendency for Britain regularly to fall somewhere in between Japan and the USA.

The book details ways in which Americans and Japanese find each other's behaviour irritating, rude and even distasteful. It relates how Americans cause offense in a number of ways when in the company of Japanese. These personal foul-ups include such offenses as sitting on the desk while at work or when teaching in front of a class; chewing on a pen or pencil; talking or laughing too loudly or excitedly when in public; chewing gum in certain social situations, eating while they walk down the street; drinking from bottles and one thing guaranteed to annoy almost all Japanese people: getting overtly physical and assuming it is fine to be on first-name terms with superiors. Blowing your nose into a handkerchief is also a social gaffe.

On the other side of the fence, Japanese cause varying degrees of offense to Americans when they make a horrid slurping noise when eating noodles or drinking coffee. Americans complain they eat too fast, which is rude. (A good example of just how much this is a question of degrees is that I never noticed that Japanese people tend to eat so quickly until someone mentioned it to me. I am an extremely fast eater.) They also tend to talk with their mouths full of food, something that is regarded as pretty bad form in many Western countries. Some Japanese repeatedly snivel disgustingly rather than getting it over by blowing their noses (in the belief that to do so publicly would be rude!) Vomiting and urinating in public are usually socially unacceptable in the West, especially when done so openly and with such little sense of shame or embarrassment. Sucking air through their teeth, closing their eyes at business and other kinds of meetings (and therefore seeming to have fallen asleep) pushing and shoving on trains and in other crowded places, being so infuriatingly vague and so on.

That's quite a list. It's best to always keep in mind how such things are measured in degrees. I have met extremely tactile Japanese, really uptight and formal Americans and English people who have no problem with publicly relieving themselves in the street after a few drinks down the pub. Here we are dealing with averages and means and are obliged to recycle the trusty old phrase "in general" once again.

So why do these actions, seemingly innocuous to the overwhelming majority in one culture cause reactions ranging from minor irritation to outright disgust in the other? I see the answer as relatively straightforward. Psychologists have coined the expression "cognitive dissonance" to describe a kind of mismatch between our expectations and the fact of what actually transpires in any given situation. This can, for example be the awkwardness felt when two people that you like equally as friends can't stand each other. You care about them both, but they can't abide being in the same room. Two plus two suddenly doesn't appear to equal four and this can be a really disconcerting experience.

In America, most of this would be considered no different from the behaviour of children who don't know any better. Likewise, the actions that Japanese dislike in Americans also strike them as being immature. In both cases, the observer is seeing adults performing like badly raised children and it is just too much for them to shrug off. An American child is regularly reminded to eat quietly, or not so fast; likewise, Japanese learn from an early age that sitting on desks, or being too informal with a senior figure is unacceptable.

Indeed, it is interesting to recall the comment attributed to General Douglas MacArthur during the early days of the Occupation after World War Two. He likened the Japanese to a nation of twelve-year-old children. It would surely have surprised him to learn that in all probability, there were plenty of those among his hosts who were having precisely the same thoughts about his little entourage!

You might expect to find that Britons more or less line up with Americans against the Japanese when it comes to what is and isn't regarded as "proper." This isn't always the case.

Smoking

Many Americans are outraged by smoking in public to an extent that is incomprehensible to most Japanese and until the past decade, to many British people. In Britain, attitudes have calcified steadily since the turn of the century, until around 2007 there was rarely the kind of Puritanical over-reaction that has become all too familiar in contemporary America.

A few Japanese often appeared to think they had the God-given right to smoke anywhere they please and "No-Smoking" signs were routinely ignored. By the late 1990s, there were more smoking restrictions in Britain than in Japan, but less than in many parts of the United States. To a far greater extent, British people tended not to complain anything like as much as Americans when somebody lit up. British pubs often had "No-Smoking" sections, but I remember seeing people emerge from them, pick up ashtrays and return to their seats. I recall a very witty sign in a wine bar in my hometown that read: "Yes we have a no-smoking area – You can chose not to smoke anywhere you want to!" In 1999 around 29% of Britons smoked, compared with about a quarter of Americans and 35% of Japanese. Ten years later, this was about 22% in the UK to around 30% in Japan.

By 2005, the PC brigade was making threatening noises about a blanket ban on smoking in public in the UK, including bars and pubs. In 2006, the Government passed a bill that in the summer of 2007, effectively banned yet another pleasure in the name of the politically correct thought police that increasingly call the shots. Numerous pubs have closed since and many smokers have chosen to drink cheap supermarket beer at home rather than endure the stupidity of being banished outside to get their nicotine fix.

The Japanese are far more sensible. They have no smoking times in some restaurants and on stations, the area around most stations is non-smoking and separate sections for smokers and non-smokers are commonplace in most restaurants. In all, they seem far more adult about it that the wild over reaction that characterizes the health fascism rampant both in the UK and USA.

Get your Feet off the Table and Other Table Manners

Americans will sit on, or put their feet on a desk. This is less acceptable in Britain; it's just too informal for a lot of people. Likewise, regarding chewing gum, another habit that in Britain is frowned upon in "polite" society we have yet another activity that some are calling for to be banned.

Granted, Britons and Americans alike often share a strong dislike of those that eat noisily. Many British people find noodle slurping just as gross as Americans. A few years ago, in one of the Monty Python films, there was a scene that would have been incomprehensible to the Japanese, yet sickeningly funny to British (and other Westerners.) In the short sketch, an impossibly obese man sits in the centre of a crowded restaurant slurping his soup, tea and whatever else the harried waiter rushed to bring to his groaning table. His fellow diners become increasingly overcome with disgust, until at last the gigantic man of bad manners manages to explode from over eating.

Indeed, when enjoying breakfast in a London Hotel a couple of years ago with my Japanese wife, she commented how eerily silent the room was. It was full of people steadily consuming their food without speaking or making a sound. Eating too fast or talking with a mouthful of food is also unacceptable at most British dinner tables.

However should an American drink from a bottle, there will still be those mainly older Britons who will be more than a tad offended. This is not nearly the taboo it once was, but still is regarded as being somewhat low class; confined mainly to beer-swilling louts in pubs.

Self-effacing, who me?

American's tend to blow their own trumpets more than the typical British person. Here, the British tend to be annoyingly like the Japanese in being so irritatingly self-effacing. The same "grin and bear it" attitude that the Japanese call "gaman suru" (literally, "to endure".) There was an amusing article on the BBC Internet at the end of 1999 about how over half of the Britons surveyed reckoned they would hide their feelings from family members when given a Christmas present that is not appreciated.

I have heard it said by American friends many times in the past that they see both the Japanese and English as being so vague and indirect. They also reckon that in both cultures, there seems far less of a spirit of adventure than back home. One American acquaintance believes it is a downside of the education systems of both countries and the Welfare State, which encourage what he described as a culture of dependency.

Of course, there are plenty of ways in which Britons are closer to their American cousins. Both share the strong sense that "work" and "play" should be kept separate. This is something that the younger Japanese are beginning to accept. It's not that they don't work hard, just that hanging out with colleagues in bars after hours, or going to hot springs together with other company members on a weekend is not most Westerners idea of a good time. (Nor is it for many of the Japanese who feel obliged to go along with the majority.)

British people can be just as sarcastic as Americans often are said to be. Indeed, many Japanese people complain that they cannot understand Western humor for this reason. I find this strange as much of what passes for comedy on Japanese television seems regularly to be based on subjecting the victim/guest to little more than cruelty and abject humiliation.

So What do Americans Think Anyway?

Former Senate Majority Leader George Mitchell "I don't want to take anything away from the British and the Irish. They are warm and wise and articulate. But sometimes you get the feeling these guys are so articulate they could go on talking forever. Americans are more likely to say: 'Enough already, let's get the thing done.'" He was referring to the Northern Ireland peace deal, in which he played a major role. He could just as well have been describing the Japanese with their endless meetings and discussions of minor points of order. Another American working in Britain commented "They (The British) worry endlessly about rules and procedure, you know, doing things the way they've always been done." Does this remind you of another nationality we've been speaking of? (From the Washington Post of January 18th, 2000)

The late Edwin O Reischauer, the former US ambassador to Japan also saw similarities between the character of British and Japanese people.

"The Japanese are figuratively, as well as literally, an insular people, like the English but in a very different way. The British are conscious of themselves with a certain air of self-satisfaction, which is by no means wholly unjustified. Japanese self-consciousness contains a large degree of embarrassment and the fear of being thought of as inferior. Perhaps the difference is that between a people isolated enough to feel slightly set apart and a people so isolated throughout their history as to have feared that they did not belong at all."

Broadly speaking, I believe Reischauer was right, although I doubt somehow that the Japanese are particularly fearful of not belonging. They share with the British a high degree of self-containment, part of which obviously comes from being an island nation historically able to keep their neighbours at bay. Britain has not been successfully invaded since 1066 and until the US occupation of 1945-52 and subsequently the presence of several US bases, Japan had never seen a foreign army on its soil, save for the foiled invasion of the Mongols back in the thirteenth century.

I would suggest that instead of having any feelings of inferiority, the Japanese are quick to point out how "This is Japan and that's the only way you can do it here." Some older Japanese still seem to cling to the belief that they are a unique people. This often makes them appear arrogant or insensitive to other cultures and sometimes, just plain silly.

On the other hand, the naturalized civil rights campaigner Dr. Debito Arudo believes the Japanese have an inferiority complex when it comes to the West. The 19th Century education pioneer Yukichi Fukuzawa (1835 – 1901) argued that Japan should "quit Asia and enter Europe."

"So that's what happened" continued Arudo. "Over several decades, Japan industrialized, militarized, colonized and adopted the fashions and trappings of "Western civilization". Japan sought recognition and acceptance from the West…but that didn't happen." Few Japanese regard themselves as being part of Asia and yet they are not specifically "Western" either as a result.

In the late 1990s a major Japanese car manufacturer set up a factory in the north of England. They created a lot of ill will by trying to force the employees to perform group exercises every morning before work and to sing the company song. Such practices are common in Japan, but most Westerners feel they are being treated like children, or that their intelligence is being insulted when expected to take part in such (to them) idiotic activities. Just a little research on the part of the Japanese investors, followed by some adjustment to their usual manner of doing business would have saved them so much trouble.

That's the way we do it here.

A Japanese writer, Itasaka Gen in his generally informative book "100 Tough Questions for Japan" frequently was able to give illuminating responses to queries about various aspects of Japanese culture. However, whenever he was stumped, he resorted to the same banality as anyone else.

He defended the Japanese custom of noisily sucking noodles up like human vacuum cleaners with the curt "Japanese food should be eaten following rules applied to Japanese food." He also made some rather sorry reference to the fact that noodles are hot and need to be cooled by taking in air at the same time. There is no necessity involved. I can and do eat noodles without making a sound and manage not to burn my mouth either. Indeed, if we take his absurd advice, then we should all be eating curry with our hands, as this is regarded as being the "proper" way for many on the Indian subcontinent. There is no such underlying reason, it's a custom and that's all there is to it. Sometimes enduring the revolting spectacle of unwitting Japanese attempting to eat pasta as they do noodles I recall Itasaka-San's advice and imagine he would be rather flummoxed.

Britons can be just as foolish as this when it comes to rules and customs which foreigners find absurd. Remember the old etiquette when it comes to tea drinking. We are supposed to extend the little finger when holding the cup, or some such nonsense. Elbows must not rest on the dinner table because it's "bad manners." There is no logic involved here at all. In this we can be just as dogmatic and childish as the Japanese. We insist: "That's how it is done," (and the inference is that if you don't know that, then you clearly aren't "one of us.")

Regional Rivalry

In Britain the sense of regional rivalry between North and South still exists to some extent although many would counter that a lot of it is decidedly tongue in cheek. Northerners accuse Southerners of being snobbish, pretentious or soft, for example. On the other hand, southern people might dismiss Northerners as being ignorant or rude. Then there were the stereotypic images of granite-faced Northerners in cloth-caps walking their pet whippets. Southerners were lambasted for being shallow, greedy yuppies supping cocktails in pretentious wine bars and talking about their portfolio of stocks.

In Japan, they have something much the same. Tokyo people regard the citizens of Osaka as being rude, while Osaka folk think Tokyo is largely peopled by snobs. Then there are regional food rivalries. In the North of England, they have their "mushy peas" (mashed green peas) and "black pudding" (a kind of sausage containing pigs blood) that most Southerners eschew. Likewise in Japan, there is "natto," fermented soybeans, the taste is very vaguely like baked beans marinated in Marmite. People in the Tokyo area often love natto, but it finds far fewer takers in and around Osaka and the Kansai (Eastern plain) Area in general. This kind of silliness is probably worse in Britain, on balance.

The effect of television has, to some extent, helped to smooth out the edges of regional accents in both countries, but not by much. Tokyo Japanese has replaced Kyoto and Osaka as the "standard dialect" to such an extent, that a pronounced Kansai accent can be seen as a handicap when job-hunting. In England, what is called "Essex English" has taken over from the Received Pronunciation of the Royal Family as the norm for much of Southern and Central Britain. Once considered a mark of education, those who speak with the plummy tones of the Queen are often mocked for sounding stuck up or pompous. The "Estuary dialect" as it is also known falls somewhere between the English of working class London and of more educated tones. The former PM John Major is a good example, with his "I wunt to go to London."

Animal Rights and Wrongs

When it comes to the attitude towards Animals, both countries are pretty similar. Britain is of course rooted in the Christian belief that humanity is the master of the world and all living things upon it are there for our use. Hence we have the cruelty towards animals and the wholesale rape of the planet that can be justified by scanning through the Scriptures. In Japan Buddhist edicts formerly forbade eating meat, but some feel that this never stopped the Japanese attitude being similarly abusive.

Japan continues to hunt whales, to the disgust of much of the rest of the world. Even Russia has scaled back the catch to a small number per year, perhaps worried about the threat of sanctions and boycotts. Japan cannot be swayed by such concerns. Until 2005, Britain maintained the 300-year-old tradition of foxhunting, which almost two thirds of the British public (myself included) found distasteful.

If Japan were to end whaling, it would please many foreign critics. It might also win Japan some much-needed international goodwill. The ban on foxhunting pleased a majority in Britain. It was very much a minority activity since less than half a percentage point of the population either hunted or followed the chase on foot. It is doubtful that anyone much outside of the UK gave a damn either way. A ban was finally enforced in early 2005, but it remains possible that should the Conservatives ever win a future election outright they would reverse this.

A Mori opinion poll confirmed my impression that a lot of Japanese couldn't care less about whether or not they have whale meat on the table. Conducted in May 2000, it showed that 55% had no opinion or were indifferent, while less than 20% actually supported resumption of commercial whaling. Most under the age of thirty have hardly ever eaten whale in any case and few would choose to even if it were readily available the poll showed. In 2014 under 5% of the Japanese population admitted to regularly consuming whale meat.

They object more to what they see as prejudice and double standards by the rest of the world. Likewise, even in the most conservative heartlands of the British countryside, polls show that nearly 60% of the people were in support of a hunting ban, as against over 80% in the cities. In the same manner as the Japanese regarding whaling, they feel slighted at the attitude of city politicians, outsiders who ignore real problems such as rural poverty and run-down bus services.

They have a point. Modern politics in the UK seems to have degenerated into a tepid stew of social engineering and gimmicks rather than tackling the real issues that are not so easily swept under the carpet. Over 100,000 country people demonstrated in London against what they saw as neglect and arrogance on the part of the government in early 1999 and a larger number in 2002 when the foxhunting issue was again being hotly debated.

Of course there is hypocrisy on both sides. Pro-whaling countries such as Japan are seen to be showing that they couldn't care less about the feelings of anyone but themselves. The anti-whaling fraternity is often less vocal about the issue of battery farming and other practices that are just as obviously cruel to animals. Whaling was revived by the Occupation forces after World War Two. It would hardly exist today but for MacArthur's efforts to find a cheap source of protein. The irony of this seems to be lost on the American and European protesters.

As for foxhunting, its supporters' claim that it is a form of culling is pathetic. It is indiscriminate killing and nothing else. Without grants and subsidies funded from the taxes of city people, the rural community couldn't survive. Many feel it is only reasonable that those who pay for something, being the urban taxpayers, have a right to demand at least some say in how things are run. Opponents of foxhunting were often hypocritical too, pretending not to be anti-elite, when many of them openly hated the aristocracy and saw the foxhunting issue as an excuse to have a go at what they regarded as the arrogance of obnoxious and pompous upper class twits.

With or without a ban, whaling in Japan is in terminal decline in any case. The average age of whalers is now over 60. Many of their sons are unwilling to continue the tradition, preferring to enter a less arduous profession with a more secure future. If commercial whaling were resumed, it is doubtful that the industry could survive in Japan. Many young Japanese admit they find the taste of whale to be unpalatable. Likewise in Britain, foxhunting had been slowly declining for years, although ironically the ban might have revived interest for the time being. Increased urban sprawl and the steadily strengthening animal rights lobby would perhaps have seen an end to this vile activity regardless of whether or not the prevaricating Blair administration finally got around to outlawing it. The possibility of a foxhunting ban was used as a carrot dangled in front of the radicals just as the issue of abortion is exploited in the USA by the Republicans to placate the extreme religious right.

Food, Glorious and Otherwise

Regarding food, you might think that no two countries could be more dissimilar than Japan and Britain. The American humorist Dave Barry quipped "English food is like industrial fuel; it will keep you alive in the short term but it will kill you in the long term!" He also said "English food is fine, so long as you like the internal organs of some animal sautéed in fat and dumped on a dish in front of you."

Among Continental Europeans, British cooking has long been little short of a joke. They sneer at the soggy vegetables, greasy meat, chips (French fries) with everything and daunting pies with the consistency of Pre-Cambrian fossils. Some say the obsession with overcooking everything can be traced to the 19th century "Mrs. Beaton's Cookbook." It allegedly recommended that all vegetables be boiled for at least 45 minutes. Britons have one of the highest rates of heart disease in Europe and yet one of the lowest percentages of smokers. Most doctors regard the diet to be a contributory factor.

In complete contrast, Japanese food is arguably the healthiest national cuisine in the world; its only bad points being a lack of roughage and too much salt. Indeed, if you replace white rice with brown, that is basically the macrobiotic diet favoured by some lovers of health food (which is based on traditional Japanese food.) Japanese food means a lot of rice, some fish or tofu, not a lot of meat and plenty of vegetables.

The fundamentals of British and Japanese food are similar and not at completely opposite ends of the culinary spectrum. Both are simple and rely on only a few basic ingredients. In Britain, that is three vegetables, being typically potatoes, carrots and green peas, some meat, or sometimes fish and of course tomato ketchup. Lots of tomato ketchup. In Japan, they need only rice some soybean product like tofu or miso soup, fish, or sometimes meat, a few pickles and of course soy sauce, plenty of soy sauce. Japanese food is typically fried in corn oil, whereas traditional English food used animal fat, although recently corn oil is becoming more popular.

Japanese food doesn't hold all the aces, though. In Japan, they have what is called "shoku-pan" or table bread. It is tasteless, soft, lacking any trace of fibre, with the consistency of silly putty. Granted it is a matter of personal preference, but to this writer brought up on crusty whole-meal loaves of brown bread, shokupan is inedible garbage. So why do the Japanese prefer such atrocious bread? Possibly this is due to their dislike of having to chew anything for long. Since the Heian Period, the Japanese have favoured soft foods, that being one reason why brown rice is unpopular. White rice was originally reserved for the aristocracy. Thus white bread was perhaps seen as being suitable for those of more refined palates.   My Japanese friend, Rie who I quoted in the chapter on education said: "Generally speaking, I like English food (she is atypical here as many Japanese visitors are less than enthusiastic) but one thing I couldn't stand was the awful bread." I rest my case about it all being a matter of taste!

The first main difference here is in presentation. A Japanese meal is set out beautifully, each food item or dish with its own little bowl. How a meal first appears is just as important as how it tastes. Often a British meal is unceremoniously dumped on one big plate. The staple foods of both countries are quite similar, namely rice and potatoes, both of which are basically starch. Neither is native, each having been introduced from overseas. The potato arrived from America in the 1600s, but was scorned as a food item right up until the early 19th century. It was used primarily as animal feed and sometimes even sold on freezing winter evenings to passers by that grasped a hot baked potato between gloved hands to warm them then later discarded it.

According to the latest research, settlers that crossed over to Japan from the Upper Yellow River in China introduced rice cultivation. The beginning of wet-rice growing in paddy fields marked the end of the hunter-gatherer Jomon Period and the start of the Yayoi Period when the Japanese switched to farming around 300 BC.

Some would say that Japanese and British eating habits are growing closer. Those of the British are improving (they could hardly get much worse) while those of the Japanese are rapidly going downhill with the brakes off. There are actually not so many Japanese people who eat only Japanese food except perhaps for some senior citizens, Zen Buddhist monks and perhaps a few traditionalists here and there.

In Britain, there is far more variety available than even twenty five years ago, mainly thanks to increased trade. Stir-fry dishes and pasta have become far more popular and curry is said to have practically taken over as the national dish. Most supermarkets have a bewildering array of exotic canned and dried foods from around the world. The downside of this is that people routinely buy something they haven't a clue how to prepare and end up throwing it away or ruining it. Every year, millions of pounds are wasted in this manner across the land.

Vegetarianism has gone from a cranky hippie fad in the late sixties to more or less mainstream respectability in the early 21st century. Estimates vary, but it seems that almost one Briton in ten now abstains mostly or totally from meat and fish. If the definition includes "semi vegetarians" or those who have given up most meat but still eat fish and sometimes chicken it's probably nearer 12 to 15% of the population. Some non-vegetarians have given up beef or at least cut their consumption down. This is partly due to health concerns, especially over the "Mad Cow Disease" that hit the headlines in the early 1990s. Vegetarianism increased in many countries, especially in Germany, Britain and Australia and to some extent in America.

It's interesting to note that in France, the number of vegetarians is reckoned to be less than 1% of the population. French food is like Chinese in some ways, in the large variety and in the presentation. Maybe that is part of the reason. In Britain, or Germany, the meat is staring right at you. In France, China and Japan, it is often much better disguised, or at least mixed in with the vegetables and other ingredients so it is more subtle.

Junk food may be ubiquitous in Britain as in much of the West, but for various reasons in Britain, some people are attracted to a flesh free diet. This does not automatically lead to a better diet. Some people replace the meat with more chips, snack foods and other junk leaving them no better off and with more calories. Then there was the counter-trend of the rather controversial Atkins diet, favoured by certain celebrities, that consists of meat and not much else.

By contrast, Japanese people consume more and more meat every year. Worse, purveyors of utter garbage ranging from chains such as McDonald's and marginally less unhealthy local imitators such as MosBurger have ballooned in popularity. Fast food has caught on more in Japan than almost anywhere. The reason seems to be that traditional Japanese food such as noodle dishes can be prepared in a soba restaurant in a few minutes. Likewise sushi can be in front of the customer in about the same time. The idea of eating a meal in a rush that is quickly prepared is nothing new to the Japanese. It's just an unhealthy modern version of an old custom.

Obesity is becoming an increasingly serious problem in Britain due to more sedentary lifestyles, car use and junk food. By 2014, the Overseas Development Institute, a UK think tank reported "In the UK, 64% of adults are classed as being overweight or obese. The report predicts a "huge increase" in heart attacks, strokes and diabetes."

In Japan there are similar trends emerging. One man in three is now classed as overweight. "If Japanese continue this lifestyle, you'll see a lot more people with diabetes," said Doctor Fuminori Katsukawa, of Keio University Sports Medicine Research Center in Tokyo.

One quarter of Japanese who had a checkup in 1998 were found to be suffering from some form of liver trouble. Western food and increased drinking were the main culprits in the words of the Japan Hospital Association. Japan may well hold the world record for longevity at the moment (83 for women and 78 for men) but this is unlikely to endure if the Japanese diet continues to overload on saturated fat laden junk.

Japanese attitudes towards vegetarianism range from incomprehension to outright hostility. Even those who eat fish, but no meat are treated as if they are in need of aversion therapy. In Britain, so long as they don't pester others to join them in their dietary choice most vegetarians are tolerated, sometimes even respected. A book appeared a few years ago in Japan urging older people to eat pork for their health. No less than a practicing doctor gave this advice! It's hard to imagine this in the West, where doctors are forever trying to persuade their patients to reduce their consumption of meat and fat.

Of course there are exceptions. In July 2000, a nutritionist in Britain raised more than a few hackles with his suggestion that humans need to make red meat the basis of their diets. He was slammed not only by vegetarian groups but also by the government's own advisor on good diet habits. He defended vegetarianism as being one of several healthy choices of diet. On the other hand, some UK doctors recently warned that strict vegetarians can run the risk of having too little protein in their diets. This can cause health problems later in life.

Back in the mid-nineties, when I told some women I taught that I take a regular multi-vitamin supplement one asked me whether or not I was sick. Another opined that taking vitamins was a waste of time and money since all I needed was to eat at least 34 food items a day. If this advice sounds like the kind of "Eat carrots to help you see in the dark" kind of wartime homily, that's because that's precisely what it is! During the Second World War, the military-led government carried out research to see if Japan could become self sufficient in food by eating all kinds of wild plants. The Japanese still clung to such ideas well into the nineties. Perhaps yet another effect of an education system that teaches them not to question anything but merely to memorize facts in order to pass tests. While the Western world has been popping vitamin pills for years, supplements have only caught on in Japan near the end of the 20th century.

I once asked a student, a middle-aged woman what was her favourite food. In class, we had been practicing asking each other about our likes, dislikes and favourite things. She looked blankly at me for a moment and replied. "I don't have a favourite food, I can eat anything." This is more a reflection on society than on her tastes. Japanese people learn to subdue such things as food preferences in the need to conform. I also knew a woman who bemoaned the fact that she couldn't stand some foods and wished she could learn to tolerate them, presumably so she would not stand out when eating with friends. Such self-denial is difficult for those raised in a Western country to relate to.

Criticism or Insult

Another way in which the Japanese differ from the British is in their inability to take criticism from outsiders. Again, this is another example of degrees, since some Britons will be pretty defensive, even about such things as the food. Offer even the mildest critique of some aspect of Japan to a Japanese person and they will frequently take it almost like a personal insult. They are incredibly thin-skinned in this way. The funny thing is that in private, among themselves, they are just as scathing about problems in their own society as any other nationality, but on the whole, they don't like to hear it from outsiders.

In contrast, British or American people will usually be open to at least some degree of debate about their homeland. (This may have changed in the USA of late.) My feeling is that the 250-year isolation of Japan inculcated a high degree of ritualized and regulated behaviour to the extent they could conceive of no other. Since the mid 90s, this has become less pronounced as problems with the moribund economy and in society as a whole have seen Japanese people increasingly coming to question every aspect of their country.

Class System

The British class system is well documented, with "class distinction still a part of life in this stratified nation." Even the way you talk in Britain "speaks volumes about you- your economic status, school, ancestry and such." This is also true of Japanese, in a different way. They have a rigidly hierarchical society, with the level of politeness varied according to the relative position of the speakers to each other. Graduation from one of the top universities such as Tokyo Daigaku virtually guaranteed a lucrative job in one of the top companies. This is another way in which Japan and Britain are closer to each other than The USA, which has (in theory at least) a far less class-bound society.

Care for Tea anyone?

The British share with the Japanese a love of tea, but it hasn't always been so. "In fact, Britons were coffee drinkers before they ever adopted tea as a national beverage. The first London coffeehouse was established in the 1650s before such places became popular in the US and there were 2,000 coffeehouses in London by the turn of the 18th century. Seen as a substitute for alehouses, they flourished as political literary and business hubs until the late 1800s, when tea drinking became more fashionable." (From an article in the Los Angeles Times)

In the late 1990s, Starbucks was seen successfully expanding its coffeehouses into Britain. Many people are perhaps unaware that this is reviving an old custom, not introducing something new. In Japan, as in Britain, coffee has its devotees, but tea is firmly number one. In contrast, US tea consumption is very modest.

The way in which tea is drunk is different. Traditionally, Japanese drank green tea without milk or sugar. In Britain, people favour darker teas with milk. Actually, tea first came to Japan over a thousand years ago, but for several hundred years it was used only for medicinal purposes.

Gardening

Both the Japanese and British are famous for a love of gardening. The traditional English garden usually wasn't restricted by space, with its huge well-manicured lawns, bushes and thick beds of roses and other flowers is the opposite of the traditional Japanese garden. Once again we can see the Western notion of dominion over nature here. The English garden is above all else Mother Nature tamed.

In Japan, the philosophy behind the traditional Japanese garden is an attempt to make it look as natural as possible, to imitate rather than overcome nature. The swirling patterns in the sand are meant to suggest seas, with rocks placed here and there to represent islands. Even gardeners of bonsai, the miniature trees are striving to make them look as much as possible as they would if growing wild, only on a far smaller scale. Bonsai is said to have originated in the middle ages, when people dug up trees which were stunted from growing high up on mountainsides and brought them back to care for. Japanese gardeners have long sought to create a sparse open feeling, which is perfectly natural given just how little space they are generally working with in the first place.

Emperors and Monarchs

Both Britain and Japan have a monarchy. In Britain, it is the House of Windsor, while in Japan they have the Chrysanthemum Throne. Both families can trace their lineage back over a thousand years, in Britain to William the Conqueror, in 1066, while the origins of the Japanese Imperial Family disappear into the stuff of mythology. Both are largely figureheads. In Europe, many countries such as Italy, Greece and France are former monarchies, while in East Asia, Korea, China and Vietnam have lost their Royal Families.

In 1889, the new Meiji Constitution enshrined the Emperor as the head of state. Thus the beginnings of State Shinto and his veneration began. Until 1945, the Emperor was revered by many as a living God, although the former Emperor Showa (Hirohito) insisted that he never regarded himself to be divine. The Emperor and his family live in virtual seclusion and are seen by the public only on special occasions. Most Japanese regard their monarchy with a kind of respectful disinterest, with the possible exception of Princess Masako, wife of the current Crown Prince, who has been compared to the late Lady Diana.

In Britain, however, the Royal Family could hardly be more different from their Japanese counterparts. Their dysfunctional family life is splashed all across the UK tabloid press, with tedious regularity. Three of the Queen's four children are divorced. Until the tragic death of Lady Diana in the summer of 1997, hardly a day passed without some story putting their sorry lives under the microscope. Since then, coverage has been considerably more restrained, although often just as critical.

In the last couple of decades of the twentieth century, the image of the House of Windsor suffered, especially that of the Queen and Prince Phillip. She was depicted as both cold blooded and vindictive. She is probably the wealthiest woman in Britain and yet she is infamous for her tight-fisted nature. The legend has it that she personally counts the cans and bottles in the royal pantry to ensure none have gone missing and she is said to give inexpensive bars of soap or handkerchiefs as Christmas presents.

Prince Phillip, her consort comes in for a regular press roasting. He is portrayed as being little short of a racist and a reactionary dinosaur, a bully who his children are still afraid of and someone for whom the term "political correctness" means voting for the Conservative Party. His "spin doctors" try without much success to smooth over the ruffled feathers of whoever he has managed to insult this time with his spectacularly tactless remarks and outbursts.

He once told British students studying in China not to stay there too long or they would end up "slitty-eyed!" One of his more recent gaffes was on a visit to a factory in Scotland in the autumn of 1999, when he remarked that a faulty switch "must have been made by some lazy Indian." Usually hard-working second and third generation Anglo-Indians were unimpressed by such comments. Indeed, there were immediate calls for him to be forcibly retired from public life once and for all. Lately, his grandson, Harry has been attracting much of the same scathing press comment for, amongst other things, being caught smoking marijuana and showing up to a costume party in a Nazi uniform. Perhaps tactless stupidity is hereditary. Even Prince Charles struggles to shake off the image of a cold, aloof man who was mainly to blame for his wife's unhappiness. He is regarded by some as a weirdo and by others as just plain out of touch.

The problems the UK Royal Family faced were not only the media's doing. In trying to be more open, they have destroyed the mystique that once surrounded them. After the reign of the unpopular King George ended, Queen Victoria successfully reinvented the Monarchy as a paragon of family values. The institution was seen to be stern, remote, reliable and above all scandal-free (or the scandals were mostly hushed up!) In fact, this was much like the image of the contemporary Imperial Family in Japan.

In the years since Diana's death, the Royal Family has made strenuous efforts to restore their tattered reputation, with a fair degree of success. Charles has regained some of the popularity he lost, although he was often criticized for his continuing obsession with foxhunting and in particular for indoctrinating his sons William and Henry into taking up this revolting pastime. Diana's sons, particularly William have become pin ups and the Queen Mother remained above reproach until her death. Ironic, since it is believed that behind her sweet old grandmother image she was one of the most vicious and vindictive of them all.

The press delighted in printing photos of William enjoying a cigarette behind the bicycle sheds of his school and of Harry caught smoking cannabis in 2002. "Harry Pothead" the press dubbed him after the fictional wizard Harry Potter.

Books have appeared which suggest that the relationship between the Queen and Charles is somewhat strained. Also that Charles and his father have as little contact as possible and in private speak directly to each other only when it is absolutely necessary.

Even so, few expect there will be a republic anytime soon in Britain. Too many people remain enamoured with the Monarchy. The need to grovel before these unelected figureheads is hotwired into the psyche of the nation. Support for a republic usually stands at between one quarter and always less than a third of the population. The only poll I have ever seen on the Japanese Imperial Family showed just 16% favoured their abolition, with nearly three quarters being supportive of the Emperor system.

Ultimately in the UK, changes to the constitution may eventually see the Monarch's role more sharply defined and the last vestiges of power finally transferred to Parliament. This would be pretty much like the situation in Japan, where the Emperor is purely a symbolic figurehead.

The Imperial Family is almost always treated with deference. They never give interviews for television programmes baring their souls as Diana did a few years ago. The press is generally circumspect, except for a few cases in some women's magazines. Even when the Empress Michiko appeared to suffer a severe depressive episode a few years ago, the newspapers were restrained in their coverage. Clearly the Royal House of Windsor could do worse than learn from them.

However, it is doubtful that the British Royals would envy the Imperial Family. They spend most of their time cooped up in one palace or another and it seems they simply cannot do something ordinary such as go to a play, a restaurant, or just hang out with their friends. The current Emperor caused uproar when he once went out with friends to a restaurant while still at college. Even as a schoolboy, he was acutely aware of the thankless task ahead of him: "You can all become whatever you want" he wrote in an essay on the subject of what vocation they would like to follow once they left school "But I have no choice but to become the great Emperor of my country." The Windsors at least have considerably more freedom. While the Imperial Family themselves seem above reproach, their minder the Imperial Household Agency is frequently chastised by the media for its paranoid spin-doctoring and control freakery. It is said to make the old Blair government in the UK look positively laid back by comparison.

The year 1999 ended on a somber note for the Imperial House with the sad news that 36 year-old Princess Masako had a miscarriage. Finally she gave birth to a daughter, merely reinforcing the dilemma facing the Japanese Royal Family; none of the Emperor's grandchildren were boys. By 2005, Misako had still failed to produce a male heir and was said to be suffering from depression, often keeping her out of the public eye. The suggestion that more than one member of the Royal Household is medicated for depression is openly debated in public, but there is nothing remotely like the relentless dissection of their lives that was the feeding frenzy that passes for reporting the news in UK tabloids. There was a strong probability that they would be obliged to amend the constitution to give daughters the right of succession.

In 2005, the issue was debated by the Diet. A clear majority of the public supported the idea, although traditionalists were aghast. In antiquity, Japan had empresses, the most recent of them ruled from 1762 to 1770, but this did not quell their misogynistic outrage. This change to the Royal Family in Britain has already been made, although it won't make any difference for quite a few years, since the first and second in line for the throne are both male. The wife of the second son of the Emperor bore a son in 2006 and that effectively ended the debate for the foreseeable future.

In the second decade of the 21st century, articles in which various members of the Imperial Family made mild but pointed criticisms of each other might be the prelude to the end of the era in which they are above reproach. The Japanese press seems increasingly to resemble the UK tabloids with its endless rehashing of theories on which members of the Imperial Family are on antidepressants and so forth. We shall see what happens in due course.

Let's go for a Drink!

Japan and Britain share a love of drinking and a drinking culture. In Mainland Europe and Asia, this varies from country to country. Korea and Taiwan, for example have similar drinking customs, while in Europe, Germans are renowned beer lovers. The French and Italians are regarded as being big wine drinkers, but much of this goes on in their homes. In Japan, sake is used even in some religious rites and is drunk by the bride and groom from three little cups at a Shinto wedding.

About 40 percent of Americans are either non-drinkers, or only have the occasional glass of wine or Champagne at Christmas time. The number of teetotalers in Britain is about 12% and perhaps 5 - 7% in Japan. Beer arrived in Britain soon after the Roman Invasion. In Japan, they were drinking rice wine (sake) at the beginning of recorded history. Beer became popular in the late 19th century following the re-opening of Japan to the West. Japanese beer is generally a lighter, larger type, while much British beer is darker and bitterer in taste (as its name suggests.)

The traditional pub, which was often family-run and the "izakaya" of Japan are very much alike in atmosphere. Often they were the social centres of their communities. Going for a drink after work or on weekends is a part of the culture in both Japan and Britain. In Japan, business is often done over drinks. This was true in 90s Britain too, but it was more likely to be at lunchtime rather than in the evening.

To be visibly drunk in public is often frowned on in the United States, due in part to the killjoy attitude of the Puritanical religious communities who have so much influence and power. In Britain, it is slightly more acceptable, or perhaps, tolerated. In Japan, there is almost no censure of such behaviour. It may come as no surprise that Britain and Japan are among a small number of developed industrial nations where the intake of alcoholic beverages has steadily increased rather than remaining level or slightly falling. One in twenty Britons are reckoned to be alcoholics, about the same number as in Japan. Some 25% of Britons are said to "self medicate" with fairly heavy home drinking, which is also commonplace in Japan.

Regarding drinking, both Britain and Japan share similarly foolish customs. In Britain, there is a tradition that when a group of people are in a pub together, each person takes turns to buy what is called a "round" or a drink for every other person. Anyone who wants to go slower than the rest either has to skip buying their own drink when it is their round, or leave the unfinished pints on the table. Those who want to drink faster are also forced to slow down if they are among moderate drinkers. In Japan, a group of drinkers will settle the bill at the end of the session in most cases. This also penalizes anyone who drinks and eats just a little, as they will be paying more than their share and once again, the heavy eaters and drinkers will get off lightly.

Both countries also have some downright stupid customs regarding drinking styles. In Japan, they call it "ikki-nomi" or basically "down in one gulp." This is common especially among university fraternities who pressure their members to down drink after drink in this fashion. Occasionally it leads to tragedies, such as the freshman university student who died from alcoholic poisoning after such a session a few years ago. His father started a campaign to try and stamp out this activity. In Britain, we can be just as irresponsible with our drinking contests and the "yard of ale." This is a nearly meter-long glass of beer, which must be drunk in one go. It seems, as I have observed before that idiocy knows no national boundaries.

Perhaps it is not surprising that since the mid-90s a lot of English and Irish style pubs have sprung up in and around Tokyo. They are popular with the locals and the expatriate community alike. One major difference is that the Japanese like to eat food with their beer, while most British people prefer just to drink. Even that may be changing, as in the UK having a bottle of beer especially real ale with lunch in the pub has gained in popularity.

Healthcare and Such Matters

The Japanese national medical insurance system is pretty similar to the UK Health Service. There is nothing surprising about this; Japan is one of many countries around the world that was inspired by Britain's pioneering 1945-51 Labour government's healthcare policies. Payment is based on income and for that everyone is entitled to basic healthcare. In Britain in the late 80s, about 6% of GDP went on healthcare as against nearly 9% in the United States. Prior to the introduction of "Obamacare" in America, about a quarter of the people had no medical insurance. I leave it to you to decide which is more efficient. The USA surely has the best medical know-how in the world and yet one of the most unequal healthcare systems.

The Conservative administrations in Britain from 1979-97 did their best to undermine the Health Service, but failed in their not-so-covert plans for privatization. The Health Service is strapped for cash and not in such good condition as of old, but remains ingrained into the fabric of British life. In Japan, medical care is generally pretty reasonable, although the standards vary from one hospital to the next.

In both countries, the drawback of easily affordable healthcare is what economists call the problem of "common resources" meaning something that is free or inexpensive tends to be over-used. Aristotle said: "What is common to many is taken least care of, for all men have greater regard for what is their own than for what they possess in common with others."

This means that in Britain and to a far greater degree, in Japan people trudge off to see their doctor often for the most trifling of ailments. It is standard practice for English workers to get a doctor's sick note and take several days off work. There are bound to be a few who abuse the system. The same thing happens in Japan. I know of a man in perfect health who hasn't worked for ten years and more. He claims his back and neck are excruciatingly painful, gets the necessary documents from his obliging healthcare provider and then goes off to play golf, after collecting his disability benefit.

The Japanese already have something akin to a phobia regarding dirt and germs. This may have its roots in Buddhist and Shinto ideals of ritual purity. Taken to extremes, we have the obsession in Japan with hygiene and a morbid fear of illness. Some Japanese with colds will don surgical masks in the belief they are helping slow the spread of disease; an absurd over-reaction. Such a gesture is seldom very effective, surgical masks are intended to protect the wearer from free floating germs, not the other way round. Whenever somebody sneezes, the pressure sends the virus through the gauze almost as easily as a mosquito passes through the strings of a tennis racquet. Some of the cheaper masks are little more than glorified coffee filters. It wouldn't be the first time and place where people have made themselves look stupid for nothing.

The Japanese are probably among the most heavily medicated people on the planet and yet at least half of the bewildering array of sprays, pills and tablets are barred from sale in the USA. This is simply because they fail to meet the standards set by the Food and Drug Administration. It has also left many of them with very low resistance to germs. Doctors in Britain and Japan have been the targets of criticism for over prescription of medication and in particular antibiotics. Some Japanese routinely rush off to the clinic for an injection whenever they have even the slightest cold. Both Britain and Japan have more than their fair share of incurable hypochondriacs. "Experts have warned of the dangers of creating an environment in which threats to health are overemphasized." Alarm bells have been sounded both in Japan, the USA and elsewhere.

In the late 1990s, on an Indonesian island, several Japanese went down with stomach ailments leading to fears that there had been an outbreak of cholera. In fact, it was nothing more than mild food poisoning. This was due to the Japanese tourists having no resistance to the bacteria that passed harmlessly through other foreign visitors and locals alike.

National Holidays

The Japanese have national holidays just as in Britain. Japanese New Year's Eve and Day are pretty much like Christmas in Britain. On New Year's Eve, most families watch variety programmes on TV and go to the shrine or temple at midnight. Then the following day, they visit relatives and eat and drink a lot of special food, known as "osechi ryori." This is not so different from what many British people do on Christmas Eve and Christmas Day. Presents are traditionally given twice a year, the mid-summer gifts (o-chu-gen) and the end-of year- presents (o-seibo).   At the same time as these presents are given, most Japanese also send cards.

There are those that complain the Japanese have adopted Christmas as a purely commercial venture without any interest in or understanding of the religious significance. This smacks of hypocrisy as in many countries of the West, none less than in Britain, this is all Christmas has come to represent for a lot of people.

New Year's Eve in Britain is traditionally a time of going to parties, or pubs and sometimes of seeing in the New Year in the town square. The Japanese do this several times over December with their "year-end" parties known as "bonenkai," so it's not surprising that they have had enough of drinking by New Year's Eve.

The Japanese have "O-bon" in the second week of August. This is where they believe the spirits of their ancestors return. They make offerings of food and light incense on the family shrine. This is quite similar to the "Day of the Dead" which is held on November 2nd in such countries as Mexico and Spain. It is also vaguely like the original meaning of Halloween.

Let the Train Take the Strain

As everyone surely knows, the train was invented in Britain. The first steam locomotive was built by Richard Trevethick in 1808 and used to haul coal in South Wales. In 1829, Stevenson's Rocket won the contest to be the first steam train to operate a passenger line between the northern towns of Stockton and Darlington. Soon there were scores of railway companies with their tracks crisscrossing the land. Japan built up its extensive network of railway lines beginning in the late 19th century. The first train line in Japan was completed in 1872 and ran between Tokyo and Yokohama. It was built by the British engineer, Edmund Morel. The Yamanote Line in Tokyo is a loop line, like the Circle Line of the London Underground, but not a subway.

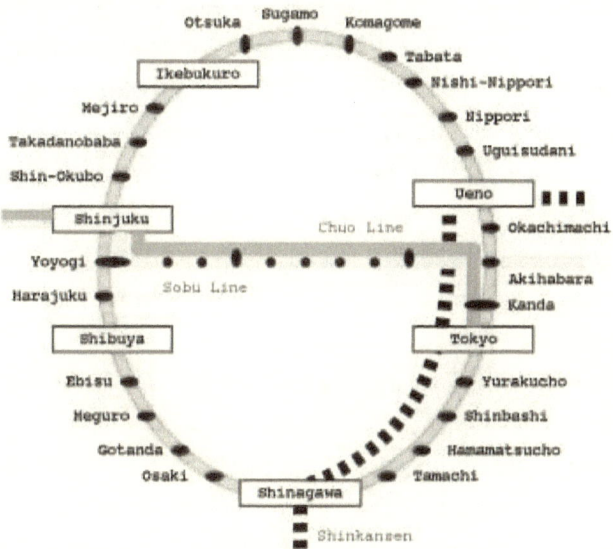

Yamanote Line Map

That's where the comparison ends. If a train is more than a couple of minutes late in Japan, there is a public apology over the loudspeakers. Britain's trains long had a reputation for being a national disgrace. Trains are frequently delayed and sometimes canceled altogether. The carriages are dirty and old. A cabinet minister once likened them to "cattle trucks."   The electronic timetables on each platform usually show two times for the next couple of trains due. One is the scheduled time and believe it or not, the other gives an estimate of the train's probable time of arrival! This can be anything up to half an hour later than scheduled in some cases. It is said the service has improved in the past few years, however.

Left – Stephenson's Rocket   Right – First Japanese steam train (1853)

The reasons for this are simple. There was under-investment by successive governments and cuts in the 1960s to many lines and on to the aggressive promotion of "car culture" by the Thatcher government in the 80s. It all served to undermine Britain's railways. It is said they have improved somewhat in the new century, but are still far below what many would regard as being satisfactory. Meanwhile, Japan goes on building Bullet Trains and only a suicide on the line will make a train late. The British can only dream of such things.

The Japanese Mother-in-Law and the British Mother-in-Law

Elsewhere I have described how the Japanese mother-in-law has a reputation for bullying her son's wife one that in some cases appears to be justified. However, in a recent survey carried out by the BBC and posted on their Internet page, it seems that a lot of British mothers-in-law disapprove of their son's choice of bride and a sizeable minority confessed to "disliking" or "hating" them. It went on to describe how a fair number of daughter's in law had much the same feeling about their husband's mother. Also, that many families disliked Christmas, as they dreaded getting together with their relatives, knowing there would be all manner of arguments and conflicts. It is not surprising that the UK divorce rate is said to peak in the months following the Christmas holidays!

Noise annoys, sometimes

One way in which the British and Japanese are at opposite ends of the spectrum is in their relative tolerance for noise. The Japanese seems to be as impervious to noise as the British are sensitive to it. In Japan, it is routine for "sound trucks" to blare out their moronic messages, be they rightists demanding that Russia return the Northern Isles to Japan or some form of advertising. Many shops have recordings of some pop song cranked up to excruciating levels, it seems. Even on the trains, there are endless, generally superfluous messages. Some of them remind us of which door to exit by and others exhort us not to leave our umbrellas behind. Few of them are genuinely needed. Some see this as evidence of an authoritarian mindset. I agree, but to me, it's just another example of the belief that "if something is good, then more of it must always be better." A visiting American psychologist commented that such an excess of noise pollution contributes to mental illness and greatly increases stress among those forced to endure it, even those who are oblivious of the racket around them. Existing laws could be used to stop some of this pollution, but they simply aren't enforced in almost all cases.

There actually is a "Group to Think about Loudspeaker Noise" in Japan, but it has a mere fifty or so members. Apart from making periodic complaints to Japan Railways about the horrible noise, they can't exactly claim stunning success in the campaign to persuade their fellow Japanese to give up on the loathsome cacophony all around them.

In Britain, complaints about noisy neighbours abound and there are strict regulations regarding the permissible level of decibels. There is also the Noise Abatement Society, with considerably more than fifty members! That's one of the other differences. In Britain, people actually get up and complain, while in Japan, they have been raised to conform and not to disturb the harmony of the group. That is ironic really, since noise pollution is a major disturbance to everyone's harmony, much of which could be eliminated at the flick of a switch, quite literally.

Traditions and Customs, in closing

Many things we regard as being traditions going back in to the mists of time are in fact often relatively recent. Take Christmas for example. The custom of sending Christmas cards began in Britain around 1843, not long after the first stamps were issued. The "traditional" red-suited Santa was popularized by American department stores at the turn of the 20th century, where they would have employees standing outside dressed as "Father Christmas" to attract customers. Even the Christmas tree was practically unknown outside of Lutheran Germany until Prince Albert persuaded his new bride, Queen Victoria to have one in the 1840s. The inspiration was said to have come to Martin Luther one icy winter night when he saw the stars twinkling through the branches of a pine tree.

Kabuki is as old as the plays of Shakespeare, but many Japanese customs are surprisingly recent in origin. The "traditional" sumo with its ranking and yokozuna grand champion is only a hundred years old. Christmas has been emphasized in the last couple of decades, but only as a sort of "lover's day" where young couples have a romantic Christmas dinner together. "Kami shibai" or slide shows for the kids only go back to the 1920s.

Arguably the most irritating device under the sun, the cell-phone, is a very recent phenomenon. In 1994, only a few Japanese had one, but by 2002 this had risen to over seventy percent, about the same as in Britain. What one critic called "the most impolite invention ever" has rapidly become indispensable and anyone under twenty five probably couldn't imagine it any other way.

A brief outline of my theory of cultural comparison

While writing this book, a few points occurred to me and I include them here. It is in the attempt to clarify my impressions of culture and how to approach the often-challenging task of comparing one with the other. I don't claim this is an exhaustive list and by no means is it supposed to be earth-shatteringly original, but it might put a few things into perspective. Although it is aimed specifically at the comparison of Japan and Britain, some of these points could apply to other cultures as well. I should emphasize that these are subjective observations and represent my own interpretation of reality.

1.   It is often a question of degrees. One culture will emphasize some things over others. One crude analogy that occurred to me is when we vary a recipe. The ingredients are more or less the same, but in different proportions, with one flavor emphasized over another. The Japanese focus on form and presentation often to a greater degree than in the West. This may make them appear obsessive or excessively perfectionist.

2.   The Japanese tend to assume (just like Americans are often accused of doing) that if something is good, then more must always be better. They are nominally Buddhists, but don't seem to remember one of the central messages of the Buddha that of taking the middle way in all things. Thus you will find air conditioners turned up to the highest setting and explanation and information overkill, such as on the trains that a lot of the time is plainly superfluous.

3.   Japanese society is arguably one of the most autocratic democracies in the world, or the most democratic authoritarian state anywhere on Earth. In social settings, particularly within the family, this is basically the concept of threat without any force to back it up. People will obey out of fear of rejection or ostracism, but anyone who finds the courage to stand up to their tormentor will usually be left in peace, since in many ways, Japanese society resembles one based on bullying and intimidation. As with bullies anywhere, they are only strong so long as their victims fail to fight back. Some writers have defined Japan as being the only truly successful Communist country in the world. The incessant use of loudspeakers, what university professor Yoshimichi Nakajima refers to as "cultural noise" or perhaps more accurately when he describes it elsewhere as "Stupid and moronic broadcasting." He believes this is used to keep people passive and to hammer them into conformity.

4.   Meetings. The Japanese are forever holding meetings. This is a throwback to the old days where they had to coordinate the harvest and other communal activities. What they call "nemawashi" is often translated as "consensus" in English. Often, this is really more a case of the person or people in charge telling everyone what has been decided, everyone complies, with more or less no comment and even less complaint and they call it coming to a consensus. In Britain, this is called "Winning the argument."

5.   In the cautionary children's tale of "The King's New Clothes" a couple of con artists trick the king into buying clothes that only a wise man can see. The king is too proud to admit he can't see anything and so he parades along the Royal Mall naked. None among his on looking subjects are willing to stand out

by showing their ignorance either, until one little boy calls out "The King hasn't got any clothes on!" People who grew up outside a culture can sometimes see their host country more objectively than those who know nothing else. Certainly, they are often better able to make comparisons. Japan and Britain too, in many ways often resemble the King and his non-existent garments. Everyone can see there are problems, but nobody wants to stand up and draw attention to themselves so they all go on pretending everything is normal. Recently, it seems more and more little boys are starting to realize that maybe there is something amiss with their naked monarch.

SOURCES

(1) Ugly Americans, Ugly Japanese

(2) "Survey" From the BBC Internet

(3) Introduction to Psychology (Pages 331, 334-5)

(4) A "lout" or a "yob;" an uncouth young man, prone to violence

(5) Japan- The Living Tradition (from Notes~"The Japanese feel they are Special People"

(6) Itasaka Gen "100 Tough Questions for the Japanese" page 69

(7) Debito Arudo's article in the Japan Times July 2014 - "Complexes Color Japan's Ties to the Outside World."

(8) Daily Yomuri news article

(9) Ditto

(10) Morton – History of Japan

(11) Los Angeles Times

(12) Yomuri article and BBC Internet Health Homepage.

(13) Obesity Quadruples to Nearly One Billion in Developing World - article from BBC News 3rd January, 2014

(14) UK tabloids, until the late 90s most were slavishly supportive of the Conservative Party. Usually lowbrow newspapers thin on real news, heavy on sex and scandal.

(15) Daily Yomiuri articles

LITERATURE

Unless there is some great long lost masterpiece that history has forgotten we can safely assume that the first modern novel was completed around 1008 by a woman in the service of the Imperial Japanese court. She is known only as Murasaki Shikibu, "Murasaki" being a nickname, something like our "Violet" which she may have earned by giving this name to one of the principal characters in her book. So, meet Violet the Heian-Era party planner, who wrote a seriously long book on the side. Some scholars believe her real given name may have been Takako. "Shikibu" was her official title, meaning the person who dealt with the day to day organization and preparation for the various festivals and social events. The aristocrats of the imperial court surely looked forward to them as eagerly as we do Christmas, Halloween and carnivals. Her lengthy work is known as "The Tale of Genji" (Genji Monogatari in Japanese.) Knowledge of her

life is so fragmentary that we only know that she was born around 975 and died either in 1014, or more likely, between 1025 and 1031. Records also show that she was married for a couple of years before her husband passed away, she may have had a son and that her father was a provincial governor. The image here shows a 16th Century painting of Murasaki Shikibu.

Genji was not the first Japanese book. This was the Nihongi, or "Chronicles of Japan from the Earliest Times to AD 697" to give it its official title in English. It was completed in 720. It was written using Chinese characters and must have been tremendously difficult both to write in the first place and to read. The earliest major work of literature written in the native Japanese "kana" script was the Tosa Journal, an account of the voyage back to Kyoto from the Tosa of the title. It was first circulated around the Imperial court in 935. The official who wrote it was a man, but he wrote it pretending to be a woman. At this time, women tended to concentrate on writing in kana, leaving the Chinese classics to the men. The Tosa Journal was probably an appeal for people to take works written in native prose seriously.

In Britain, following the Norman Conquest and for some time thereafter, a similar situation existed regarding literature. Most books were written either in French, or Latin. Sir Thomas Moore's "Utopia," was published first in Latin and only translated into English some years after his death in 1535. Educated people simply didn't use English when writing. Even by 1500, some estimates suggest that only between ten and twenty five percent of the male population was literate to some extent. French was the official language of Parliament until 1362.

The first work of English literature actually written in English was "The Canterbury Tales" of Geoffrey Chaucer (1340-1400) published in 1387. It is a collection of stories told in turn by a band of people brought together while on a pilgrimage to Canterbury, the site of the cathedral and the spiritual centre of the English church. Many of these tales are ribald in nature, others cautionary and marked the beginning of a purely English literary tradition.

Thus it took some three hundred years for English to reassert itself both in the spoken language and written form. A slightly longer amount of time elapsed between the introduction of Chinese writing in the sixth century and the acceptance of literature written in the kana script by the middle of the tenth.

When comparing the style of classical Japanese literature with that in the West, one significant difference soon becomes apparent. There is an unfinished quality to many Japanese works, a characteristic largely absent from Western classical literature. The only exceptions were books left incomplete at the time of the author's death, such as Dickens' "The Mystery of Edwin Drood." Japanese novels often lack the dramatic action common in the West and typically have less plot or story line. Instead, they give the impression we are dropping in on a group of people. We linger with them for a while and then take our leave with no definite idea of what will happen to them after we are gone.

In this light, Japanese literature can be seen as far more realistic than its counterpart in the West. We usually see a "happy ending" as being a prerequisite. Even in modern literature, the tale generally ends on a somewhat upbeat note. In the classics, the hero inevitably got the girl, the knight slew the dragon and the king became a wise and benevolent ruler.

Once again this is in part due to religious influences. Buddhism stresses the impermanence of the world, nothing lasts for long and we are doomed by misdeeds in past lives to suffer setbacks and losses. In the West, the Christian tradition holds that we have but one life and if we are virtuous we will both be happy and will ultimately enjoy everlasting life in the Kingdom of Heaven. Never mind that life isn't like that. Western literature can be seen as escapist, while Japanese attempts to create a mood, to reflect the world as it is, much like in art, which traditionally strove for realism, sometimes minimalist, but mostly realism.

A cursory glance through some of the early works displays this unfinished quality quite clearly. The Kagero Nikki (The Gossamer Journal) written about 970 AD ends in mid-sentence: "Late on the eve of the new year, there was a pounding outside..." It is as if the writer, a bitterly unhappy woman who writes movingly of her lonely life simply loses interest in her diary. She tosses it into a corner then answers the knock at her door.

The Pillow Book of Sei Shonogon (used as the basis for the film "The Pillow Book" in 1995 starring Ewan McGregor) is a collection of anecdotes, lists and the writer's opinions laid out in no particular order. It isn't even remotely chronological. It can be dipped into at random without the reader suffering any loss of comprehension. It was written around the year 1000, a few years before the Diary of Murasaki Shikibu, which is also fragmentary.

Even "The Tale of Genji" appears to be unfinished. Scholars have long debated this possibility. The late Ivan Morris, a British expert on Chinese and Japanese literature believed that only a few pages at most were missing. Considering the conflagration that engulfed Japan at the end of the 12th century, it's a miracle that any of it survived. Perhaps the lack of a rounded conclusion in most of the classics encouraged the tendency to leave novels open-ended, which has continued to this day. It is said that Japanese compare this to the excitement of waiting for the next installment of a television drama. Others say that it is like a traditional screen painting where the viewer is expected to fill in the blanks made by intruding clouds and to use their imagination to picture what may be occurring beyond the line of vision.

Murasaki seems to have written her novel piecemeal, passing each chapter around for the other courtiers to read as she finished it. She surely kept a detailed family tree of the scores of characters who flit in and out. Murasaki never once made a mistake with the age, family relationship or in any other detail of any single one of them. That was no mean achievement for a novel that in its English translation runs to over eleven hundred pages.

The inconclusive nature of most traditional literature has endured among modern authors. Yukio Mishima, one of the better-known Japanese writers outside of his own country closed the semi-autobiographical "Confessions of a Mask" by leaving the central character in a dance hall. A homosexual, he is engrossed in sensual fantasies, eyeing up the men and we are to presume, about to lose his virginity. We never find out, as the book ends as suddenly as if someone turned out the lights before we finished the last page.

Likewise, at the finale of Yasunari Kawabata's "Snow Country, the reader can safely assume that Komako, the geisha and her lover, Mr. Shimamura are going to part company for the last time. However, we cannot be sure whether Yoko, one of the principal players is still alive or dead after having fallen from a balcony. It seems to depend on which character's eyes we are seeing the tragedy through. In Ikku Jippensha's novel of travel, "Hizakurige" there is virtually no continuity or plot. It simply has the two dissipated heroes travelling on from one inn to another along the Tokaido Road, between Edo (better known these days as Tokyo) and Osaka. The book was originally written in parts. Jippensha's intention was to write a kind of comic travel guide. Once again, there is no real ending as such. At the time of his death, he had been planning yet more travels for his two characters.

Ikku Jipensha and Tobias Smollett

To illustrate some of these points I selected four books. Two are Japanese and the other two are British. These are the "Tale of Genji", "Tom Jones" by Henry Fielding, "Hizakurige" by Ikku Jippensha," and lastly, "The Expedition of Humphry Clinker" by Tobias Smollett. Smollett penned one of the greatest, yet almost forgotten classics of English literature. It is a novel mostly about travel.

Smollett (1721-1771) was in the last year of his life when he saw "Clinker" published. At the same time in Japan, Ikku Jippensha was just six years old. "Hizakurige" dubbed "Shank's Mare" by its English translator Thomas Satchell, first appeared in 1802 and the last part was published in 1831, the year of Jippensha's death at the age of 67.

In "Clinker," a party of characters, some serious, others comical led by a gout-afflicted squire, one Matthew Brambell, sets out on a journey. Initially, they intend to go just from South Wales to Bath, but on Brambell's urging, they decide to carry on to London and eventually make a meandering trip around the country, passing through the north, to Scotland and back down again almost to within sight of the fictitious Brambell Hall in Glamorgan, South Wales. Along the way, they have many amusing adventures, including one where they pick up the "remarkable servant Humphry Clinker" who eventually turns out to be the squire's long lost illegitimate son. Brambell's sister acquires a husband, a bizarre Scotsman who also joins their little group while they are passing through the Scottish Highlands. Apart from this, there is little in the way of plot.

Smollett uses his characters to poke fun at many of his contemporaries, just as Jippensha attacks the swaggering samurai and especially the grasping priests, for whom he seems to have had almost utter contempt. "Clinker" unfolds as an ingenious series of letters and journal entries made by the various members of the squire's party. This novel has the inevitable happy ending, with three couples married or about to be and only the squire still single, but with the obvious delight in being reunited with his son, Humphry.

In "Hizakurige," we meet the two loveable clowns Yaji and Kita, who are also beginning a long journey across their country, but this time, chiefly on foot. In Japanese, the title means a kind of contemplative journey, rather like a pilgrimage, although neither Yaji nor Kita comes across as being remotely pious! "Hizakurige" has even less of a plot than "Clinker." Yaji, who is 40 and Kita who is 24 are both natives of Edo (Tokyo). They set off on their journey, passing through one town after another, forever seeking to slake their seemingly unquenchable thirst for sake, food and female company, not necessarily in any particular order.

The tone of both books is often bitingly satirical and Yaji and Kita encounter numerous adventures as do the party of Squire Brambell. Indeed, "Hizakurige" could be compared with the "Gargantua and Pantagruel" stories of the sixteenth-century French writer, Francois Rabelais in its scatological obsessions and vulgarity as social criticism.

During their meandering along the Tokaido Road, Yaji is nearly forced to eat dung by a party of travelers who he offends, much along the lines of: "Eat shit!" followed by: "No, you eat it!" They both drink from a urinal more than once, having mistaken it for a pot of sake and near the end of the story, they really plumb the depths of bad taste:

"From the bedclothes he pulled out a small chip-box.

'Why isn't that the box the old chap brought out before?' said Kita. 'The one with the sugar candy in it, I mean.'...

'Let's have a bit,' suggested Kita.

'Wait a minute,' said Yaji. The lantern was so far away he could not see very well, but he took the lid off and put some of the contents into his mouth.' It's hard,' he said.

'Let's see' said Kita, snatching the box away. He also put some in his mouth and chewed it. 'Whatever is it?' he said. 'It's like ashes.'

'It's not sugar candy,' said Yaji. 'What a strong smell it has.'

Then he began to feel rather sick and to reach, whereupon the Tanba man opened his eyes at the noise and jumped up astounded when he saw what they were doing.

'What are you doing?' he cried. 'What are you eating my wife for?'" The two buffoons had mistaken a pot of sugar candy for the urn containing the cremated remains of the poor man's dead wife that he was taking on a pilgrimage to a sacred mountain.

"Clinker" can't match this for sheer grossness, but Squire Brambell's descriptions of the hot springs in Bath are truly stomach turning.

"I went into the King's Bath...the first object that saluted my eyes was a child full of scrofulous ulcer (tuberculosis of the lymphatic glands) carried in the arms of one of the guides...suppose the matter of those ulcers comes into contact with my skin, when the pores are open." and "It is far from being clear with me that the patients in the Pump Room don't swallow the scourings of the bathers, in any case what a delicate beverage is quaffed every day by the drinkers, medicated with the sweat and dirt and dandruff and abominable discharges." We get the impression that Smollett and Jippensha would have delighted each other with their descriptions were it possible for them ever to have met.

Jippensha fell afoul of the censors early on in his career, as did Henry Fielding and for similar reasons. Smollett had to be at least a little careful of who he slandered. We can only wonder how much more brutal they might have been in a freer environment. Smollett really went to town in his gruesome descriptions of the dreadful food in London:

"I saw a dirty barrow-bunter in the street, cleaning her dusty fruit with her own spittle; and, who knows, but some fine lady of St. James's Parish might admit into her delicate mouth those very cherries, which had been rolled and moistened between the filthy and, perhaps ulcerated...(mouth of the seller.)...The pallid, contaminated mash which they call strawberries." and "table-beer, guiltless of hops and malt, vapid and nauseous...(a) rancid mess, called butter, manufactured with candle-grease and kitchen stuff...fresh eggs, imported from France or Scotland." He also described the milk: "frothed with bruised snails, exposed to foul rinsings...spittle and snot and tobacco-quids from foot-passengers."

In "Tom Brown" there are also descriptions of the food. Fielding relates how Tom had "over two pounds of beef and as many of pudding deposited in his belly" at the time he got into one of his many fights. Fielding died of complications related to gout aged 45 and this was no doubt worsened by such eating habits. Smollett barely lived to his fiftieth year. If the poor were sometimes close to starving, then the upper classes in contrast seem to have been doing their best to eat and drink themselves into an early grave.

Yaji and Kita seem to have enjoyed better food, notwithstanding some little accidents such as the one detailed above and the following mix-up while having some sake.

"He handed the cup (of sake) to Kita who drank it off at a gulp. It seemed to him to have a very strange, salty taste and made him feel sick, but he said 'Thank you.'" It was one of those occasions mentioned earlier which involved mishaps with urine, this time being when poor Kita drank from a pot in which Yaji had shortly before relieved himself!

This kind of "toilet humour" is far more popular in Britain and Japan and much less so in the United States. Naturally, there are exceptions. Eddie Murphy can be pretty explicit, when for example, in his hilarious live video, "Raw," he relates a series of amusing impressions of well-known celebrities defecating. On the whole, Americans tend to be intensely uncomfortable when discussing, for example, the state of their bowels, toilet matters and such. This shows even in the language. Americans refer to the "rest room" whereas in Britain most people say "toilet." One word for the same little room in Japanese, "benjo" translates as "excreting-place."

Both Smollett and Jippensha were satirists, using gross and scatological images to expose the hypocrisy of their worlds. Jippensha, in particular resembles Rabelais in this regard. Jippensha was a little less specific, but Smollett often attacked famous individuals, especially when the party reached London and spent some time among the pompous members of high society there. Many of them were only thinly disguised. Indeed, modern day historians can even now identify most, so there seems little doubt they could recognize themselves when the book was first published.

Britain and Japan were pre-industrial societies at this time. The overwhelming majority of the people worked on the land, although urban populations had increased considerably. Smollett was in fact a country squire himself and used the character of Brambell as a mouthpiece for his own opinions, criticizing what he saw as the shortcomings of his world. In just the same way, Jippensha created the travelling twosome Yaji and Kita to poke fun at situations he deplored and at the kind of people he had contempt for.

Now, let's consider Henry Fielding's "Tom Jones" and "The Tale of Genji" by Murasaki Shikibu. There are some similarities, although less than in the previous two books. Both novels are extremely long. "Jones" runs to over 800 pages and "Genji" in the translation by Sir Arthur Waley is more than 1100. Dare I say that both writers could really have used a good editor! For anyone not familiar with "Tom Jones" they could do worse than find a copy of the film version, starring Albert Finney in the title role, which one reviewer described as "Fielding without the boring bits."

In both cases, the central character is a young man who is adored by several women and has a number of romantic liaisons. Genji is presumed to be of comparatively low birth, which precludes him from ever rising beyond a certain level in his society. Tom Jones is also believed by everyone to be of not just low, but of outright common stock and the child of an unwed mother to boot.

Henry Fielding

Genji has an affair of sorts with his stepmother, the Lady Fujitsubo, while Tom is presumed to be having some sort of unsuitable liaison with a woman who everyone believes to be his mother. Eventually it transpires that she is not. Tom then discovers that he is in fact of blue blood and therefore free to marry Sophia, his true love.

Both Tom and Genji have one woman they give their heart to. For Tom, it is Sophia, the daughter of his revolting neighbour Squire Western and for Genji it is Murasaki (Hence the nickname of the writer.) This doesn't prevent them from having regular dalliances with several other women along the way. Tom has at least five close encounters of the romantic kind, while those of Genji are too numerous to mention.

Another parallel in the two stories is in the way that both men are exiled from their homes for what we might politely refer to as an "indiscretion." Genji is ordered to spend six months on the lakeside of Suma, for much the same reason that Tom's benefactor Squire Allworthy throws him off the estate. Tom's estrangement lasts only a couple of weeks, but while Genji does little more than sit on the veranda, mournfully pondering the infinite, Tom has a variety of adventures. He goes to London, has an affair with a disgusting middle-aged woman with rotten teeth and finally wins the hand of Sophia in marriage.

Here, the similarities between the two novels end. Genji leads such a static life; indeed many people would judge him to be nothing short of bone-idle. I recall not one occasion where he accomplishes anything more strenuous than lifting a pen to write down a poem he has composed, or attending whatever festival, dance or drinking party that has come around on the social calendar once again. Tom gets into several fights, falls into the canal, breaks his arm while saving Sophia whose horse has gone out of control and much more. He is basically an action hero. Fielding intended the novel to be a comedy, although much of the humour is lost on a modern day reader. Nowadays, punning references to the classics in Latin can elicit only blank stares from even the most educated of individuals and the jokes about foxhunting for example, would no longer be funny to the majority of British people who consider the practice distasteful.

Henry Fielding (1709-54) is remembered as being the writer of "Tom Jones" and also the burlesque "Tom Thumb" about a tiny little man. He also helped to organize the first police force in London, known as the Bow Street Runners. He was, among other things, a lawyer. Smollett actually attacked Fielding in writing and it is quite likely he was the anonymous "fierce critic" of "Tom Jones and its filthy author." There were those in the straight-laced world in which both men lived who felt that the book was promoting immorality. Nonetheless, it was a great success when first published in 1748.

Comparing the worlds of Genji and Jones demonstrates the rigidity of both societies. They were glacially slow to change, bound by strict rules of convention. "Parents were the best judges of matches for their children." Squire Western in "Tom Jones" harshly delivered these words to his daughter but they could just as easily have been lifted from "The Tale of Genji." Everyone knew their place and everything would be fine just as long as they kept to it.

There are parallels in what each society considered to be handsome or proper in a man's appearance. Tom is said to be "fair of skin," and this is coupled with his description as being "a pretty young man." This could of course just be an example of change in usage of language, much like Victorian writers who sometimes referred to women as "handsome." Genji also has white skin, made whiter by the use of powder and makeup.

The description of the unsavoury Captain Blifil in Jones is quite similar to the account given of the provincial figure, Prince Higekuro (Literally "Blackbeard") who tries to win the hand in marriage of Tamakazura, one of the beautiful young ladies featured in the story. Both men are held in contempt for their heavy black beards, swarthy complexions and large limbs. They seem more like the contemporary ideal of masculinity than the effeminate Heian courtiers, or even the 18th century gentleman with his silk blouse and powdered wig. Both during the Heian Period and at the time Fielding wrote "Jones," gentlemen wore perfume. Their manner was often less than what would be regarded as altogether manly in the contemporary world. The notion that a suntan was a mark of a common labourer only began to change in Britain in the 1920s, when it became fashionable. Tanning caught on in Japan in the last few decades of the 20th century and lately it is once again declining in popularity.

In both societies, we get the impression of gentry with an awful lot of time on their hands. In Genji, we see people who while away the hours with poetry reading parties. They also had events where they composed a verse off the cuff, then challenged the next participant to better it. They also went on moon-viewing excursions, generally no further than their elegant gardens and had cherry-blossom viewing parties. This last of these customs has endured to the present day. Then, as now it was more an excuse to get drunk under the trees than for any serious appreciation of the flora. The brief period when the cherry and other blossoms appear and the accompanying flower viewing or "hanami" as it is known in Japanese is eagerly awaited every year

In "Jones", we see a similar situation where the gentry fritter away their time hunting various hapless forest creatures in the name of sport, listen to a daughter play their favourite piece of music on the harpsichord, get drunk in the afternoon with their friends, or some combination of these. Obviously someone must have done the day-to-day work of running the estates, but in "Genji" they are scarcely mentioned at all. Indeed, Genji complains openly to Murasaki on one occasion that all these tiresome official duties are keeping him from what he regards as the more relevant task of composing poetry for the Battle of the Seasons contest.

Tom visits the home of one of the supporting characters, the wily gamekeeper Black George, but Fielding describes not at all the obviously squalid condition of his home. Fielding seems "indifferent to the filth and squalor and stink of London" (unlike Smollet.) "We visit Tom in his prison, but we are not told what it is like." In much the same manner, when Genji is sent into exile by the lake at Suma, he scarcely ever interacts with the local peasants except once when "One day, some fishermen arrived with cockles to sell... Genji sent for them, he questioned them about their trade...it was a story of painful, unremitting toil and though they spoke in a jargon (dialect?) which he could only half understand, he realized that their feelings were, after all, very much like his own." We can see in both cases how there was so little contact between the gentry and the peasantry. Tom Jones' friendship with the gamekeeper is somewhat frowned upon, in part because he is disreputable, but also for the reason that he is so low on the social scale.

When we turn to the characters of Tom and Genji, we find they are surprisingly similar. We might expect Tom to be tough, unsentimental, with a personality to match the athletic adventurer that he is. Indeed, they are both romantic, sensitive souls. Genji can shed tears at the beauty of a sunset. By now, we should be accustomed to seeing him in such a light, but what of Tom? One of the women in Sophia's employ related the following story.

"He (Tom) came into the room one day while I was at work and there lay your Ladyship's muff on a chair and to be sure put his hands into it.... and then he kissed it ~ to be sure, I hardly ever saw such a kiss as he gave it...he kissed it again and again and said it was the prettiest muff in the world." This is far from the only time Tom waxes romantic.

On another occasion, when he is on the road, pursuing Sophia who has run away, Tom and his would-be Sancho Panza, the painfully unfunny Mr. Partridge gaze up at the night skies and Tom utters the words "I wish I was at the top of this hill, it must certainly afford a most charming prospect especially by this light; for the solemn gloom which the moon casts on all objects is, beyond expression beautiful, especially to one cultivating melancholy ideas." That sounds a lot alike Genji when he comments on the beauty of the moon while staring up from the veranda around his palace.

Both characters conspicuously fail to conform to the traditional image of the stiff-upper-lip Englishman, nor the impassive emotionless Japanese. In his book "The World of the Shining Prince," Ivan Morris argues, "Genji and his companions lived in an age when the virtues of male impassivity had not yet come to be valued. Tears, far from being a sign of weakness, showed that a man was sensitive to the beauty and pathos of life." Tom Jones is a little less willing to let others see his grief when his benefactor appears to be on his deathbed. "Here his words choked him and he turned away to hide a tear which was starting from his eyes." It was also commonplace for men to exchange kisses on parting, "a hearty buss" being a smacking kiss. A similar custom still persists in some parts of Continental Europe.

Not one of these four authors argues that society itself is in some way deficient. Murasaki and of course Sei Shonogon in particular both find fault with people who commit social gaffes, who are vulgar, or who simply go against what is deemed to be right and proper. Even Fielding appears to be generally satisfied with the status quo, although he accepted the need for reform. He was instrumental in establishing a red-coated police force (known as the Bow Street Runners) in London and was an advocate for rooting out corruption. He loathed hypocrites; indeed Tom Jones can be seen as an extended attack on the hypocrisy of his time. "We are made very much aware of the class system throughout Tom Jones, but the system is, on the whole, accepted; Fielding's protests are reserved rather for the snobberies which class generates." All of these writers seemed unable to make any connection between the inherently unjust nature of their social systems and the hypocrisy they affected to dislike so much.

Jippensha in "Hizakurige," like Smollett in "Humphry Clinker" also directs his wrath at what he sees as its facile and hypocritical aspects. Once again, he is attacking individuals within his society rather than the structure of society itself. Smollett time and again excoriates bad food and lodging, Jippensha too, but more often than not goes for the priests, who he regarded as being thoroughly corrupt and the samurai, for whom he seemed not to have a lot of time either. Both stop well short of calling for any radical overhaul or revolutionary changes.

Both had good reason to be wary of the censors and yet we can't escape the feeling that they essentially supported keeping things much as they were. This applied even to Smollett, although he called for some measures to alleviate the suffering of the poor, particularly city dwellers. The lives of the common people are touched upon from time to time in Heian literature, more so in books by Smollett and Fielding, but the squalor and abject poverty are ignored completely.

Fielding was, after all, writing a comedy, not a work of social protest. Murasaki had even less capacity to find fault with her world. It was based on the social structures of the Chinese court and she was in no position to be able to conceive of another. Jippensha could always look back a few hundred years and recall the civil wars that had preceded the orderly society in which he lived, hardly a desirable alternative. In Murasaki's time, there was minimal contact between the tightly knit Heian court, made up of perhaps 500 or so individuals and the lower strata of society. Even in Fielding and Smollet's century in Britain, the ruling classes tended not to socialize with those lower than themselves on the social scale and like the Heian court, the aristocracy inhabited a relatively closed world, albeit one spread more evenly across the country.

The lives of the masses in Heian times were "nasty, poor, brutal and short," to quote Hobbes. They were not so different from those of the poor people we encounter in "Jones," or anywhere else for that matter. They were illiterate, lived in hovels and worked long and hard. Only the occasional festival, wedding, funeral, or some other such event provided a break in their monotonous lives. In Heian Japan and in Tom Brown's England, they were blinkered by superstitions, totally controlled by the need to produce food, much of which they saw carted off to feed the aristocracy. In Japan, the masses were even banned from the pleasures of sake and instead brewed their own rice whisky, known as "shochu" which is still popular in Japan to this day.

All things considered, the first translator of "The Tale of Genji," Sir Arthur Waley's choice is less of a surprise. "As one critic remarked, (Waley) doubtless unwittingly, selected for his new milieu an English 18th century country house." Perhaps this might not have been so unwitting after all. Despite the obvious differences there are several congruencies between the two societies.

The sense of isolation and self-containment that we find in "Jones" is stronger still in The Tale of Genji. The characters of the Heian court express not the slightest interest in what might be going on beyond their glittering capital. Genji was exiled for several months to Suma and was miserable to be "so far" from home and yet it is not even two hours by local train from contemporary Kyoto. Even in his day, Suma was only a few days ox-cart ride away at most.

Likewise, Squire Brambell at the end of "Clinker" expresses the earnest desire that he will never again set foot outside his own neighbourhood. Brambell would have understood the Heian courtiers being equally adamant that they wanted to stay put in Kyoto, the centre of their world, indeed, for most of them, the whole of the world. "I am so agreeably situated in this place, that I have no desire to shift my quarters." These are the words of Brambell, but could just as easily have been uttered by Genji as he contemplated his lakeside exile.

This aspect of aristocracies, the tendency towards isolation, is typical throughout history. The same thing can be seen in the royal families of Europe who are thoroughly inbred and intermarried.

In Tom Jones, too, we see how little interest most of the men and especially the women of the gentry expressed in news from the "outside world" of London. "Indeed, the conversation, if it may be called so, was seldom such as could entertain a lady. It consisted chiefly of hollowing, singing, relations of sporting adventures and abuse of women and the government." Does the government being listed last perhaps suggest that it is of even less interest than women in these "gentlemen's" eyes?

The position of women in both of these societies also had similarities. If anything, their standing in the Britain of the 18th century was possibly even worse than that of the ladies of the Heian court. In Tom Jones, we hear Squire Western roaring at his daughter, Sophia "For his part, he (the father) should insist on the most resigned obedience from his daughter." Later he states "Marriage...it is a match between two kingdoms, rather than between two persons. The same happens in great families such as ours." This could just as easily have been one of the fathers of the Fujiwara clan, the power behind the throne in Heian period Japan giving orders to his daughter regarding her arranged marriage to someone who would further the Machiavellian plotting of his family.

Women in Heian Japan were of course dependent on their husbands and were often left alone for long periods unless they were the principal wives, polygamy being the norm for the aristocracy at the time. During the Meiji Era, the new constitution stripped away what few rights women had. Only since the end of the Second World War have Japanese women enjoyed more rights and power than they had one thousand years ago. In 18th century Britain, women could inherit land or a house, but if they married, it became the property of their husband. Even if they divorced, they could not reclaim it.

It would be a mistake to try and glamorize the women of Heian times. They lived lonely, closeted lives. For most of the time, they were shut up behind screens to preserve their privacy and keep from being spied upon by men. They spent their days immobilized by their voluminous many – layered kimonos. Some historians have compared them to women in conservative Muslim societies.

"Tom Jones" offers a somewhat similar impression of the late wife of Squire Western, who is described as having led a "vegetable existence." "She was never interrupted by her husband who was engaged all the morning in his field exercises and in the evening with bottle companions. She scarce indeed ever saw him but at meals...Thus she was the perfect mistress of her time...Western at length heartily hated his wife." We can imagine her moping around the huge house, reading, doing some embroidery and gracefully going to seed in the country. Much in the same way that the Heian ladies must have sat about poring over their poetry, calligraphy or some other diversion which they were able to find to fill their aimless lives with.

Despite being surrounded by the sea and there being plenty of rivers, lakes and pools, few of the characters appear to be able to swim a stroke. The ability to swim was fairly uncommon in either Japan or Britain when these books were written. Even in 2012, a survey in the UK showed 40% of children did not know how to swim. In Tom Jones, for instance, everyone was relieved that "the water was pretty shallow in that part" when Tom fell in the canal. Likewise, in "Clinker," the maid Winifred admits "The first time I was mortally afraid" when obliged by her mistress to join her in the large bath. Squire Brambell can swim a little, but only Humphry Clinker himself appears to be truly proficient. This becomes obvious when the carriage is swept away by the river and he is the one to go in and out of the water, pulling everyone to safety one by one.

In Hizakurige, Yaji and Kita complain about the cost of being carried across the river. "That's dear,' said Kita.

'Well, just go and look at the river then', said the waterman.

'It is running fast' said Yaji. 'Don't let us fall in.'

'It is deep,' said Yaji. 'Don't let us fall in.'..."What would happen if you were to let us drop?' asked Yaji.

'You'd be carried away by the current and drowned, that's all,' said the waterman."

Finally, the endings of these stories show sharp contrasts. The last pages of "Humphry Clinker" see everyone about to be happily married, or settled comfortably. In comparison, we simply take leave of "Hizakurige" and its two heroes Yaji and Kita. We are left with the impression that as soon as our backs are turned, they will be up to yet more of their adventures in bad taste. The first part of The Tale of Genji ends with the death from illness of Murasaki and Genji heartbroken. We are made to assume that either he pines away soon afterwards or perhaps withdraws from the world into a monastic life. The second book begins some years after his death and details the lives of his and his friend's sons. It is this book that has the abrupt "unfinished" ending.

Tom Jones, in contrast, ends in the most contrived fashion imaginable. It is as if the author has taken his characters and drawn them out of a hat at random to decide who will marry whom. For example, it has the ludicrous pairing of Tom's friend, Mr. Partridge who is so embittered and mistrustful of women after his betrayal years before at his first wife's hands with Molly, the promiscuous gamekeeper's daughter. Besides, he is some thirty years her senior, a more improbable match is hard to conceive of. Genji concludes with an aura of ennui and realism, one that is entirely lacking in the final part of Tom Jones.

The literature of Japan and the West demonstrates little similarity in style. It inhabits opposite ends of the spectrum and yet the characters share much more in their feelings and cares. Perhaps this shouldn't seem so unexpected, for after all, when we pierce the veneer of culture, we can see the essential sameness of people everywhere.

SOURCES

(1) Kagero Nikki (page 167)

(2) "A Companion to Britain in the Late Middle Ages" S.H. Rigby pub Riley (for literacy rates in Medieval England)

(3) Sarashina Nikki

(4) Pillow Book of Sei Shonagon

(5) Murasaki Shikibu Diary

(6) Ivan Morris – The World of the Shining Prince (p.299)

(7) "Hizakurige"(Shank's Mare); "The Expedition of Humphry Clinker"; "The Tale of Genji"; "Tom Jones"

(8) "Gargantua and Pantagruel" by Francois Rabelais

(9) Humphry Clinker (p.45) and (page 122)

(10) Tom Jones (p.210)

(12) Hizakurige (p.242)

(13) Tom Jones (introductory notes p.xi)

(14) Tom Jones (p.227)

(15) Tom Jones (p.358)

(16) Tom Jones – (Introduction page xix)

(17) Tom Jones – (pages 274, 227, 271, 273,126)

(18) Humphry Clinker (Pages 313-17)

(19) Hizakurige (pages 87, 111)

(20) Survey in Daily Telegraph 2nd November 2012

MARRIAGE

In the early summer of 1981 I was planning my first visit to Japan. I obtained a pamphlet from the Japan Tourist Board in London. It was one of those "Meet the Japanese" type publications that seek to introduce foreigners to their society. In it, were featured the Sato family. They were supposed to represent a "typical" Japanese family. The husband was around 42, his wife about 38 and their two children, a boy and a girl, were about twelve and fourteen respectively. Naturally enough, it was informative, giving many details. These ranged from the kind of meals Mrs. Sato served her family, (typically rice and fish with miso soup,) to the job Mr. Sato commuted to every day (an office in central Tokyo, about an hour from his home) and the school life of the children (seemingly quite demanding.)

Outdated images: Above – 1950s Japanese family dinner
Below – British Family in 1940s listening to the radio

The pamphlet was equally revealing when I read between the lines. Mr. and Mrs. Sato were said to have met through the services of a go-between; theirs was an arranged marriage. Mr. Sato spent a lot of his evenings drinking in bars, but wished sometimes that he could return home earlier, so it said. The children were supposed to be extremely busy with their schoolwork and other obligations. In all, it seemed the family didn't spend an awful lot of time together. It even mentioned that divorce was very uncommon in Japan and that although Mrs. Sato sometimes felt her life was hard, she would never think of leaving Mr. Sato, who she "appreciated" for his hard work and sacrifices.

The problem with this picture is that it is well over three decades out of date. Moreover, the Japanese are starting to divorce far more than before. The rate has increased rapidly. By 2010 it had reached 36%. Divorce is now as commonplace as it was in Britain in the early eighties. The apocryphal Mr. and Mrs. Sato might well be among them now that their children are grown and they no longer have any excuse to continue with their marriage.

In Britain, the number of failed marriages seemed to have leveled off at 45% by 2014 and single parents are no longer a rarity. Almost a third of children were growing up in a family without a father, or with a step-parent. The right of a woman to initiate divorce was legalized during the 1945-52 Allied occupation of Japan, while in the UK it was made far easier in amendments to existing laws in 1969.

The difficulty facing the writer at least attempting to be objective is to resist stereotyping and pigeonholing the Japanese. Whenever a Westerner, particularly a man, writes about marriage in Japan this can be difficult. Some tend towards the extreme view that all Japanese men are sexist, misogynistic swine. The women are poor downtrodden and weak little things, at the mercy of these boorish creatures. The reality is that there are indeed plenty of Japanese husbands who fit this bill, but such men exist in abundance in every society.

An acquaintance of mine back in Britain once told a horrific story about her friend who endured a live-in lover who periodically beat her senseless if she didn't make his dinner just as he liked it. She could sometimes be seen in the Indian all-you-can-eat buffet with her doggy bags, scooping up the leftovers. She said that as he liked curry dishes, she was safe for the next couple of days since she would re-heat what she was taking home with her. As Nietzsche said "Convictions are more dangerous enemies of truth than lies." Hampered by such ideas, it's not surprising that attempting to get to the truth when considering marriage in a foreign culture sometimes fails. One of the best books on the subject, especially with regard to marriages between Japanese and Westerners, is Karen Ma's "The Modern Madame Butterfly."

Hong Kong resident Karen Ma suggested that among other things, many Japanese men are just as henpecked and harried as their Western counterparts. Their boorish behaviour in public is a front, intended only to persuade those around them that they are the ones in control. In reality, many men who can afford it stay out at night, or work as long as possible to avoid their wives, who they know will start nagging them as soon as they set foot in the house. There is even a medical term in Japanese to explain this phenomenon which translates as "the fear of returning home syndrome."

I considered the experiences of two friends. I added one or two minor details from similar stories gleaned from other people only to fill a few gaps. Essentially though, it is a reasonable description of marriages in Britain and Japan that both failed. I decided on the names Ray and Reiko. In both cases many aspects of their marriages seem typical.

Reiko, a Japanese woman and Ray, an Englishman were born in 1961, within a few months of each other. Reiko in Tokyo and Ray near London. They met their spouses at work and both tied the knot at twenty, after only a brief courtship. Eventually their marriages soured, ending in divorce. In Ray's case it was after nine years together (which is about the average length of time a marriage survives in Britain.) Reiko ended her marriage in 1996, after almost fifteen years with her husband. Both admitted that their marriages had been a mistake. They simply hadn't taken the time to get to know their partners and worse, they weren't in the least bit compatible.

"A good marriage is based on a talent for friendship. When entering a marriage, one should ask the question: do you think you will be able to have good conversations with this woman right into old age? Everything else in marriage is transitory but most of the time interaction is spent in conversation." This is advice once again from Nietzsche, who although he remained single, was a keen observer of human relationships. It seems that in Ray's case, he simply gave up trying to relate to his wife, Reiko too, seeing it as being an exercise in futility trying to have any meaningful dialogue with her husband.

Ray's marriage was typical in the West. He met his wife when they were twenty, working in the same company. After a whirlwind courtship, they were married and settled down to their new life together in a house near their workplace. Reiko went through an "O-miai" or arranged marriage where she was introduced to her potential spouse who was five years her senior and his parents by a go-between. This was only to satisfy convention, as they already knew each other from the office.

Reiko admitted that she didn't feel any special attraction towards him, but always considered that her primary role in life was to be a wife and mother. She was pretty conservative in much of her thinking. She chose him as much as anything for the same reasons as he did her; namely to fulfill a role expected of them by their parents and society at large. Reiko nearly backed out of the marriage altogether after meeting her future in-laws, finding them so sour and intimidating.

The go-between was probably someone from the company such as her immediate superior, or maybe the branch manager. A Japanese arranged marriage should not be confused with one in some countries where the parents decide who their children will marry. More than one choice of potential spouse is offered and either party is free to back out at any time. However, if they do this too often they are said to risk earning a reputation for being difficult or choosy and might find it harder to entice a suitable partner as a result.

Newlywed Reiko went to Guam on her honeymoon, four ghastly days, she said where her husband barely uttered a word, sulkily refused to hold her hand when they were strolling around and couldn't even manage to consummate their marriage. This deed came some two months later when he just forced himself on her one night. The instant he was finished, he pulled away then spent an age in the bathroom, showering and gargling. (She found this hurtful right from the start. He routinely did this after sex, making her feel as if she were dirty.) Reiko was too intimidated by the stern unsmiling creature to complain. Ray and his wife had a week in Continental Europe, which they appear from all accounts to have enjoyed well enough.

Ray was happy at first, but he sensed that things were going wrong little by little, as they communicated less and less, hardly ever had sex and worked so hard that they had little energy left to even try and talk much. From day one, Reiko knew her husband was a cold, humorless man, whose only interests seemed to be his job, golf (usually work-related) and visiting his parents. Every morning his first word to her was "Tea!" as in "Bring me my...!" He was an absolute "Momma's boy," who would come running whenever his mother called, or send Reiko off to wait on her if she so required. He expected Reiko to cook a meal for his visiting mother once when she could barely stand with influenza and was weeping with pain. They clearly didn't care in the slightest that she was so obviously suffering.

Early on, Reiko had made some attempts to show affection, trying to initiate intimacy in bed for instance. Even trying to cuddle him resulted in an icy brush off. It was as if he found her physically repulsive. Apart from the irregular occasions when he desired sex, they never made the slightest physical contact. As always, he simply initiated it with the minimum of fuss and withdrew to the bathroom a few minutes later. Once their two children were born, their sexual relations became far more occasional, much to her relief.

This is something many foreigners notice after being around Japanese for a while, very few of them will purposely touch another person unless they are drunk, or it is absolutely necessary. This includes family members and is often consistent even when relations appear to be otherwise very good. It is a learned, cultural response and should not be regarded as a sign that the person in question is invariably cold.

Reiko eventually learned how to reject his crude advances altogether, which after a few years effectively ceased. Simply by turning away or by saying she was too tired he gave up without a murmur. She increasingly elected to sleep downstairs, or with the children to avoid him. This withering away of a sex-life seems commonplace in Japan after the children come. Not just Japan, perhaps, as recent research in Britain shows that after they become fathers, many men suffer a loss of libido and feel that their wives are preoccupied with the baby. In Britain, a BBC survey in 2005 showed that a large number of respondents preferred sleeping to sex, as they were exhausted from their workload.

Clearly in both marriages, there was a near total lack of meaningful interaction between the couples. With Ray and his wife, this was certainly not the case in the beginning, but steadily became so, while in Reiko's marriage, days passed with little more than greetings exchanged between them.

By now, a casual observer might wonder how, or more to the point why Reiko endured fifteen years of unhappiness, brightened only by the arrival of her two children. Once again, there was absolutely no support from her husband; he couldn't even be bothered to take leave from work on the day his first daughter was born. He simply dropped by the hospital for less than fifteen minutes on his way home to see the newborn baby. He also pressured her to give up working. She complied.

From what she said, he appears to have had a similarly distant and domineering relationship with his children. She said they and their father didn't talk much beyond the usual formulaic exchanges and inquiries as to how school was going. Indeed, the children were just about the only regular topic of conversation between them.

Reiko genuinely entered into married life believing if she fulfilled her role as dutiful wife and mother, then they would come to love each other. This does happen in some instances, but in her case, she couldn't have been more mistaken. As the years passed, he increasingly took her for granted. He was stingy with his money, giving her barely enough to pay the bills, which is atypical, as over 70% of Japanese husbands hand over the whole paycheck and live off an allowance. Reiko reckoned that he simply had no idea how much she needed and she was too afraid of him to ask for more. Of course, it could also have been just another way of exerting the maximum control over her. Without sufficient money, she could only go out occasionally. She took a part-time job in secret to make ends meet, always fearful that he would discover this. Incidentally, she also concealed from him that she smoked; he didn't notice a few extra cigarette butts in the ashtray, considering that he himself got through over a pack and a half a day. In contrast, Ray and his wife shared the costs of running their home. They didn't have any children. He reckoned that even if they had, it wouldn't have made much difference in the end.

I became acquainted with Reiko through being her English teacher for a fairly short time. It is my opinion that quite a few Japanese, especially married women whose speaking ability is sufficiently high unconsciously use their language lessons as a substitute for psychoanalysis. They often have nobody else to open up to and leave the class feeling much lighter. However, I got the strongest impression that when she related these sad tales, there was no hint of self-pity or an attempt at gaining my sympathy.

Far from it, Reiko regarded the shortcomings in her marriage to be largely her fault. Obviously she was in part to blame for her sorry plight. I remember asking why she didn't complain more, or try to express her misgivings to her husband. Reiko shrugged, shifted in her seat and told me that would only create bad feelings and besides, it wouldn't work. It's unfair to put all the blame on her spouse, even if we accept that he sounds like a pretty unpleasant individual. She simply didn't even try to protest, or explain how unhappy his attitude was making her. Her husband was also a product of his pampered upbringing, of his society.

He probably regarded his behaviour as normal, or unconsciously was using his own father as a role model.

She confessed once that after only a few months of our private one-hour a week lesson, she knew more about my preferences, opinions and ideas than her husband of (then) nearly fifteen years. She had only become acquainted with the foods he disliked by a process of trial and error. Generally he would eat his meals without comment. However, he would soon let her know if he didn't like something and she made a mental note not to prepare the offending food item again. She replied to my expression of surprise by telling me that in her experience, Japanese husbands hardly ever praise their wives cooking, or thank them for anything at all.

Reiko did begin to react to her husband's rudeness though. He routinely called her stupid, both to her face and when talking to others. After a few years of this, she suddenly lost her temper and challenged him, asking why he had married her in the first place if he thought her to be such an idiot. He retorted that he had only been making a joke.

When it came to relations with their in-laws, Ray had no great problems. Reiko on the other hand was not so fortunate. Her husband's parents lived in the country to the east of Tokyo. They were quite wealthy, very conservative, polite to a fault, but even colder and more self absorbed than their son. Her father-in-law appeared to be a silent, very distant man, she barely mentioned him in our conversations. Her mother-in-law was thoroughly nasty. She would always have some judgmental comment ready about Reiko's hair being too long, her clothes being showy, her food very poorly prepared. I get the impression though that she could have visited them dressed in funeral black with a short-back-and-sides haircut and the miserable woman would still have found something fresh to complain about.

She told me that the most hurtful thing about these disagreeable people who she found herself obligated to was not their disdainful attitude. It was more the fact that when it came down to it, they didn't appear to care in the slightest whether she wanted to visit them or not. Her presence was superfluous and even her husband never put the slightest direct pressure on her to come. She just assumed that she was expected to endure one weekend a month at their home. He seldom accompanied her when she visited her family and when he did, remained almost silent the whole time. He never once joined Reiko on a visit to her relatives in the country.   Reiko was also appalled when she discovered that her husband had given his mother a key to their house without even mentioning it to her. Once again, she said nothing.

It almost goes without saying that her husband never lifted a finger around the home and even when Reiko was pregnant; he wouldn't so much as make himself a cup of tea. Of course, this attitude is not unique to Japan by any means. Her in-laws fawned over their new grandchildren, but continued to treat Reiko as little more than a servant; it seems their affection jumped a generation. Reiko was a paradigm of the Japanese saying that the womb is a borrowed object.

Reiko's husband rarely joined her and the children on weekends when they went out, preferring to stay slumped in front of the TV, or to go off and play golf. It was quite different if his parents were involved, then he enjoyed splashing lots of money around in expensive restaurants. This was galling to Reiko who was always kept under such tight financial restraints. For several years, her budget only stretched far enough for her and the children to have some donuts and soft drinks a couple of times a week with one or two other mothers. He mumbled complaints whenever she went out seeming to expect her to wait on him hand and foot. Her husband was an absolute tyrant, albeit a non-violent one in his home. He never hit her, but she was already so afraid of him that she usually bowed to his selfish and unreasonable wishes.

In Ray's case, he was the one more likely to have problems with his mother-in-law, if the traditional view of families in the West is to be believed. In fact, they seem to have had a pretty smooth relationship, judging from what he told me. The reverse was traditionally the case in Japan, with the bride being treated cruelly by her sadistic mother-in-law, or so the stereotype goes. From anecdotal evidence alone, I would conclude that in a lot of families, especially among the older generation, this is unquestionably true.

The writer Hiroko Mizu in "Marriage with the Japanese" reckons that "In rural areas where family bonds are strong, some Japanese traditions may still remain, but relationships between mothers and daughters-in-law are contemporary." Perhaps this is true now, but I recall story after story of the downright unpleasantness directed at wives by their husband's mothers who will never accept that anyone could be good enough for their precious little boy. Even the most understanding of men is going to feel he is caught between a rock and a hard place in such a situation, seeing his mother and wife coming to blows.

Here we have a problem of trying to get to the truth. Some critics say Japanese women get off on complaining to sympathetic Westerners in English conversation lounges about how lousy their men are. I concede there must be an element of truth in this. We must also consider the cultural tendency for Japanese wives to moan on about their husbands. This is what Japanese women have told me. So are we going around in circles here looking at a "chicken and egg" situation that doesn't even exist?

There are two reasons for me to doubt this. Firstly, many of my students, Reiko included, were most definitely neither trying to get my sympathy, nor just bringing their feelings out in the open. They mentioned details of their family life so casually and often reacted with surprise when I expressed my disgust, or shock at some aspect of what they told me. Secondly, many of them, even Reiko became quite defensive when I went as far to say their husbands sounded like a sorry bunch of losers. They were merely relating things as they saw them in a wholly matter of fact way, just as if they were discussing the state of their health, or what they had prepared for dinner that night.

In all honesty, it's hard not to conclude that there is often genuine and intense dislike within Japanese families. This is to a degree that few would imagine from the polite exterior they show the world. They become so convincing that they manage to more or less delude themselves into believing the lie that they are one stable and happy family. In Britain, there must have been something similar up until perhaps the late sixties and early seventies when the divorce rate began to rise. Taking the example of my maternal grandparents, both of whom were born around 1900, we can see a situation in some ways similar to the one Reiko endured, with the additional pain caused by infidelity.

My grandfather was a somewhat eccentric individual and it seems entirely probable that my grandmother detested him. He engaged in extramarital affairs and occasional one-night stands, one apparently even during their honeymoon! Near the end of his life, she had exacted a kind of revenge. She had a long-standing affair with the next-door neighbour, one of their mutual friends, seemingly without my grandfather having the slightest idea. One weekend morning, she followed him in secret, doubting his story that yet again, he had to work on a Saturday. Her worst suspicions had been justified. She looked on as he met a young woman on a street corner and watched them get into a taxi. Why did she endure this? Divorce was legal then as now, but the option was rarely taken up. There was so much shame involved and it was this as much as anything else that kept so many unhappily married couples together. Until very recently, in Japan it was the same.

Reiko did start to stand up to her in-laws a little as time passed. On one occasion, her mother in law tried to coerce her into taking care of her while she had some minor illness. (She sounded like an outright hypochondriac.) Reiko refused, bluntly telling her husband that she didn't want to go there and be a nursemaid as she was very tired and unwell herself. Amazingly, to her, he dropped the subject with hardly a murmur. She also ignored her in-law's hints that they wanted to move in so she could look after them.

This is a key point when trying to understand the nature of relationships between Japanese people and in particular among family members. If anyone within the family has the courage to stand up to another for whatever reason, the person whose request or demand has been refused will more often than not just back down. The sky will not fall in on them after all. In interpersonal relations, Japanese often appear incapable of dealing with any great degree of dissent. They are raised to expect those under them to obey and to be subservient to those who are above them on the social scale. Perhaps complaints will be made and it is said that there is always the threat of ostracism although would being ignored or avoided by her mother-in-law have been such a tragedy for Reiko? Clearly though, this would have made her relationship with her husband even worse.

I met one or two of Reiko's friends and her mother on occasion. They mentioned her family life and said that she and her husband were like a couple of strangers to each other. They preferred not to visit her home unless her husband was away since he was always so cold and unfriendly. He didn't appear to have close friends of his own, which is typical of many Japanese men. They simply don't have the time to maintain many real friendships due to their heavy workloads. One of my former Japanese students, a man in his late twenties complained that he and his old school mates hardly ever find the time to meet up anymore.

It is easy to be critical of such soft targets as Reiko's husband, but we should not lose sight of the fact that many Japanese men lead utterly thankless lives. They surrender their salary to their wives and many have no more spending money than school kids. They rarely have any social life apart from increasingly sporadic work-related drinking, or the occasional game of company-funded golf. Many are married to wives who are exacting and shrewish, forever complaining even when the man tries to help out at home. Nothing is ever good enough for their perfectionist spouse who regards them as a supply of money and little else.

Perhaps it's no wonder that middle-aged Japanese men have one of the highest suicide rates in the world.

I abruptly lost touch with Reiko. I had already given notice to quit the school, as I had found a better job. Reiko had suddenly stopped coming to classes shortly before that. I didn't have any idea why, the manager of the school just mentioned "family problems" without being specific. I had also been out of contact with Ray for several years and met up with him after about a ten-year absence on a visit to England. At about the same time, I ran into Reiko as well, purely by chance for the first time in about nine months. I had another part-time job near the old school, so there was always the possibility of our paths crossing.

She was walking with her mother. She looked thinner; her hair was wavy and longer. She told me that she had divorced. I was really surprised and on her suggestion, we went to a coffee shop where she told me the rest of her story.

Reiko had been thinking about divorce for years, she said. She had often told herself that she would wait until her children were grown up then get out of her loveless marriage. She had improved her financial position a little more by working from home, doing some selling and a little piecework. Her husband didn't seem to have objected to this as it came across as more of a hobby than anything else and besides, she was still in the house, where in his eyes she belonged.

Her husband had been just as selfish and inconsiderate as ever. On one occasion, a few months before she finally left him, Reiko was involved in a minor accident, which left her with whiplash. She was not seriously hurt, but in a lot of pain for a few days. She returned from the hospital on a Sunday and he casually mentioned that he would be going out drinking the following night. He added, it was just business. Once she would have been angry, but she no longer cared.

Not long after that, Reiko just came out with it. She couldn't remember why she chose that particular moment. She just faced him across the dinner table and told him straight. The children had gone to bed. She said something to the effect that she didn't love him, she had never loved him in all probability and that she wanted him to divorce her. She wasn't asking for any money, just her freedom.

His reaction was to laugh in her face and walk out of the room. She persisted and eventually he became angry and refused to speak. She brought up the subject on several occasions over the next couple of months and each time got the same stonewalling reaction. A psychologist would say her husband was in denial, knowing there was a problem, but refusing to face it.

They also argued frequently after that, or more specifically she lost her temper with him and he stormed out. She said to me that when she told him she thought he was so cold, he retorted that he was shy. The Japanese use this catchall term to describe almost any behaviour that anyone else would simply condemn as immature, rude or selfish. Not unlike the way that Westerners bandy about those tired old clichés that he or she is "sensitive" or the old standby "highly strung."

Eventually, he conceded that there were problems in their marriage, but blamed it on the stress he had at work, or being over-tired. He was too undeveloped emotionally to see that his selfish attitude and arrogance *was* the problem. He begged Reiko to let them make a fresh start, but she told him: "It's too late for that, it's over." I remember she told me that in Japanese, so I could get more of a feel for how it must have come across. Her furious, dark expression when she relived that moment must have taken her husband by surprise, seeing that until that time she had always been so passive. She so rarely registered any negative emotions when in his company, that once again I should emphasize that to be fair, he was only half to blame, given that for years, he appeared not to have had any real sense that anything was amiss.

My old friend, Ray told me on our reunion over a few pints that he had divorced. He realized that he wanted to part from his wife and suspected that she was having an affair. When he confronted her over it, she calmly admitted that indeed she was. They then proceeded to terminate their marriage with about as much ease as is possible in such situations. They managed largely to avoid the rancour that often accompanies such an undertaking. After selling the house, she moved back with her parents and he bought a small apartment with his share of the money. Since his divorce, in fact, Ray has kept in touch with his ex-wife and they even exchange Christmas cards. She has since remarried and eventually he did as well, although his second attempt at wedded life also ended in failure.

In Reiko's case, she could see it was hopeless. The tension between her and her husband was becoming ever more unpleasant. She tried to explain to her children what was happening. One morning, just out of the blue, she decided to leave. Her husband had coolly announced during breakfast that they would all be joining his parents at a resort in the hills the following Saturday. Maybe it was this she conjectured; the thought of yet another wasted weekend in their disagreeable and thoroughly boring company. Once again, he hadn't even bothered to check if she had already made alternative plans. She had angered him by replying that she wouldn't be going, but he could take the kids if he wanted to.

That same morning, she got one of her friends to bring round her station wagon. Then she and the children loaded it to capacity with as many of their things as they could and went off to her mother's home. She stayed there for a while. That night, her husband returned to an empty house and realized where she must be. He came up to her mothers' begging her to return.

Reiko related this part of the story in detail so I could picture it clearly. Her mother, whose opinion of her soon to be former son-in-law was unprintable, would have been sitting there glaring at him malevolently. Forget what you have heard about the Japanese never showing their emotions, she makes it only too clear how she feels about somebody, especially when she dislikes them.

Her husband had been so arrogant and superior most of the time, but was now shattered, whimpering like a child who had lost his mother. The idea that she would actually carry out her threat to leave had presumably never occurred to him. When he told her he would be lonely, this set her off. She gave him a lecture through clenched teeth about how she had been lonely for fifteen miserable years and that he had never once shown her the slightest consideration, just ignoring it when she was sick or tired. Then she just told him quite quietly to go back to his home. There was no point in their talking any more.

For the next six months, they lived separately, something he agreed to as it would maintain the impression to outsiders that there was nothing wrong. During that time he stuck to the story that Reiko was nursing a sick relative and no doubt hoping she would come back. She said that he phoned her a few times, but never gave the slightest indication that he cared one jot about her, or that he accepted that he might in part be to blame for their separation. Eventually he caved in and agreed to sign the divorce papers after Reiko threatened to drag it through the Family Court.

Reiko and Ray ended their marriages relatively smoothly. If Ray's wife had wanted to, she could have contested it. They would have gone through the courts and probably have wasted a lot of time and money. The same is true in Japan, where the "Katei Saiban" or "Family Court" handles such cases. In Britain, if one party is opposed, the couple must complete a two-year separation, after which, the court will generally grant dissolution of the marriage. In Japan a three-year separation can be followed by an automatic divorce.

In Japan, at present, if one partner does not consent, then in theory they will never get divorced. In practice, the courts come into it less than in many Western countries. The Japanese have the very wise custom of trying to resolve such matters out-of-court if at all possible. Reiko's case is quite typical. The wife walks out and after a few months reflection, the wife (usually) contacts the husband and they proceed with the divorce, or occasionally are reconciled. If they decide to go ahead and end their marriage, they will have a meeting.

Ironically, this meeting is much like the o-miai. Indeed, the soon to be ex-in-laws are sometimes present. Reiko's parents-in-law refused to get involved with it and have had no contact with her since the day she left their son's house. Two family friends attended and they did most of the talking, as Reiko's husband had obviously primed them. He sat staring at the tabletop for much of the time. He promised to pay support for the children. He was stingy to the end; the figure he agreed to was far less than what she needed.

They also agreed that the children could spend one weekend a month with him. The children began making excuses after a while and contact between them and their father withered away to the occasional email. Even as he signed the paper ending his marriage, he asked her to at least consider returning to him. She actually laughed out loud as she told him there was no chance of that happening. Reiko has since found a job and lives in reasonable comfort. She married again a few years later, but the chances of her ex-husband doing so seemed rather remote. Surprisingly, he did remarry in 2002, much to her surprise. Until recently, few women divorcees and even fewer men in Japan remarried. To many people they were considered "damaged goods." This attitude is changing though.

So, why is divorce rising so rapidly in Japan? In Britain, we have become accustomed to the fact. By 2014, the rate was about 47%, sitting between the US at around 53% and Japan's figure, which by the end of 2010 had risen to 36%. Between 1970 and 1997, the percentage of Japanese divorces more than trebled.

There are several factors, but for which Japan would probably have a similar rate to Britain, if not the US. One of these is what is known as the "katei-nai-rikon" or "In-house divorce." Under this arrangement, a couple who can no longer abide each other sleep in separate rooms, have absolutely as little communication as is humanly possible and for all intents and purposes resemble two room-mates on bad terms rather than husband and wife. Outwardly, though, they go on with the pretence, appearing at weddings, funerals and the occasional family gathering. Reiko and eventually Ray both seem to have had something pretty close to this situation. So then, what are the reasons why these unhappy people chose not to end what has become a marriage on paper only?

These vary from not wanting to hurt their children, to worrying what society would think of them, to the wife realizing she would be living on the poverty line; to the husband's fear that his position at work would suffer and he would be passed over for promotion. A cynic would add that another consequence of this would leave the wife without money to squander in department stores, one reason why some wives are said to endure their marriages, just so long as they can go shopping for brand name goods.

Nobody can say for sure just how many Japanese marriages fall into this category; people are hardly likely to go around telling everyone. Others might easily be judged to have a "katai-nai-rikon" marriage, but not regard it as such themselves. One clue came in a recent poll that surveyed how much time spouses spent talking every day. It showed about ten percent were what the paper dubbed "silent marriages" where there is effectively no communication whatever. This could mean that as many as one tenth of marriages are "In house divorces". By simply adding "katei-nai-rikon" to the total number of divorces, it equals the UK figure. The divorce rate has risen by 26.5% in ten years according to the Japanese Health Ministry.

Another reason is the difficulty women face in raising children alone. A single mother receives about ¥45,000 a month per child in state support. This is about $400 US, or £300, far from enough. If she leaves her husband, the law says he is supposed to support her, but in practice relatively few do and the authorities are not particularly strict in trying to enforce payments, unlike in Britain or the US, where new laws have been enacted to try and crack down on "deadbeat dads" as they are known.

Yet one more factor, in both Britain and Japan keeps the divorce rate lower. It is the tendency for people to live alone. In the Tokyo Metropolis in 1999, surveys showed that 46% of residents lived by themselves for a variety of reasons. Some were elderly, others students or men working away from home, but a fair number were people from their twenties to middle age and beyond who had never been married. In the UK, about 30% of adults live alone, while 32% of men and 24% of women have never been married. Many commentators have observed both in

Japan and Britain that more and more people are simply avoiding commitment, living insular, self-absorbed lives and see no benefit in being married, quite the contrary, it all seems like just too much hard work. If these people were to marry, some would surely end up swelling the ranks of the divorced.

Many young Japanese, women especially, are delaying marriage or even giving up the idea altogether. They can see no point in trading in a life where they have lots of cash to spend, a not terribly demanding job and the chance to indulge in foreign travel and dining in fancy restaurants. In comparison they regard the role of wife and mother as being a rather lonely and unglamorous one. Quite a few men are choosing to stay single for similar reasons. They only have to look at the drudgery their own parents endured, or to accept the fact that in some cases, there is little more between their parents than pent up frustration and bitterness to make them think twice before committing themselves to marriage.

Some in Japan have blamed the influence of Western movies and images for raising women's expectations unreasonably. They cite the romantic Don Juan types, or the loving and demonstrative husband they seem to regard as being typical of movies and literature from the US and Europe. They believe that Japanese women have watched such programmes, read such literature and got it into their heads that they can expect the same, thus undermining the family in Japan.

Japanese TV also shows men often in such a light, once again harking back to the "Genji" image of the ideal man perhaps. If we look at Sunday TV in Japan, for example, we can see two shows; both cartoon stories about family life in Japan, they run in the evening, back to back. Both illustrate points we have already covered.

The first, "Sazae-san" is a sort of Japanese "Dagwood and Blondie" with the central character being Mrs. Sazae, the head of an extended family, all of whom have the names of various kinds of seafood. Her husband, Masuo, is the ideal partner. He is kind, thoughtful and above all considerate and has the sort of qualities that would surely be welcomed by women in any society. They all get along happily in their simple fantasy world.

The second show, "Chibi Maruko Chan," is vaguely like Japan's answer to "Peanuts." The main difference being that there are also adults. The stories are set in the mid-seventies. Maruko is a nine-year-old girl whose father is, in contrast to Masuo, a more realistic depiction. Her father is portrayed as being generally kindly towards Maruko.

However, in one story, Maruko's mother is sick and he sulkily refuses to lend a hand, "I have my work and your mother has hers" he snaps when Maruko tries to get him to help with preparing dinner. On this occasion, he comes across as decidedly inflexible and self-centred, demonstrating what was by then typical insistence on the rigid division of labour. Nevertheless, the stories are always light-hearted and he gets his come-uppance. Just as soon as he catches a cold like the one that laid his wife low, he comes in whining like a five-year-old, expecting everyone to feel sympathy for him.

Chibi Maruko Chan and Family

The late Machiko Hasegawa, who started drawing "Sazae San" comics in 1947 never actually married. Her Masuo character was as much an idealized image of a man as Hikaru Genji who appeared a thousand years before. In the early versions of the comic, Masuo is dominated by his wife and is seen as being quite passive and easily controlled. Sazae-San was regarded by some conservatives as being borderline subversive in its day.

"Chibi Maruko Chan" was based on the girlhood memories of its author, Momoko Sakura who started drawing them when she was around thirty. Maruko's father is of course supposed to be entertaining; both programmes are after all aimed mainly at children. They are popular with all ages, much like "Peanuts" or the Disney characters in the West. In the two fathers, we can see one who is an idealistic image of the kindly parent and the other who at times can be rather infantile and selfish. Both types exist in Japan and elsewhere.

Divorce is now commonplace in TV dramas as well. In one TV show about a love affair between a female high school teacher and one of her students, her father slaps her mother during an argument and she walks out on him. Later, we see her meeting her daughter and she reveals that she has sent divorce papers to her husband and is only waiting for him to sign them and return them to her. This being TV land, they are eventually reconciled, but it seems to illustrate that far from being a taboo subject, divorce is increasingly accepted in Japan as part of life.

There is yet another programme worthy of mention which is "Couple Counseling" where families from Hell would be featured, their identities concealed, who poured out their grievances to a panel of celebrities who attempted to give them advice. It was not unlike the Jerry Springer Show in the United States. By the end, in many cases, they had signed the divorce papers in front of everyone. This show was cancelled when it transpired that some of the "couples" were in fact not really married and just staging it to make money. Nevertheless, it demonstrates once more that there is no longer any big deal in Japan about ending an unhappy marriage. This attitude has changed markedly in the last ten to fifteen years.

When we look at Western images, it's perhaps hard to understand how Japanese critics can make claims that they present such wonderful examples of ideal men. "Gone with the Wind" is perhaps the most famous romantic movie in the world and a clear favourite with women in Japan, yet the character of Rhett Butler is surely no role model. He is a hard drinking gambler, incapable of remaining faithful to one woman who frequents brothels. In one scene after returning home late he drunkenly boasts that he could crush Scarlet O'Hara's head in his hands. There are numerous characters in Western movies, TV programmes and literature, many of which are just as cold and inconsiderate as Japanese men are said to be. In "Love is a Many Splendoured Thing," another romantic classic, the William Holden character is attempting to divorce his wife while having an affair with a Eurasian doctor. Traditionally, men in Japan and let's be perfectly honest, just about everywhere else, have not been what most would call demonstrative. In Britain too, there has long been a prevalent attitude among men to keep their feelings to themselves and to refrain from opening up to anyone. The late movie actor Toshiro Mifune made the catchphrase "Men are silent" famous after he used it in a 1960s TV commercial. To many Japanese, this summed up the ideal man in three short words. The traditional marriage in Japan was not a love match. In this, Japan was typical of much of the world. There are those who argue that the Western idea of romantic love is a construct born of literature with no basis in reality.

In Japan, there is a saying that some might find mildly insulting. "My wife is like air," something that I need, but never give a thought to. Women have their own saying: "A good husband is healthy and absent." We should also keep in mind that there are cultural factors that can prevent us from seeing the big picture.

One of my former students, Mr. W was around sixty-five. He was clearly happy in his marriage and once described his wife as "His best friend." Yet when she was hospitalized for a few days once, he remarked glumly to me that as his maid was also away on vacation, he would have to eat out all the time. My suggestion that he should simply open a can of sardines and cook some rice met with amazement and almost anger when I persisted. Here is a man whose company manufactures complex medical equipment and who can demonstrate the use of such machines as CAT scanners and stomach cameras but who hasn't a clue how to operate the essence of simplicity itself - a rice cooker.

The idea of getting his own food ready never occurred to Mr. W for a moment, but clearly it would be a mistake to view him as some kind of chauvinist who regards cooking as something beneath his dignity. He often talked about his wife in class, which is comparatively rare for Japanese men. Perhaps the idea of working full-time outside the home would be just as incomprehensible an option for his wife to consider.

There has long been a highly divided sense of gender-role in Japan, which became even more pronounced after the Second World War. The Journalist and author of "Housewife's Blues," Shigeo Saito put most of the blame for this on the "salaryman" lifestyle and the "corporate culture" that arose out of the ashes of World War Two. After the oil crisis in the early seventies, this became even more pronounced and coincided with a steady rise in the divorce rate. Men were obliged to work long hours; leaving them too burned out to even try having much interaction with their families.

The wife was expected to take care of everything in the home, from housework to making the rent or mortgage payments and choosing furniture. About three quarters of men who are what can be described as "salarymen" or white-collar office workers on fixed salaries, hand over all their money to their wives and live on a fairly meager allowance, like a Western child being given pocket money. In fact, most of them don't even see their salary since it is paid directly into their bank accounts that the wives keep hold of.

In return most men worked up to twelve hours a day, sometimes longer when we factor in the afterhours drinking which was really an extension of office hours.

Some men have quite literally worked until they dropped; dead that is from "Karoshi" or "death from overwork." This is a term that was coined in the late eighties. Once they returned home, they would not have to do anything. Often, their wives even laid out their clothes for the morning, ran a bath for them, waited on them hand and foot. Not many traditional Japanese men would dream of lifting a finger to do any housework. Even making tea would be seriously beyond some of them.

With some, this is obviously sheer laziness. Others who would be quite happy to help out hesitate through fear of being scolded. When I first moved in with my common-law-wife, it was a day-to-day battle whenever I tried to do anything for myself. At first she seemed almost embarrassed at my offer to do the dishes, or hang out the laundry. As time passed, she came to accept my help and she assured me, even to appreciate it. I am certain that had I shown less determination, I would soon have given up and slipped into the role of an unhelpful husband who shouts for his dinner and won't even make a pot of coffee. It seems pretty safe to say that many men, Japanese or Western would find it all too easy to become lazy slobs if they were continually pampered in this fashion.

Women are raised to accept the fact that once married, their role is to be supportive to their husband so he can work excessively long hours at the office. Indeed to paraphrase Karen Ma of "The Modern Madame Butterfly" we can see that one major contribution to Japan's economic miracle was in the gender division.

Men only had to crawl out of the futon in the morning (knowing their wife would put it neatly away) and collapse into it at night (once again, neatly set out for them along with their morning clothes) and thus were able to focus all their energies on their jobs. This allowed them to work excessively long hours and endure all manner of petty minded, unreasonable demands from superiors and employers. They enjoyed an advantage over their Western counterparts, rather like sprinters being given a head start.

While this may have helped them win the economic war abroad, at home it was a different matter altogether. They spent so little time at home that their wives began to create their own little worlds of meeting friends, doing the social rounds, karaoke parties and the rest. Their husbands were no longer the centre of their lives, if they ever had been in the first place. Most crucially of all, they took almost total control over the raising of the children.

The extended family has largely disappeared since the 1945-52 allied occupation of Japan. The number of households with in-laws living with their son or daughter and their family falls by an average 15% every year. Nuclear families have become the norm. This is true too of Britain, where since the rebuilding of bombed out cities that went on after the War and into the sixties, smaller housing units suitable for nuclear families sprang up and the number of such families rose steadily.

With nobody else to interact with in the home, many mothers became what the Japanese call "kyoiku mama" or "education mothers." The vicarious pleasure they get from devoting themselves to the education of their children, especially their sons became their overriding passion. In November 1999, a gruesome case where a 35-year-old mother strangled her neighbour's two-year-old daughter and buried the body on her parent's farm shocked the nation. Her motive appeared to be jealousy that the neighbour's child had passed the entrance test to a prestigious kindergarten while her own daughter had failed it. This horrible tale illustrates graphically just how preoccupied many mothers in Japan seem to have become with education.

Indeed, a casual Western observer might conclude (as I did long ago) that some of them are more than just a little obsessive. Their children are packed off to the "juku" or cram schools every evening, on top of various music lessons (often the piano) swimming school and of course English class. This is on top of the considerable amount of schoolwork and extracurricular activities they also have to get through. It is no wonder that most Japanese children, in a recent survey, complained that they are nearly always tired, feel under stress and have no free time to do anything they want to do.

The juku started out a few decades ago with noble enough intentions, as vocational training schools for students hoping to get into, for example, technical colleges. They seem to have evolved, or perhaps that should be degenerated into places solely geared to getting kids through their exams and into good universities. Many children say that they like the more individual attention they are given at juku and the teaching methods are more effective.

The kyoiku mamas take such enormous interest in their children's education that they spend quite a lot of time at their schools. The Japanese Parent Teachers Association often appears to be a somewhat unpleasant organization that imposes wholly unreasonable demands on mothers. It is highly bureaucratic and invasive. In fact, one Japanese high school teacher of my acquaintance described it as "a kind of Mafia." I didn't often hear the teachers say anything especially positive about it in the schools where I worked. Many of them were weary of the continual complaints they are at the receiving end of. The PTA manages to subject the mothers to all manner of time-wasting nonsense. I spoke to mothers that strongly resented, even disliked the PTA and yet they rarely or never complained directly. They were paranoid that their children would be bullied if they did.

It's not only in education that many mothers invest so much of their time and energy. It goes without saying that the bond between a mother and son is very close in almost any society. In Japan, this has become very pronounced. Japanese mothers usually sleep in the bed with their babies and often share the bedroom with their sons until they are in Elementary School or beyond. Many even take baths with them, this too can continue almost until the onset of puberty. Most Westerners would regard such behaviour as abnormal to say the very least.

Girls are raised with stricter discipline on the whole. They, after all, are being taught to fulfill their expected role of wife and mother. Boys are allowed to get away with almost any misbehaviour. You only have to look at them out with their mothers to see this in action, with the little brat repeatedly acting up and being scolded in the mildest of tones, or not at all.

Psychologists have broadly classified the home atmosphere in which a child is brought up into three patterns. The first of these, the autocratic pattern, is where children are strictly raised: the second is the permissive pattern, where they are given little or no discipline; the third is called the authoritative/reciprocal pattern. In this kind of home, parents discipline their children "but they also encourage the child's independence and allow a good deal of verbal give and take." Researchers have concluded that children raised in the permissive pattern were "not particularly independent...seemed very immature and lacked social responsibility...here, as so often, the happy medium seems to be the best approach." Try telling that to a typical kyoiku mama and you would no doubt be met with an expression of utter incomprehension.

This clearly plays a part in causing family dysfunction. In the words of Chie Nakano, a Japanese sociologist and author of "Japanese Society" "most wives adopt the role of mother rather than wife with their husbands." Just as children take their mothers largely for granted so Japanese men tend to do the same once they are married.

126

Whether they are aware of the fact or not, it is women themselves who have indirectly caused the very problem that many of them blame on men. By spoiling their sons rotten, they are discouraging them from developing into well-rounded adults. It is not all the fault of women. They are reacting to an often unhappy or lonely situation and are caught up in what is basically a vicious circle.

By their obsession with education and their relentless pampering they are raising their sons to become just like their fathers, that is to say, work-centred and uncommunicative men whose wives sometimes give up trying to have a relationship beyond frozen language and occasional sexual intercourse. Many men in Japan, to put it simply are growing up to become pampered little mother's boys. Indeed, the Japanese themselves seem quite aware of this tendency. They have even coined the term "maza con" (or "mother complex") to describe this oedipal phenomenon.

"There is evidence that the parental pattern experienced when the child was three or four is related to the way the child behaves in later years." A mother and son that I formerly taught English to were a good example of this. For about three years, I would first have the women for a one-hour private lesson, followed by the child for another hour. The mother would tolerate the most unbelievable rudeness from her son, who was nearly twelve the last time I saw him. He seemed not to have the words "please" or "thank you" in his monosyllabic vocabulary. He would sometimes burst into her lesson demanding money for candy. She almost never protested, often stopping the class for several minutes to find her purse and pander to her obnoxious offspring. Once that boy reaches adulthood and if he marries, it is entirely within the bounds of possibility that he will expect the same uncomplaining service from his wife that he has always known from his passive mother.

Until recently, I couldn't imagine seeing such behaviour in a child much over five back in Britain and even then it would have been followed by a stern rebuke from one or both parents. It now seems that many parents in the UK have become as useless and ineffectual as their Japanese counterparts when it comes to discipline or instilling good manners and self-reliance.

If it is true that the first three or four years of life are so vital for later development, then it has to be said that Japanese mothers are doing their sons a real disservice. Unless they can try and instill in them some measure of independence then it is hard to see how the cycle will be broken. The husbands will continue to be selfish and silent, the wives resenting this, pampering their sons excessively and turning them into the same kind of men as their fathers. Just from anecdotal evidence alone, it is easy to conclude that a lot of men in Japan (and quite a few of the women too for that matter) do not seem to progress emotionally much beyond the level of dependent children when it comes to relationships. This seems to be especially true of the most highly educated men, Reiko's ex-husband for one.

A professor of Tokai University, Kogo Tsuji, suggests that the collectivist nature of society in Japan may be another factor. Such a society is one that is based on interdependence. Obviously, this is only relative, since everyone is dependent on others to some extent; it is just a matter of degrees. The husband depends on his wife to cook and clean for him, in fact to do just about everything while he is home. In return, the wife, despite her illusory power over the household purse depends on the husband financially.

In Japan, it seems that in the past, plenty of women were content to live in this fashion; their husband was little more to them than a supply of money. In turn, the husband barely gave his wife a thought, regarding her service as being natural. In the West, we often forget that in many ways, this was typical throughout the world. All that happened in Japan was that the post-war years saw such tendencies exaggerated and taken to the extreme.

Comparing the home life of the "salaryman" family in Japan with that in Britain, the Japanese white collar worker comes across as being similar to the traditional image of working class manual labourers and factory workers. The chauvinistic attitude that: "a woman's place is in the home" is more often found among less well-educated blue-collar workers than the typical middle class professional.

A lot of men in Britain (26% in a recent poll) would never consider cooking and many more balk at the idea of doing housework. These men come in from work and expect their dinner to be on the table and don't like it if the wife tries to get them to help with the dishes. On the whole, the better educated the man the more likely he is to help around the house, which seems to be the opposite in Japan. Moreover, younger men in both Japan and Britain tend to be more helpful and are more willing to lend a hand.

In Britain, about 70% of women have at least a part-time job. Often, this is necessary, as the husband's salary is just not sufficient by itself. The number of women working in Japan has also risen, especially part-time. The reasons are varied. Some do it for a hobby and others because their husband either doesn't make enough money, or like Reiko, who was barely given sufficient funds to pay the bills. Men in Britain generally keep, or share control of the finances and often have a joint bank account with their wives.

Usually discipline of children and decisions regarding education are made jointly. Actually, in Britain, until recently, most parents had little regular contact with the schools, unless they wanted to, or only when some problem arose with their child and there were fewer choices to make.

In Britain, until the late sixties, divorce was uncommon, many women and of course men too endured miserable marriages. There was such a stigma attached to getting divorced that the shame kept them together. This was the case in Japan too, but it has changed. Now, polls show that a clear majority of Japanese people think it better if a couple cannot live happily together then they should part company for good.

Communication may be the key to a happy marriage, but in Britain and much of the West, it hasn't stopped the divorce rate from soaring. There is also a growing problem of domestic violence in the UK and in Japan, which has caused many families to break up. Britain now has one of the highest divorce rates in Europe and the longest working hours. More than a few commentators have linked the two. In the relentless pursuit of consumerism, many couples have lost sight of why they got married in the first place. Domestic violence is also rife in Japan, something that was formerly concealed by the secrecy and denial that many couples lived with. Greater openness and a new law aimed at protecting victims of domestic violence have brought this issue out into daylight.

Returning to Reiko's story, we might well ask why someone like her husband even considered getting married in the first place. Clearly an unsociable and selfish person who prefers his own company, had he been born in say America or the UK, he would have been much more likely to remain single. He would have faced less pressure from his parents and society as a whole to marry.

Clearly all he required was a substitute mother to wait on him. Furthermore, he knew that to some extent, his precious promotions hinged on his conforming to the societal norm of being married and pursuing the dream of buying his own home. Some companies pass over men who are in their thirties for promotion if they are still single and regard them as being less reliable. More likely it means that it is less easy for employers to control single men than their mortgage-strapped married colleagues.

Reiko was not a wife to her husband in the Western sense of the world. There was no love between them. It was a social contract, just as if they were employee and employer, or perhaps rather unequal partners in a business. Reiko once said that she believes people in Japan often marry primarily to please their parents, not because they feel any inclination to do so by themselves. This was certainly the case both with her and her husband, who in many ways had a very typical marriage, although his (perhaps unwitting) stinginess and extreme coldness are a little unusual. Reiko's story is typical of many women who married from the early-seventies to the late-eighties and now find they are stuck with a man who they barely know and from whom they get nothing except money. It works both ways, as the husband is also trapped in a loveless union from which he senses he gets nothing tangible. Many husbands regard their wives as "lazy," and in a fair number of cases, it must be admitted that they are.

Once her former husband had divorced, many traditionally minded Japanese would have regarded this as a sign of failure. While Ray and his ex-wife are still on reasonably good terms, Reiko and he have no direct contact. Reiko heard that he transferred to another branch office, perhaps to escape from the sniggers of his colleagues. His chances of further promotion were seriously diminished. This might seem unfair, as his obvious shortcomings as a husband do not reflect on his ability in the workplace. Perhaps this was the reason why he eventually remarried, that and the need for a housekeeper.

At least you would think not. So much importance is attached to such things in Japan. This appears to be one of the main reasons why men are sometimes unwilling to agree to divorce. Totally focused on their work, if their colleagues and superiors perceive any weakness in them, they see this as being far worse than being seen as a pathetic excuse for a husband by their own wives.

Another woman of my acquaintance who divorced her husband of only three years challenged him to tell her what was more important to him, his wife or his job. In Japan this is a standard way for a woman to initiate a bust-up with her husband or boyfriend. He regularly returned home after midnight and had almost ceased speaking to her. When he just stared at the floor mumbling after she had gone on demanding to know whether he actually loved her at all, she simply left the room, picked up the two suitcases she had prepared prior to this confrontation and walked out of his life forever. She had built up tremendous resentment of him, but in all probability, he had not had the slightest sense that he was doing anything wrong.

If shame was all that was keeping many people together both in Britain and

Japan, then it is a loss of shame that will increasingly see them end their marriages. In Japan, simply getting control of the paycheck is no longer enough for many women, but was it always so bad?

SOURCES

(1) Karen Ma–The Modern Madame Butterfly (Pub. Tuttle)
(2) "Ray" and "Reiko" are composites, but the majority of their experiences are based on two acquaintances of mine, with some minor details altered to conceal their identities.
(3) Friedrich Nietzsche -"Human all Too Human" pages 195 and 199 (Pub. Penguin)
(4) BBC Internet
(5) Hiroko Mizu–"Marriage with the Japanese" page 103 (Pub. Hiratai Books)
(6) BBC Internet
(7) See Wikipedia "Divorce Demography" to compare divorce rates around the world

MORE ON MARRIED LIFE

I once heard tell of a survey carried out in the mid-nineties that covered 151 countries from around the world. I was never able to track it down to verify its origins. It compared married couples, in particular how well they communicated with each-other and how helpful the men were around the home. Not surprisingly, Japanese men did pretty poorly, coming in second to last, ahead only of their Korean brothers across the sea. Even in Japan, Korean men have a reputation for not making very good husbands. Men in the UK and America were in the top twenty-five or so. Among Asian countries, China and The Philippines did the best, coming in the top twenty.

Interestingly, there seemed to be little or no correlation between how well or badly the couples scored and the divorce rates in their countries. The problem with such a survey is it might well have been culturally biased, failing to take many factors into account. Nonetheless, it seems to confirm the chronic lack of communication within many marriages in Japan and how the "salaryman" lifestyle has amplified this.

A middle aged woman, Harumi, who I taught English to told me the sad tale of her mother. She died suddenly following a heart attack at the age of seventy five in 1999. Shortly before her death, she confided in Harumi that the one dream she had left was being able to go to her husband's funeral. She looked forward to the day when she could feel that she was finally rid of him forever. They had had comparatively little contact for the final ten years of their marriage as he was confined to a hospital bed for most of that time. Harumi was only half-surprised, she said, as even she regarded her father as being an utter chauvinist.

The post-war politician, Shigeru Yoshida, for example, returned home late one night from the Japanese Diet or parliament and greeted his wife with the usual grunt. Never mind that only hours before he had just been elected prime minister of his country, he didn't bother even to mention it. His wife only found it out the next morning in the newspaper headlines.

The traditional attitude of Japanese men towards their wives could be summed up as a kind of arrogant indifference bordering on contempt. While a wife is necessary, she is not something to be given much thought to, rather like a piece of furniture in many ways. They regard women as being inferior and thus not worthy of being shown any respect. They should be dutiful to their men and keep their opinions to themselves. Once again, this attitude is by no means unique to Japan.

When I expressed this view to Reiko and other women, they tended to agree with me, although they felt I was being rather harsh. I couldn't see any difference in this position than my own feelings for my computer. I depend on it for Internet news, e-mails and for my writing. Once recently when both the Internet link and the e-mail function were down due to a glitch, I was at a real loss. Even so, I wouldn't for a moment say I have any affection for my little machine. I use it daily and need it, but never once have felt any sense of gratitude towards it.

The corresponding attitude of the "English gentleman" might be regarded as a similar arrogant sense of superiority, tempered with the belief that women are weak and need the protection of their "gallant" men. They can't be expected to have the strength of men and must have doors opened for them and need to sit down on trains and buses, as they will be too tired to stand; that sort of nonsense. An English gentleman may give the impression that he is being considerate but to many people, this attitude is just as chauvinistic as the traditional boorish image of the Japanese male.

It is not solely the fault of men that divorce and marital strife are increasing in Japan and the UK. Many Japanese women are adamant they will quit work once they marry and until they have children, are pretty indolent, if truth be told. It's not always the men who insist on this as a precondition of marriage either. I know of international couples who have parted company because the foreign husband resented his "lazy" wife who not only lounged around at home all day, but nagged him to hand over all his salary into the bargain. This is something that many Western men simply will not even consider. During my marriage, my Japanese wife and I reached a financial compromise. I gave her about 60% of my salary, used what I needed for my daily expenses and put the rest in the bank, with the understanding that if she ran short of cash, she only had to ask.

Most Western men demand at least some say over what is done with the money and major decisions over financial matters typically are made together. However, working-class families in Britain often resemble those of a typical "salaryman" family in Japan. The wife will get her husband's "permission" to do something, but it is often just a formality. She is only giving him the chance to exert his "authority" in the home. In the case of my family, my mother always chose the place for our family holidays since my father was usually too busy to join us anyway.

So, have relations between men and women in Japan always been so miserable? More to the point, is it the fault of advances in women's education and increasing presence in the workplace? The answer to the second question is probably a qualified yes. Women have the choice if and when they marry. Marriage is now an option, not a virtual obligation. Also, education has opened many doors for them. A clear majority of young women nowadays would not endure a marriage to someone they did not love in the way their own mothers and grandmothers sometimes did.

In answer to the first question, here are a couple of quotes from a woman complaining that her husband was forever absent and he hardly ever spent time with her. "He continued to pretend that nothing was amiss and sent laundry and sewing for me to take care of." … "I saw him as rarely as ever. The child, who was beginning to talk, took to imitating the words with which his father always left the house: 'I'll come again soon...' I was sharply conscious of my loneliness as I listened to him. My nights, too, were lonely; there was indeed no time when I was completely happy".

This might be a bored homemaker in contemporary Japan bemoaning the fact that her husband is always off somewhere and she feels so neglected. This would be correct, except that this extract comes from the "Kagero Nikki" written more than a thousand years ago! In this diary, the unnamed Heian lady pours out the bitterness and frustration she feels towards her usually absent, often-inattentive husband, from whom she had become virtually estranged by the end of the book.

Bear in mind that she was a "second wife" of a fairly important court official who in fact probably kept two or three women such as her each in their own home. The Heian aristocracy practiced polygamy. The "Kagero Nikki" woman went on to say that she wanted a husband of her own "Thirty days and thirty nights a month." If many Japanese women are discontented with their married lives, then it looks like this is nothing new. Just that in the past they had no choice but to endure their unhappiness.

Looking at one of the earliest Japanese literary characters from well over a thousand years ago, we can see that the love of a man for his wife was not an entirely alien concept. The Japanese Aisaika (Doting Husband) Society, recently formed to try and counter the rising divorce rate by a man whose wife ditched him due to his workaholic ways, The group declared that "The Honorary Chairman of JAO is Yamatotakeru-no-Mikoto who is known, from the myth of Nihon Shoki, as the first man to publicly announce himself as aisaika to the world.

According to Nihon Shoki about 1900 years ago, when he heard of the sudden death of his wife named Ototachibana Hime, Yamatotakeru cried openly for his wife, shouting "How I love my dear wife!" Since then, Yamatotakeru has the image of the first "aisaika" and we are holding him as Honorary Chairman of JAO."

Should anyone take such literary figures as Hikaru Genji from "Genji Monogatari" at face value? Here is a man who clearly adores the women in his life and there are a fair number of them. He even takes pity on a plain, comical princess with a huge red nose, setting her up in a wing of his palace and appearing not even to demand any sexual favours in return. (Judging from the unflattering description of her, it's not hard to see why!) Genji is devoted to his true love, Murasaki and never really recovers from her death. We readers are left to assume that he dies around the age of fifty, from heartbreak.

"Genji himself broke down completely...day and night Genji wept until it seemed that a vale of tears hung between him and the world." So was Genji typical of Heian men, or was he just an idealized creation of Murasaki Shikibu? Perhaps he was a bit of both.

Murasaki is said to have based Genji on Fujiwara no Michinaga, the powerful leader of his family at the time. Ivan Morris, a renowned scholar of Chinese and Japanese literature states: "Genji and his companions lived in an age when the virtues of male impassivity had not yet come to be valued. Tears, far from being a sign of weakness, showed that a man was sensitive to the beauty and pathos of life." Men in the book are described as helping women in their heavy kimonos climb down the steps of their ox-drawn carriages and in many ways seem far more considerate than their modern counterparts.

Indeed, at the beginning of the "Tale of Genji" the reader listens in on the hero and his friends as they discuss love and the meaning of life. They are most open in their manner, almost confessional. Even when compared with "progressive" men in the West, they seem very forthcoming with their feelings; so much for the cold and unemotional Japanese.

Down the ages to this century, once again it's hard to escape the conclusion that the contemporary dysfunctional family is some kind of aberration. Even in modern Japan, a lot of couples are contented, as they are anywhere. Many men in Japan are nothing like the cold, selfish creature that Reiko married. Sadly though, her story seems to be all too common.

A recent survey by the Tokyo metropolitan government found that "A third of women had been physically abused by their partners at least once. More than half of the women felt that their partners abused them mentally by ignoring them or patronizing them." Also, child abuse has been on the rise, up 30% in fiscal 1998 according to the Health and Welfare Ministry. "The number of cases has increased annually by 30-50% in the last four years."

A pair of twins "Kin san and Gin san" (Their names mean "Silver" and "Gold") are in the Guinness Book of Records as being the oldest surviving twins in the world. They were born in 1892 and became instant celebrities after appearing in a TV commercial when they were one hundred years old, or one hundred and one years in the old reckoning system. Gin san celebrated her 108th birthday on August 1st 2000. Kin san passed away in January 2000 and Gin san the following spring.

An interview with the twins was featured in the occasional column that Elizabeth Kiritani wrote in the Daily Yomiuri Newspaper. American-born Kiritani, a long-term resident of downtown Tokyo asked them about their attitudes towards marriage and modern lifestyles. She was expecting them to be pretty conservative.

On the contrary, their thinking was remarkably progressive and modern. They had been farmer's wives and in their world, a rigid division of labour simply didn't exist. Women worked alongside men in the fields and in turn, husbands would sometimes lend a hand in the kitchen when the wife was taking care of a baby. They could see nothing wrong with young women who spurn the idea of marriage in favour of a career. One of the twins said, "As long as they can support themselves, why not?"

They were rather less sympathetic towards the "professional housewife" who stays home, focused wholly on her children's education and various hobbies. Gin san and Kin san reckoned that a lot of such women were just bone-idle. They didn't see how their husbands could have any respect for them.

Tomiko Higa is an Okinawan homemaker and writer of a fairly short autobiography: "The Girl with the White Flag." In her simple but moving account, she relates how she survived the American invasion of Okinawa in the closing days of World War Two. She wrote in detail of her mother and father. They were farmers who had lived for generations in Southern Okinawa, descended from samurai. Her parents were known as the "Mandarin duck couple." This is a Japanese expression for a devoted husband and wife who are always together, just as Mandarin ducks are said to be.

She described her father as being strict but fair. He never failed to administer punishment along with an explanation for the reason why. He was clearly devoted to his wife, Kame. "Father began to play the shamisen (A stringed instrument like a banjo) and I listened enthralled. Then I suddenly glanced at Mother, who was beside me and noticed that she had fallen asleep. I looked toward Father to let him know, but he seemed to be already aware of the fact, for he was looking at her tenderly as he played. He abruptly stopped playing and said, "Tomiko, we mustn't let your mother catch cold. I'm going to put her to bed, so would you lift up the mosquito net? "All right," I replied and went in and lifted up the edge of the net and held it as high as I could, standing on tiptoe. Father lifted Mother up in his big strong arms and gently laid her in bed. "She's fast asleep," he whispered as he brushed aside the hair that had fallen over her brow.

Later when her mother was sick "Father came and helped her rinse her long hair. After he had rinsed it over and over again, he took a comb and combed it for her. It was typical of their great love for each-other."

After her mother's death from meningitis shortly afterwards, Tomiko Higa recalled how her father "would steal out more and more often into the garden alone at night and stand gazing up at the moon." Clearly he was grieving for his beloved wife. There was nothing cold or unfeeling about Mrs. Higa's father.

He seems light years away from Reiko's self-absorbed spouse. Indeed, Reiko told me once that her grandparents had enjoyed much the same warm loving relationship. She spoke fondly of her grandfather who would get drunk at family gatherings then sing and dance for everyone while her grandmother pretended to be embarrassed. Once again, they were country folk. She suspects that is one reason why her former husband wouldn't have anything to do with them. He was essentially a snob who undoubtedly felt that mixing with such people was beneath his dignity.

It was only in 1964 in Japan that the urban population exceeded that of the countryside for the first time. In Britain too, the move to the cities that had been underway since the Industrial Revolution accelerated after WW2. There is ample evidence both anecdotal and otherwise to suggest that the "salaryman" lifestyle and the "grab and go" of modern Britain have both contributed greatly to the estrangement people feel not just from each other, but also from themselves. People who are so busy that they can barely fit everything in to their schedule are left with little or no time to even try having much of a relationship with their families.

Another factor that might help keep divorce lower in Japan is the company transfer, known as "tenkin" in Japanese. Larger Japanese companies routinely force their employees to relocate often at short notice. Ostensibly, the excuse is this gives them experience in different aspects of the business. This is often nonsense, since they will be doing pretty much the same work wherever they are. The real purpose seems to be a kind of modern day continuation of the Edo Period policy of "sankin-kotai," where the Daimyo or regional governors were forced to come to Tokyo for fixed periods then to leave their families in the capital when they returned home. This ensured that they would be unable to plot against the Shogun by keeping them on the move a lot and by holding their families as hostages.

The "tenkin" appears to serve much the same purpose, allowing the company to exert a far stronger level of control. Their employees are treated as little more than indentured labourers; the property of their employer. Workers are far less likely to form strong bonds with their colleagues and also less able to protest against their dire working conditions when they are shunted about like cattle. They are responsible for paying off a mortgage and putting their children through the expensive school system and they know they are chained to the company for life, especially those who have borrowed money from their employer to buy a house.

Some wives welcome the transfer of their husbands, as they often stay behind. Reiko was very relieved to have her husband off her back for a couple of years when he was transferred up north. Some husbands seem to be pleased too, as they can re-live their freewheeling bachelor days. The "tenkin" is an inhumane practice that in this age of e-mail, faxes and conference phones is surely as anachronistic as it is mean-spirited. It is questionable whether people even need to be physically in the same office for most of the time.

Another factor that could be contributing to rising Japanese divorce rates is the reduction in overtime and the decline of the after work drinking parties. Men could formerly hang out boozing with colleagues increasingly have found since the late-nineties that their companies will no longer foot the bill for them to waste so much money in pricey hostess bars. The economy turned down in the early nineties and overtime rates fell with it. Suddenly men who managed to routinely avoid their families were increasingly forced to return home earlier.

In the late 80s, one of my jobs was with a company near Tokyo Station, teaching English to a group of businessmen every Friday evening. I noticed that at around 5pm, when our two-hour lesson was about to begin, a fair number of men were usually hanging around, smoking, sipping coffee, reading magazines and whatever else they could think of to kill time. Few of them seemed to have any actual work left over. I asked the four men in my class why those others simply didn't go home.

The reaction was a surprise to me. They told me in all seriousness that the other men were waiting for the English lesson to end so everyone could go out for a drink together. Failing that, they had no choice but to go home and play with their kids and even worse talk to their wives. At first, I thought they were joking around, a couple of them probably were. As time went by, I realized some of my students there actually dreaded the prospect of returning home too early.

Quite a few couples in the past decade have promptly separated when the husband received his retirement bonus. Both parties came to the swift conclusion that they are virtually strangers to each other. Neither can see the point in spending the rest of their retired lives in the company of a partner who they often barely know and in more than a few cases actively dislike. I read in the agony column of a newspaper recently of a man who retired and on the same day his wife announced she was seeking a divorce after 29 years of marriage. He was shell-shocked and couldn't understand what he had done wrong. After all, he had left her alone, not bothered her and now she was telling him that she had a lover and wanted to end their marriage as soon as possible. The columnist, another man, advised him to give her what she wanted, as he had probably neglected her for years and what else could he expect?

Even in 2014, things do not appear to have changed that much in Japan. According to a poll for the Yomiuri Shimbun Newspaper: "married Japanese women feel they do about 80 percent of household chores and tasks involved in raising children, according to a recent survey by the National Institute of Population and Social Security Research.

This figure for 2013 was down marginally from the previous such survey conducted in 2008, but indicated that many women still feel they carry a heavier burden than men when it comes to child-rearing and housework. According to the survey, 41.6 percent of wives are dissatisfied with their husband's lack of involvement.

Meanwhile in the UK: "eight out of 10 married women still do more housework than their husbands, according to the research by think-tank Institute for Public

Policy Research (IPPR), while just one in 10 married men do an equal amount and 13 per cent do more". Only one husband in ten does an equal share of the housework in the UK.

Interestingly, in the United States "a 2007 survey by the Pew Research Center indicated that 62 percent of Americans ranked "sharing household chores" as "very important for a successful marriage"—a big jump from the 47 percent who answered the same way in 1990. Sharing housework ranked higher than factors such as adequate income, shared religious beliefs and children".

Traditionally in Japan, love was not a pre-requisite for a happy marriage and many looked for romance outside it. In Britain, a survey showed that about 10-15% of married couples admitted to having affairs (and the survey concluded that some of the rest were being less than forthcoming!) According to the findings of a 2008 poll by the Ministry of Health, Labour and Welfare, more than 20 percent of married men (aged 16-49) had had extramarital sex within a year of the survey. For women, the equivalent figure was 11 percent. I would conclude just from anecdotal evidence alone that the figure for wives could be considerably higher. An American acquaintance told me that his Japanese wife of three years met some of her old school friends and they all admitted to cheating on their husbands at least once and were surprised that she hadn't yet done the same. I know of numerous married Japanese women and seemingly contented men who have embarked on furtive romantic liaisons in the past five years.

Traditionally it was often accepted that Japanese men would have a mistress. I remember a story about a homemaker who always packed a box of condoms in her husband's suitcase whenever he went on a business trip by himself to Thailand! On the other hand, wives who were found to be unfaithful were branded as fallen women and made to suffer. Japan was not alone in this inequality of the sexes.

One final contributory factor in the rise in divorce could be the sharp decline in the o-miai, or arranged marriage. Some would say, though that the o-miai, which can be incredibly formal, has probably changed and nowadays is often not much different from a "double date" where a couple introduce two mutual friends over dinner or coffee. An o-miai used to be the norm, but by 1989, those marriages that came as a result of one had fallen to 27%. By 1997, this figure had fallen still further to a mere 14%. At this rate, the custom will probably be consigned to the history books sometime in the 21st century.

With Western-style love matches becoming common, expectations have risen on the parts of both men and women. Love was regarded as being a possibility that would grow out of their union, desirable yes, but by no means inevitable. Now, men and women demand more from their partners and while some young couples are coping just fine, many others are inevitably finding that their marriage falls far short of their ideal.

Both young men and women alike are said to be far more selfish and spoiled than their parents and grandparents were. They seem less willing or able to "gaman suru" as the Japanese call it, something like the "grin and bear it" attitude that was prevalent in Britain until fairly recently.

Even in the West it's best to remember that the concept of romantic love is relatively recent. "When did love enter the picture? Later than you might think. For much of human history, couples were brought together for practical reasons, not because they fell in love. In time, of course, many marriage partners came to feel deep mutual love and devotion. But the idea of romantic love, as a motivating force for marriage, only goes as far back as the Middle Ages. Naturally, many scholars believe the concept was "invented" by the French. Its model was the knight who felt intense love for someone else's wife, as in the case of Sir Lancelot and King Arthur's wife, Queen Guinevere. Twelfth-century advice literature told men to woo the object of their desire by praising her eyes, hair and lips. In the 13th century, Richard de Fournival, physician to the king of France, wrote "Advice on Love," in which he suggested that a woman cast her love flirtatious glances—"anything but a frank and open entreaty."

There was no golden age of wedded bliss either in Japan or anywhere else outside of escapist literature and Hollywood for that matter. Japan's post-war success came at the expense of the family that was once the cornerstone of this essentially Confucian culture. The same thing seems to have happened in contemporary Britain. People may be more affluent than their parents, but can devote so little time to building relationships with their families that many break up. It seems that the simple farmers may have had far less material wealth, but often had more meaningful, even contented marriages than the wretched state that many find themselves in both the Japan and increasingly Britain of the 21st century.

SOURCES

(1)   Quote taken from the Japanese Aisaika Organization's website.

(2)   "The Gossamer Years"(Kagero Nikki) Translated by E. Seidensticker Page 95 (Pub. Tuttle)

(3)   Ivan Morris "The World of the Shining Prince" Page 145 (Pub. Tuttle)

(4)   Japan Times- May 1998

(5)   Daily Yomiuri - 1995

(6)   "The Girl With the White Flag "By Tomiko Higa pages 22-3(Pub. Kodansha)

(7)   BBC Internet

(8)   Quote from the WeekMagazine.com

(9)   Yomiuri Shimbun poll – August 10th 2014

(10)   Who Does the Housework?   familylife.com

EDUCATION

During the mid to late 1990s, there were dire predictions in the Japanese media about what was termed "classroom collapse," and equally gloomy reports on the seemingly relentless rise in juvenile crime. In Britain, since the seventies much the same grim pronouncements have been made. There were warnings about the collapse in morale among both teachers and students; similar problems with crime among teens and pre-teens have long been the fodder for headlines. Students are said to be increasingly unruly.

There was a case in Britain in 1996 where the teachers at a state school in Nottingham went on strike to successfully demand the removal from the school of a 13 year old boy who was so violent that he was deemed as being effectively impossible to teach. They eventually came to a compromise where it was agreed that the boy would have lessons in isolation from the other students in a classroom by himself and through home tutoring. The same school was in the news in early 2000 when a 13-year-old girl refused to attend classes any more due to extreme bullying. A teacher had even been assigned to her as a "bodyguard" but was forced to admit that she could not stop the bullies.

All of which goes to show that the problems facing Japanese schools are far from being unique. In some inner city schools in America they have installed metal detectors to stop knives and even guns from being brought onto campus. Some educators in Japan have called for the same thing to be tried in response to a series of incidents where knife-wielding students caused injury and on occasion death. There was one tragic story in 1998 where a 14 year old student fatally stabbed a young teacher who herself had recently returned from maternity leave. The only motive seemed to be the boy's anger at being scolded for once again being late for class.

As often is the case, in Japan, experts seem only too adept at pointing out what is wrong and equally good at suggesting the reasons behind the problem, but falling short when being expected to come out with workable solutions. This is not surprising, when you consider that most of them grew up with the very system that seemed to work well enough in the past, but now seems to be on the point of falling apart around them. Nor is it peculiar to Japan. The hapless former UK Prime Minister, John Major and his "back to basics" campaign for ethical and moral behaviour in public life was unveiled as the solution to falling standards. All it achieved was to reveal how corrupt and out of touch with reality the UK

Conservative Party had become, or perhaps had always been.

The Japanese education system is frequently criticized for a number of reasons. It is said to be too inflexible, too strict and wholly unable to deal with the problems and pressures of a changing world. This could also be sees as a paradigm of Japanese society as a whole. This may be true, but merely blaming the schools for everything that is going wrong with young people in Japan and for that matter in the UK or elsewhere is a failure to see the bigger picture.

During his tenure as UK Education Minister, David Blunkett was once asked whether he was on the hard or soft left of the Labour Party. Coming as he does from Sheffield, famous for its foundries, he compared his position to working with steel. He said that metal that was too soft easily got bent out of shape and was too malleable. Metal that was too hard was unable to bend at all and would break under too much pressure. Therefore he was on the firm left, which meant he had his principles, but was also flexible.

The education system in Japan is similar in many ways to that of the United States. This is no surprise, as during the Meiji Era, when Japan was busy catching up with the West in the fields of technology, men of vision such as Fukuzawa Eikichi (1835-1901) went first to the United States in 1860 and then on to Europe in 1862. (His head is on every ¥10,000 bill.) Part of his mission was to study Western teaching methods. He went on to found what is now Keio University. Japanese education was initially based on French models, which were later supplanted by ideas imported from the USA. The American influence was especially felt during and after the 1945-52 Occupation.

In Britain, children start compulsory schooling at five and have two years at 'infants school' followed by five years at junior high (aged seven to eleven) then five years in what is known as "secondary education." Compulsory education formerly ended at age sixteen. Full-time education is compulsory for all children aged between 5 and 17 (from 2013 and up to 18 from 2015), either at school or in some kind of training. About 60% of British schools and all state schools in Japan have student councils, largely based on the American system.

In Japan and the United States, children must begin school at seven and in America usually continue until they are eighteen. In Japan, compulsory education ends at fifteen after three years of "Middle School" but 95% go on to High School for three years. Japan's education is often referred to the "6-3-3 system" since these are the numbers of years they spend in Elementary, Middle and High School respectively. Most Japanese children start attending kindergarten from the time they are about three and more recently in Britain, where the number of student enrolments has grown steadily.

A Japanese friend, Rie told me about her experiences with kindergartens both in Britain and Japan. She went to the UK with her husband who was working in London for two years and enrolled her daughter in a local school.

"From the start," she told me. "I was impressed with the relaxed atmosphere. I had been quite nervous, having already experienced the formal way of the Japanese kindergarten. The teachers seemed quite happy to have my daughter, even though she couldn't speak more than a few words of English. I sat in on the first class and they let her choose from several activities like playing with clay, or painting. I left England after two years and I wished I could send her to such a school back in Japan. It really encouraged her to be herself and learn by doing things she liked. In Japan, you are just told what to do from the first day and that's all there is to it."

In both Britain and Japan, students are usually required to wear uniforms of some description. A number of American schools have recently begun introducing them in an attempt to improve discipline. Most private schools in Japan have the blazer, dark pants and school tie which were once typical of state schools in the UK. The uniform often worn by middle and high school boys and girls is militaristic in its design and origins. Until the late eighties, boys wore a cap, which was designed by a certain Baron Okuma at the beginning of the 20th century, with help from one of his students. This was once again based on a 19th century Prussian army officers' cap. In the last decade or so, it seems to have largely disappeared from use. The girls sometimes wear a "sailor suit," making Japan one of only a handful of countries in the world that retains such a quaint uniform. The boys in state schools wear a black jacket buttoned to the collar and matching trousers. This has been changing in some schools where they have adopted the blazer and tie look in order to appear more modern.

Japanese children have six weeks of summer vacation time the same as in Britain. US kids get about ten weeks off. Japanese students also had to attend school every other Saturday morning, at least until April 2002, when the Education Ministry introduced a full five-day week.

Japan has often been attacked for glossing over its militaristic past and forever promoting itself as a victim of the atomic bombing of Hiroshima and Nagasaki. This is undeniable; there is scant mention of the war in textbooks, but plenty about how much suffering the bombings caused. Furthermore, atrocities such as the Nanking Massacre are sometimes made out to be nothing more than an uprising by some locals in Japanese-occupied Northern China. (All the evidence suggests that the Japanese military themselves were the ones who staged an attack on a goods train in order to give them an excuse to kill an estimated 100,000 soldiers and civilians when they entered the city of Nanking in December 1937.) More than one Japanese politician has tried to deny that the massacre ever happened. This mirrors the attitude of some rightist politicians and authors in modern day Europe who try to convince us that the Holocaust is fictional.

In all fairness, there isn't so much difference in the way that history is taught in Japan and Britain. The darker side of the British Empire was airbrushed in any of the lessons I had during the mid to late seventies. I took "Modern History" as an elective subject for the final two years at high school. It never mentioned the Opium Wars, where the British were just as guilty as other Western powers of exporting opium to China spreading addiction like wildfire among the population. Indeed, Britain stepped up the cultivation of poppies in India at that time determined to take advantage of the one product that China showed any interest in buying in bulk from the West.

History as taught in Britain smoothed over the cracks pretty effectively. Indeed, it would be fairer to say that rather than to outright lie, the textbooks I was given simply ignored anything that did not impact directly on Britain. I knew nothing, for example, of the Ottoman Empire until I left school and started reading books of my own choice. The events leading up to American independence were covered in a couple of paragraphs.

In the decades since my graduation, if anything, it seems to have degenerated even further. Former Prime Minister John Major stressed just before losing the election in 1997 that British schools should focus more on teaching the history of Britain and worry less about what went on in other countries. He urged teachers to spend more time teaching children all about obscure kings from the times before England was even a single country. Nor did I expect much to change under the administration of Tony Blair. His government was far more concerned about such issues as classroom sizes and the quality of teachers.

Japanese schools have petty even childish rules that serve no purpose. These concern hair length, length of skirts, even the size of the pleats in the skirts. In some state schools this seems to have become less rigid in the past few years although it is still evident that the underlying intention is to control every aspect of the lives of their students.

Conversely though, it seems that in some ways, schools in Japan are less strict than in Britain. I amassed five years teaching experience in middle schools in Northern Tokyo between 1997 and 2002 and some of the things I saw would never be tolerated at a UK school. It was certainly an eye opening experience the first time I taught a class along with the regular Japanese English teacher.

There were around thirty boys and girls all fourteen years old slumped in their seats. About three students were sound asleep, their heads down on their desks. Two or three girls were doing their makeup, teasing hair, plucking eyebrows, their mirrors and a whole bag full of paraphernalia upon their desks as if they were at home getting ready for a date. The teacher told them to stop; most of them ignored him, or became abusive. A male student with several earrings and bleached spiky hair walked in late, swearing at the teacher when he told him to

sit down. Yet another boy promptly got up and sloped out of the classroom announcing in the most vulgar of terms that he was going home to use his own toilet, as the ones at school were too filthy. (This was actually not true) Other students were openly reading magazines, writing letters to each other, in short, anything but studying or listening

Japanese middle-school (public domain)

to their teacher as they were obviously supposed to be doing.

I was also amazed to see students wandering in and out of the teachers' room between lessons. This was another point that served to demolish my image of a stern establishment. I thought back to my years in high school. We were never permitted to set foot in the teachers' room for any reason. If we were sent there on an errand, we tapped nervously on the door and waited outside, catching only the briefest glimpse of the smoke-filled interior.

Far from being the stern disciplinarians I had imagined them to be, Japanese teachers come across more like exasperated parents trying to maintain some semblance of authority over their large, unruly family. There are stories in the press from time to time about brutal teachers of course.

One such example was a horrible accident which took place in the mid-nineties where a teacher unwittingly slammed the school gate closed on a student rushing to be on time and killed her. He had been in trouble at the school before for hitting students and received a mere one-year prison term for his crime. He was a huge hulking creature with close-cropped hair, looking more like an all-in wrestler than an educator of young minds. Even so, my impression is that such incidents are comparatively rare, hence they make the headlines.

Another way in which Japanese schools resemble those in Britain is in what I regard as a near-obsession with sports, particularly team games. British schools are pretty rigid in this regard. If you are a boy, you played football, or sometimes for a change, rugby. Girls generally went in for hockey, or tennis. Never mind if you are a puny fourteen-year-old beanpole facing off against a gigantic brute twice your size on the rugby field, you're a boy and rugby is what you play. I saw an informal poll in the Independent newspaper around summer 2000 which suggested that about 80% of girls and around half the boys in Britain actually detest school sports and would either prefer more choice in what they do, or to skip the subject altogether given the chance.

Between the ages of fourteen and sixteen, British students do usually have some say in what sport they play. The mindset rooted in the Greek idea of "A sound mind in a sound body" doesn't seem to have changed much. In the-mid nineties, John Major called for more emphasis on team sports as a way to build character. I find it astounding that so many people around the world continue to believe such things.

The administration of Tony Blair in the UK didn't seem to have any fresh ideas where the fixation with team sports is concerned. Most members of his cabinet were football fans in any case, so I quite rightly doubted at the time that much would change there. What one critic once called "the philistine creed of athleticism" will surely endure for the foreseeable future. Indeed, in July 2000 the government declared that they wanted to see a revival in "competitive sports" in UK schools.

In Britain, most schools have but one hour of P.E. every week and one afternoon of what we call "games" and that's about it, unless you volunteer to join a sports club. Many Japanese students spend far more of their time playing sports, or rather in repetitive training as members of what they euphemistically refer to as "club activities"; "bu-katsudo" in Japanese.

Students are usually required to join at least one club, although this varies from one school to another. About two thirds of boys are in sports clubs in middle school. Those who enter the "volunteer" or "photography club" for example have a far less rigorous time of it. Indeed, members of the volunteer club fulfil a useful social function such as visiting old people and doing various kinds of work in the local community. Clearly they are learning something positive from it. The clubs meet once a week in junior school, but become progressively harder and more time-consuming especially in the three years of middle school, from 13 to 15 years of age.

On the contrary, those students unwise enough to enter sports clubs, especially baseball for example, will have precious little free time until they graduate. Certainly, the baseball and karate clubs are the most brutal and demanding. Based on what I've seen and heard, many of the clubs appear to operate semi-independently for part of the time. It is up to teachers and even senior members when they meet. I saw students enter the teachers' room inquiring as to whether or not they had to attend club activities at the end of classes that day. Often they seem to go to school having no idea whether or not they have to stay behind afterwards for two or three hours in training. Many students are obliged to give up Saturday afternoons and sometimes Sundays as well for the sake of their precious "club."

Even worse, they are required to devote about half their summer holidays to endless practice sessions, making a mockery of the official six-week vacation. I can't see why the schools even bother calling it "summer vacation" since they only get from about two to two and a half weeks off in reality. They don't even seem to play that many actual games, just repetitive, tedious training. To me, the sight of a group of totally exhausted Japanese students on a sweltering summer's day with their equally weary teacher trudging home after yet another pointless session of practice is symbolic of this "mutual victimization."

The teachers lose out by sacrificing so much free time, the students likewise and in the end it doesn't even seem to turn out a nation of super-athletes as in the old East Germany. One look at Japan's middling performance in the past few Olympics demonstrates this without any shadow of a doubt. Indeed, recent surveys have shown that the average strength of Japanese students has declined in the past twenty years or so. Many students attach great importance to their club, seemingly more so than to their studies. Furthermore, they can get academic credits from putting in a lot of hours and this is another reason why parents usually endorse the system too, as it will help the children get into good high schools and colleges. It also burnishes their school report cards.

The school club isn't such a bad idea really, but it is one that the Japanese take to crazy extremes. Once again, we can see how the "more must always be better" mindset is deeply ingrained into the Japanese psyche. Many students clearly enjoy their club activities, although just as obviously others do not. In the mid-nineties, I taught English to a boy called Tooru for a while. He attempted to quit his karate club, complaining it was too strict and brutal. The teacher in charge of the club took him aside and punched him in the mouth, leaving him needing stitches. His mother protested but to no avail and the hazing went on. Clearly this sort of thing is not common, but the fact that a few teachers resort to coercion and bullying to enforce the system does not reflect it in a very good light. Quite a few teachers seem as worn out from coaching the clubs as the hapless students are from being obliged to attend practice sessions so often.

I also witnessed a boy at one of the schools where I teach attempt to quit his club. Two teachers sat with him and subjected him to the most intense psychological pressure to get him to reconsider his position. He eventually backed down. They made all manner of vague threats that he was letting his friends down and he would find it harder to graduate. If a student is really determined, he or she can resign from his club, but it takes quite a considerable amount of courage to stand up to peers and teachers alike. Students are, in fact, usually forced to quit their clubs during their third and final year of Middle and High School whether they want to or not due to the pressures of their impending final exams.

The apotheosis of this exercise in group-masochism is the All-Japan High School Baseball Tournament held in the summer and featured on national TV. One year I remember a boy being forced to pitch for so long that even in Japan it elicited some criticism from a local doctor who reckoned he could easily have done permanent damage to his arm and shoulder muscles.

In Britain, we too have school clubs, but their purpose is quite different. Membership is voluntary and students can quit without much trouble if they find the club not to their liking. They are meant to inculcate a lifetime interest in whatever activity the student chooses. In most cases, they meet only once or twice a week and never on weekends or during holidays, except for occasional sports festivals. Their popularity in Britain has increased in recent years with soccer, computer and arts clubs picking up by far the most members. Some teachers have complained of the additional workload being placed on them and one teachers' union leader charged that some parents appeared to be abdicating their responsibility by expecting teachers to take care of their children for longer than before just so they could stay at work even later.

So what is the real purpose of the school clubs in Japan? Debate on how to reform the school system doesn't usually mention them, unless it is among foreign observers. It seems obvious to me that the underlying rationale is to mould the Japanese students into good, obedient Japanese subjects. The paramount importance of the needs of the group versus the rights of the individual is stressed again and again. From the day the first grader at Middle School enters his or her club, it becomes an integral part of his or her learning process. The student is expected to sacrifice everything for the club, giving up evenings, weekends, in fact any time when either the senior members, or the teacher who coaches the club decrees.

Seen in this light, the club activities system is perfectly logical for a people whose society depends on a level of control rarely seen outside of dictatorships such as the old Communist countries of Eastern Europe or China. Picture a salaryman putting in yet another evening of overtime, enduring the endless round of pointless drinking parties and the overbearing attitude of his superior or manager. Imagine his wife subjected to the petty unpleasantness of her mother-in-law, or the loneliness she feels due to her husband seeming to be increasingly remote as he becomes still more absorbed in his work. They have learned to put their own happiness second, the dictates of the group first. The school clubs served as their first lesson in the fact that they are expected to resign themselves to their hardships for the well being of whatever group, company or family they have become a part of.

Even into university, students join clubs, sometimes with the idea of making their resume appear more attractive to potential employers. It is said that this helps to make them look like the kind of team players that Japanese companies are looking for.

Another problem facing Japanese students is the pressure they are under to pass the exam to enter high school. This is known as "juken jigoku", or literally "exam hell" by the Japanese. They sit exams, which determine the high school they will go to. In recent years some children have failed and committed suicide as a result. There were moves underway to make this less of an ordeal. In recent years, falling birthrates have largely solved this problem. Schools have lowered their entrance standards, some drastically, in order to attract students.

As the number of children falls year on year, it has become a buyer's market.

One way where Japanese schools were different to those in Britain and especially Europe is the level of parental involvement in schools. In Britain, parents will show up for an annual open evening, the odd school play and depending on the school, one or two other events, but generally will have relatively little regular contact with either the school or other parents unless they so wish. In France, it is even more pronounced with parents barred from visiting the classroom from the earliest years. One American journalist stationed in Paris commented on how odd he found the total apathy of the parents when showing up to watch a soccer game one Saturday. He estimated that perhaps only half of them bothered to turn up and many had already wandered off to nearby cafes or bars before the whistle had been blown for half time.

The Parent Teachers Association (PTA) exists in Britain, but whether they attend or not is entirely up to the parents. It is said that in some schools there is indirect pressure to shame parents into attending, but nothing like the overt coercion that is prevalent in Japan. My mother for example went to the grand total of one meeting, decided it had nothing to offer her and never bothered again. However, there are always enough parents with the time and inclination to help out with school plays and such, this volunteer spirit is a long-standing tradition in Britain. In America, parents compete for places on the PTA council and some take it very seriously.

In contrast, the Japanese PTA is something like a plant, benevolent in its native environment, but a rampant pest when introduced into a new country. Like many groups in Japan, it is used as a tool of control and for swathing everyone concerned in yet another layer of bureaucracy.

In Japan, it often seems to be the bane of many parents and teachers alike, expecting the former to give up time to attend every meeting it holds and there are a lot of them, what with the regular open classes, "fathers groups" and such. (Although at one school where I worked, the "Father's Group" appeared to be basically a drinking club, while at another, it only met sporadically.) An "open class" is where parents (Make that mostly mothers) are expected to come in and stand at the back watching a lesson. Open classes are held in Britain too, but less often.

Men can and often do use the excuse that they are too busy with their work to attend. Ironically, men often hold most of the top positions, these being largely ceremonial only requiring them to make a formulaic speech at opening and graduation ceremonies and not a whole lot else.

Women are not so lucky. They are coerced into all sorts of idiotic activities everything from making newsletters and even playing volleyball together. How team sports for the moms helps their kids learn better makes no logical sense to this writer. My wife told me that one school even used to have mothers come in occasionally to help clean the classroom, but this practice elicited so many complaints that it was eventually discontinued. Even the "passive mothers" have their limits it seems. There is certainly a lot of bullying and nastiness among the members and nearly 20% of teachers cite problems with mothers as being their chief source of stress. The parents, namely some of the more education-obsessed mothers have the real power not the teachers. My friend Reiko told me that she endured some pretty unpleasant bullying by one or two of the more dominant mothers in the PTA for a couple of years.

Mothers who refuse to tow the line are often ostracized and there is always the suggestion, or threat, that their children will be picked on at school if they do not cooperate with the often idiotic demands made of them. Indeed, many Japanese mothers of my acquaintance have told me how much they bitterly resent the PTA and its arrogant attitude. They are already busy enough without being expected to waste their time at seemingly endless and largely purposeless meetings. In a sense, we can see that the PTA in Japan is time-warped, stuck somewhere in early 1950s America, where women had the time and the inclination to indulge themselves in such things. Even the former Tokyo governor, Shintaro Ishihara once made a typically barbed criticism of the schools. He said something to the effect that if mothers had so much time for all those silly meetings, they should devote that time to more productive activities such as doing some voluntary work in the local community.

Nietzsche said, "People with a profound dissatisfaction with themselves gain pleasure in causing pain, probably their only pleasure." There are plenty of mothers who actually enjoy the PTA and the fleeting sense of power it gives them over other members. Others quite literally have absolutely nothing better to do and genuinely seem to believe that they are making a worthwhile contribution towards their children's education. I taught English to one homemaker who liked nothing better than to be elected to every conceivable committee. Without her meetings to attend and the ersatz authority she felt, by her own admission her life would be a little bit empty. All she did otherwise was go shopping in department stores or sit around the house dozing and watching TV. She saw a significant chunk of her social life disappear the year her son graduated.

Obviously, if a mother wants to stand up to the PTA, she certainly can, although relatively few seem to. It's my guess that as more women continue to work after marriage and as divorce increases, the PTA will find itself faced with more resistance by mothers who simply haven't the time to waste. The second time Reiko had a run in with the PTA was after her divorce. She told me that after being "volunteered" for membership of some committee in her absence, she shamed her PTA group into leaving her in peace. She explained that now she was a single mother, she returned home from work at 10 p.m. on occasion. There was no way she could get there before the meeting had ended. Many of the "professional housewife" types on the committee had never done a day's work outside the home in their lives. She said how some of them seemed genuinely shocked that any woman would have such a strenuous job. They simply declared her to be a "ghost member" and more or less left it at that. Once again, we can see how the Japanese can't cope when faced with determined resistance in relationships.

One or two schools have replaced the traditional PTA structure with a far less formal list of volunteers who are called upon when needed, much like the situation in some British schools. Conceivably this will be the way of the future, but don't expect change to come anytime soon.

Like my mother before me, my own experience of meetings at my stepdaughter's middle school stretched to only one. I had already resolved that I would have nothing to do with the PTA unless there was a good reason and this clearly was one of them. She had been with a group of boys who were inhaling glue and although she had been trying to persuade them to stop, she was found guilty by association. I attended the meeting called by the teachers to discuss the problem, as I wanted to show support for my new family.

Only four mothers turned up, the fifth was too busy they said. Apart from me, only one father came and he was half an hour late. The meeting itself dragged on for almost four hours, with the trio of teachers repeating themselves over and over. I couldn't see any reason why it needed to last more than an hour at most. One teacher appeared to doze off while I caught another looking at his watch more than once. Two of the other mothers just droned on about their precious little angels being such good boys and it must be the company they are keeping.

What the teachers had to say was essentially correct, that glue sniffing was wrong, but it was also clear to me that they hadn't a clue how to counteract such behaviour. I thought their reaction was basically aggressive defensive, which judging from the attitudes of those two other mothers was not surprising in the least. They are on the receiving end of the barbs and complaints of these narrow-minded individuals on a regular basis.

Another example of how the Japanese schools are still rooted firmly in the past is the visits the middle-school homeroom teacher makes periodically to the houses of the students. This is an inconvenience for both mothers and teachers alike, as they are both obliged to juggle their schedules as a result. Some of the more assertive mothers will change their appointments at short notice. Quite honestly, this idea, while not a bad one in principle really harks back to an earlier era when people had the time for such luxuries. In any case, the meeting is usually formulaic, with little genuine content. In Britain, most parents only have meetings with teachers if there is a problem, or on irregular occasions such as Parents' Evenings.

Clearly something is wrong with the schools in Japan; they are facing many of the problems that British schools have been plagued with for a longer period. By 1997, the number of primary and middle school students who were absent for a total of 30 days or more for reasons other than poverty or illness topped 100,000. Worse, the number of teenagers aged 14 to 19 taken into police custody in the first half of 1998 rose by 70,000. The years 1998 and 1999 saw further rises in the number of students being absent from school and dropping out altogether. By 2000, this had risen to 130,000. Some observers felt relief that the total appeared to be levelling off, but to others that was no real consolation.

Cases of violence in schools reported to police rose by 22.3% from a year earlier. Nearly half of these were incidents of attacks on teachers by students. The results of a government-sponsored survey also released in 1998 stated that: "juvenile delinquency is increasing and is occurring at younger ages." Probation officers noted that recent offences were more brutal and that offenders showed less restraint. "Many of the officers said that a lack of discipline and family dysfunction were major reasons for the changes."

During the late 1990s, the phenomenon known in Japanese by the term "enjo kosai" or "compensatory dating" started making headlines. This refers to where high school and even junior high school girls are basically prostituting themselves to much older men for cash. Some were making considerable sums of money. One estimate claimed that 6% of all girls aged 15 to 18 were engaged in this practice, or had done so at least once. Laws were tightened up to ban sex between men and underage girls, although the practice appears to be continuing.

In Britain, expulsion from the school altogether or suspension for a week or two is a common reaction to the problem of destructive or violent students. This is resorted to much less in Japan. I was with the Japanese English teacher trying to conduct one of our classes and persuade a particularly troublesome boy to come down off the top of the shelf where he was stretched out pretending to sleep. Eventually, he gave up and left the little wretch alone. "He will still graduate," the teacher replied to my question concerning the boy's ultimate fate with a weary smile.

In a truly horrific case in the late 1990s, for instance, a fourteen-year-old boy obsessed with torturing small animals killed and then decapitated a slightly retarded eleven-year-old neighbour and left the head on the school gates. Under the woefully inadequate provisions for dealing with juvenile offenders, this monster was probably released from the detention centre that the court committed him to before he was twenty.

In December 1999, even as I was beginning my research for this chapter, another murder occurred in the playground of a school in Kyoto. This time a seven-year-old student was knifed to death by a masked attacker who fled the scene. In February 2000, police arrested a 21 year-old suspect who managed to give them the slip and leap to his death from the rooftop of an apartment building.

Nor is Britain free of such horrors. In the early 1990s, the nation was outraged by the murder in Liverpool, Northern England of two-year-old James Bulgar, who had momentarily wandered away from his mother in a supermarket. Two eleven year old boys absconded with him and then stoned him almost to death, finally leaving the boy on a railway track to be run over by a train. The boys were released on turning 18. Ten years later, one of them appeared in the news as he had been returned to jail after involvement in child pornography and violation of his parole conditions.

According to the probation officers, such tragedies are mainly the fault of the parents and yet it is the self-important PTA dragons that are the loudest in denouncing the teachers every time there is a problem. Many of them are too narrow minded and stupid to see they are largely to blame. In their blind obsession with education, some of them resemble the kind of know-all who routinely tells his doctor what is wrong with him. Children that are indulged by their mothers will be far less able to handle discipline when they have hardly ever had any. Moreover, teachers do not know how to deal with increasingly rebellious students. A few years ago student on student bullying became a serious problem, but lately this seems to have declined, with acts of violence against school property and teachers increasing instead. "Bullying declined for the third consecutive year (in 1998) down 21% from the previous year." However, violence was still reported at a third of all schools in the same year.

One middle school teacher was so shocked when a student swore at him that he couldn't react. He was just not mentally prepared for such defiance. He had never experienced such a thing. In all fairness, some teachers have been trying to address the problem. One example came in the late 90s in Osaka, where some students staged a lock-in protest, barricading themselves into the school library. The teachers began collaborating as a group, offering each other help and back up. They also adopted a less rigid stance towards the students, concluding that: "Teachers should no longer try to jam children into the prefabricated mould, where students simply did what teachers ordered them to."

Teachers in the UK have long recognized this and more recently, in cooperation with schools, the government has set up a bullying hotline where victims can report incidents. Many schools have made strenuous efforts to crack down on bullying. Even so, schools in Britain are under-funded and some middle class parents have been taking their children out of the system altogether to have them educated in private schools. Even the Education Minister David Blunkett declared the quarter-century-old Comprehensive School model a failure. In Britain, as in Japan, teachers recently have complained of the rise in paperwork and the bureaucracy they have to deal with on a regular basis.

Even if much of the blame rests with the parents, then the schools can't be let off the hook altogether. Many Japanese students are left in a semi-permanent state of exhaustion, due in part to the excessive levels of sports and training they are obliged to take part in. Besides teaching them teamwork and helping them obtain credits towards their graduation, another purpose behind this is said to be an attempt to channel their youthful energies away from thoughts of rebellion or sex. It seems only logical to scale back the club activities. The two biggest complaints from the students themselves according to several surveys are that they have no free time and they are always tired, which leaves them irritable as a result.

Once students enter university their situation changes dramatically. Japanese higher education is harder to get into than in Britain, but graduation is much easier. Expulsion is rare in Japan, but commonplace in Britain if the student fails to maintain at least a "C" average. Many Japanese are critical of their universities, regarding them as little more than a four-year vacation for the students after the rigors of middle and high school. I once conducted a survey of attitudes towards education among Japanese people. This was as a part of my degree in Asian studies. Over 60% of those I questioned regarded Western universities as being superior and many of the rest said the sole reason they would prefer to attend university in Japan was that they could study in their native language.

I have certainly heard enough about the content of courses in Japanese universities to doubt that many of the students should be there in the first place. They are quite simply wasting their own time and their parents' money. One young woman I taught once told me she played tennis three times a week, usually went drinking about as frequently and attended less than nine hours a week of actual lectures. Worse, she often skipped on the classes that she didn't have much interest in. Even so, she graduated and landed a job with one of the major Japanese banks.

In Japan, 55% of 18 year olds go on to university or two-year-college, as against about a fifth of Americans. In Britain, the figure rose from about a quarter in 1997 to 40% by 2013. Obviously this has seen a concurrent rise in the number of drop out students, anything from 15 to 36% depending on the course. Many critics in Japan see Japanese universities as having limited educational value. In Britain, some have been saying recently that people who simply aren't capable of completing a degree course have been lured into continuing their education by the hope of landing a lucrative job in the city. This has meant that many of the more non-traditional "liberal arts" type degree courses they have enrolled in are of no use to employers. They are regarded as having been set up only to accommodate those students who would be lost if they tried to tackle a more intellectually rigorous and demanding study programme.

The irony here is that by the late 1990s in Japan, top companies and government offices preferred to recruit from the most prestigious universities and yet much of what students have learned is superfluous to their requirements, since the company will train them in whatever skills they need anyway. To the company, it seems to be little more than proof that the graduates know how to knuckle down and become obedient little drones. They could just as well have hired new workers out of high school and saved their parents a small fortune.

Even more ironic, is that my rhetorical question seems to have been answered. By 2005, it was reported in the Daily Yomiuri that increasingly, companies are hiring students straight out of high school, as their academic levels are not seen to be markedly higher after four years of goofing off in University. If this trend continues, many universities could find themselves facing serious downsizing.

Professor of Economics Takamitsu Sawa is dismissive of the cramming methods used by both schools and colleges. He notes that for instance, the average scores of Japanese English students in the "Test of English as Foreign Language" or TOEFL was only 496 in 1996, compared with 555 for Chinese. Even Mongolian and North Korean scores at 490 and 497 were almost identical, in spite of their relative isolation and far less developed economies. Even worse he noted how Japanese students languished third from bottom in a survey of the test results from other East Asian nations when it came to knowledge of grammar. This is in spite of the fact that most English teaching in schools is heavily focused on reading, writing and the rote memorization of grammar points.

Sawa also worried that the facts and figures the students spend so much time and effort cramming into their heads fail to stay put, "knowledge obtained in this way is easily lost, leaving just a void in the mind." He asserts. It reminds me of the frantic last minute cramming I went through at high school that last night before a big test and my teacher's advice not to study just before an examination because the facts wouldn't remain in our heads.

In 2000, the newspapers trumpeted the fact that the average Japanese TOEFL score had finally topped 500, but this only meant that Japan was now ahead of such countries as Afghanistan and Laos. Clearly they still had a way to go.

Ultimately, the cruelest twist of all is that in recent years, since the collapse of Japan's so- called "bubble economy" at the onset of the nineties, increasing numbers of companies have moved to end the lifetime employment system, thus rendering the "education mother" as obsolete as the mechanical typewriter. If the whole purpose of such women was to see their sons hired by the huge corporations, then the news that Nissan, for example is shedding 21,000 jobs as part of restructuring efforts must strike fear into their hearts. Press reports have expressed views pretty much along these lines. It was also reported once again that some companies are considering hiring high school rather than university graduates, as they will be more receptive to training. Or in plain English, they won't have wasted four years on an extended party and will be still in tune with the ability to cram in information.

The schools are hoping to move to a more communicative approach to teaching. My impression is that many of the teachers are up to it and it is the system that holds them back. In Britain, the main concern is with rooting out defective teachers and reducing the size of the classroom. The Blair administration introduced "league tables" to show the best and worst schools. This did not exactly endear the government to the teachers who at their trade union conference in 1999 said half jokingly "Bring back the real Tories."

In Japan, the government: "In its report on youth earlier this year (1999) called on parents to spend more time with their children. Others are urging schools to teach morals and the courts to fall harder on youthful offenders. The school system is also facing calls for a vast overhaul to cut the emphasis on conformism and allow youngsters to express their ideas and individuality. Corporations have been urged to give fathers more time to spend with their families." (Daily Yomiuri)

In 2002 The Education Ministry reduced the existing curriculum by around 30%. This was intended to give students, in particular at high school level more scope in selecting study subjects. The report also stresses the need for the changes to promote initiative and independent thinking. It is tempting to speculate just what this will do to the whole fabric of Japanese society if it succeeds in its aims!

Then fast forward to 2014 and we can read yet another story about a tragedy at a Japanese school. "A high school girl has been arrested on suspicion of killing and dismembering a classmate, Japanese police say. The 15-year-old was arrested on Sunday in Sasebo city in Japan's southern Nagasaki prefecture.

Police said the girl beat her friend and then strangled her on Saturday. She then severed the victim's head and cut off one of her hands, they said. Ten years ago, a similar crime rocked the same city when an 11-year-old schoolgirl stabbed her 12-year-old friend to death." The reason appeared to be that the friend had criticized her in internet chat rooms."

Meanwhile, in the UK, writing in the Guardian, Susan Elkin commented that "Education is in trouble in this country. And the situation has been worsening for as long as I can remember. We now send (most) children to school for fifteen years, from age three to age 18. And still they emerge with appalling, shameful shortcomings. The exam passes they may or may not hold are just a smokescreen.

The CBI regularly complains that grades awarded in school level exams are no indicator of literacy, numeracy or general ability and that companies such as Tesco (supermarket chain) have difficulty recruiting young workers of the right calibre. International ranking now puts Britain's education, once the envy of the world, sixth after Finland, South Korea, Hong Kong, Japan and Singapore. So how are our school leavers supposed to compete?"

Education is also being undermined in the UK by the existence of "faith schools" and cases such as the recent scandal in Birmingham, a city with a large Anglo-Asian population. Operation Trojan Horse was an organized attempt by Islamists to covertly co-opt schools in England. "Elected (school board) members were aware of extremist activities many months before the allegations surfaced but had made no serious attempt to address the issue, instead focusing on community cohesion and appeasement." The abject failure of the whole multicultural experiment even begins to leave some of the most ardent liberals scrabbling for excuses.

Japanese veteran high school teacher and education expert Hiroshi Sugita makes a number of recommendations on his website which are quite typical of thinking amongst many in Japan. Among other things, he suggests are "more school choices, more civilian principals, a little more difference between salaries of good teachers and average teachers, etc". He also considers that since "national laws prohibit teachers to administer corporal punishment to students and also suspension from elementary and junior high schools. In many cases class environment and school environment is becoming worse. Principals and teachers should administer other disciplinary methods, for instance, in-school suspensions, detention after school, community service, etc."

Sugita also touched on the idea of inculcating more competition between schools in the private and public sector. This theme was also central to the ideas expressed by the writer Ron Perrier. He points out that: "Students have different characters and accordingly, educational theories must be diverse. Therefore, many educational curricula should be tried in a competitive manner. However, there is no such thing in Japan. The diversity of school books and other materials is limited and there is little room for developing new educational materials and methods. Japanese education is far from vital."

Perrier echoes Sugita in calling for more flexibility as well as acceptance of diversity in schools. He cites the example of reforms at Tokyo's Waseda

University. "Four years ago,(around 2009) Waseda launched a new School of International Liberal Studies as a testing ground for "enforced artificial internationalism," as Paul Snowden, the school's dean, describes it. All classes are taught in English. The school as a matter of policy recruits one-third of its students from overseas, from countries as far away as Iceland and Uganda. The strategy seems to be working. Since it opened, the programme has seen enrollment grow at an annual average rate of 15%. "This school is dragging Waseda kicking and screaming into the 21st century," Snowden says.

Finally Chaz Valentine writing in Japan Today goes one stage further. He advocates a simple solution to the problem. "So, how to fix this whole Japanese public educational debacle? Easy. Abolish all public schools. Let private schools and private teachers compete with each other. And let parents and students choose their own education.... The solution is very easy but very hard to achieve. The reason for this is that people think the end of public schools would be the end of education in Japan. Most people worry about paying high tuition fees to private schools. But everybody fails to realize that private schools are only expensive because public schools exist. Without public schools, private schools will get a lot cheaper and affordable."

It remains to be seen how this would solve the problem. My feeling is that such a step would simply see poorer families saddled with the worst education money can buy since it would, should market forces be allowed to dictate what is available to them, be a race to the bottom to provide the cheapest schooling possible.

However, I entirely agree with Valentine's conclusion: "The current Japanese educational policies are misguided and misinformed. Eventually and unfortunately, the children pay the price for these mistakes and they are left with bad education unsuited to an uncertain future. If we really value our children's future, we should make bold and brave steps to change the current system. Because we, the human race, only advance if our children can have a better education and opportunities for themselves."

SOURCES

(1) Article in Los Angeles Times

(2) Friedrich Nietszche- "The Genealogy of Morals" Page 96

(3) Articles from Daily Yomuri Newspaper

(4) "Passive mothers" An ironic term, as many mothers are anything but passive when it comes to their children's education. In Japan, many people believe that once a woman has children she becomes very "passive."

(5) Professor   Sawa (from "Japan Times" Article)

(6) Source BBC News 28th July 2014

(7) Susan Elkin "Education is in Trouble in the UK" Guardian article 8th February 2013

(8) CBI – Confederation of British Industry, an employers' organization

(9) Patrick Wintour, "Trojan horse inquiry – A coordinated agenda to impose hardline Sunni Islam" Guardian 18th July 2014

(10) Shoji Sugita website http://www.aba.ne.jp/~sugita/103e.htm

(11) 2013 Ron Perrier website http://www.ronperrier.net – problems with Japanese Education

(12) Japan Today March 23rd 2013 "What's wrong with Japanese education?"

MYTHS AND STEREOTYPES

"China -- the cake of kings and... of emperors"

French political cartoon from 1898

Psychologists theorize that right from the beginning of our lives, we relate new information to something we already know in order to build up a coherent picture of the world. Our brain files fresh incoming data in much the same way as we categorize a piece of mail at the office. We take a look at it and decide where it seems to fit in best. Then we pop it in the accounts tray, under bills to be paid, or wherever. This is called schematic thinking.

Psychology describes "Schemas - sets of organized expectations about the way in which different behaviours in people hang together. If we believe someone to be outgoing and gregarious, we will also expect him to be relatively talkative. He may or may not be, but the pattern we perceive is partially imposed by our schema of what an outgoing and gregarious person is like."

When applied to social stereotypes these schemas are used to relate to social groups, even sometimes to whole races of people. The French cartoon above shows the various powers dividing China up between them and plays to the stereotypical image of Chinese and for that matter of Japanese. People tend to lump whole nations together and assume either consciously or unconsciously that everyone in that category will fit in to our notion of what it means to be a Greek, a Jew or an African-American, for example. Often the racial stereotyping is negative in content. Mention Jews and some will think of the less than life-enhancing foreign policies of Israel. Talk of African Americans and too often negative images of urban violence and crack cocaine fill our heads.

Take this writer as an example. An Englishman, so according to the stereotype, I should be a tea drinking, roast-beef eating gentleman, polite to a fault, who cannot speak a word of another language, who wears a cloth cap if he is from the North and who looks down on the French. In fact, the only one of these that is true of me is that I do indeed wear a cloth cap (in spite of not being from the north of England.) I prefer coffee to tea and haven't eaten red meat for many years in fact. Furthermore, I do speak Japanese to a passable degree of fluency and have absolutely no feelings of contempt towards the French. As to being a gentleman and polite to a fault, I categorically deny both of these charges!

These are lingering images of Japan and Britain; the English gentleman, the samurai warrior, foggy London Town, the Japanese love of nature. Many of the most common stereotypes surrounding Japan and Britain are either outdated, or in a lot of cases, just plain wrong.

Japanese Politeness

Obviously the Japanese seem polite in many given situations although there is always the problem of definition. Nietzsche said that language was only labeling something or rather like trying to fit everything into what we already know. Thus we label the Japanese polite. It's a convenient way to categorize them.

The second problem here is that what does "polite" mean in the first place? Are we to compare degrees of politeness within one single culture? This is meaningless since some individuals are regarded as being polite and others rude by their peers within their own society. Furthermore, what is polite, or commonplace in one culture can be judged as being at best quaint or strange and at worst as downright rude within the framework of another.

For instance, consider the table manners of the Japanese. Take variety TV programmes where celebrities sample some culinary delicacy or other. They cram huge chunks of it into their mouths, then talk and chew at the same time, something that is pretty deplorable by Westerns standards. They suck up their noodles making a vile slurping sound in a manner Westerners often find somewhat revolting. Many do the same for soup or hot drinks. Such behaviour is anything but polite from a Western viewpoint. There is also the Japanese tendency to wolf their food down as if they are in a speed eating contest. This is often frowned upon as being bad form in the West. One theory is that this goes back to the days of the samurai who ate hastily so as to be ready at a moment's notice to go into battle. The harried salaryman continues to scoff down his meals to try and keep up with his busy schedule.

The Japanese are notoriously vague in their language. This is a cultural not linguistic characteristic, as it is perfectly possible to be as precise in Japanese as in English. It's just that people aren't for the reason that it is regarded as being impolite. Westerners often find this vagueness irritating and it leads some to conclude that the Japanese are sneaky, dishonest and two-faced. In contrast the Japanese often find Westerners and their directness to be rude and threatening.

Many Japanese are often unintentionally rude when they respond in English when a foreigner attempts to speak in Japanese. Theories of why this should be range from the notion that either they cannot accept a Westerner could actually speak their language, or it constitutes a kind of nervous reaction. Nonetheless, it can create ill will. The Westerner feels insulted, or that the person he or she is speaking to regards his or her Japanese ability to be inferior. There also used to be a tendency among drunken businessmen on trains to try and very rudely start practicing English on any Caucasian on the seat next to them. By the end of the 1990s it had thankfully more or less died out.

Japanese men can also be seen urinating in public, spitting and vomiting, disregarding no smoking signs to name but a few of their habits. Indeed, even among the Japanese themselves, some of these are regarded in a negative light. The results of a poll way back in the 1960s showed that only 37% of the Japanese considered themselves to be polite.

During the late 1980s, the term "obatallion" came into vogue, based on a TV comedy programme about a dreadful old woman. "Oba" from "obasan" or middle-aged woman and "tallion" from the English word "battalion." Thus a new stereotype was born. Women thus categorized range from the merely somewhat pushy and perhaps a tad too assertive in the eyes of their peers to the downright obnoxious. They are described as being like middle aged dragon ladies, dripping with jewelry and clad in brand name goods. They are said to be overweight and very loud, pushing everyone out of the way to get to a seat on the train.

Anyone who thinks the Japanese are invariably polite should try riding trains in Tokyo. Aside from the pushing and shoving, quite a few Japanese seem to think it perfectly acceptable to take up two seats on the train. This is especially true of men who were dubbed "spreaders" by the foreign community. With their legs jutting out at close to 90-degree angles they seem to dare anyone to try and make them budge. (They do grudgingly move when made to though.)

Women are often no better, putting a bag on the seat beside them and pretending to be asleep when anyone tries to sit down. Anyone with a newspaper will happily ram it into the face or back of the head of their fellow commuters regardless of how tightly jammed the car is. As for the use of mobile phones on commuter trains, JR (Japan Railways) outright banned the practice although many ignore this rule until another commuter tells them to shut up. In Japan, you are as likely as anywhere to be blindsided by someone, or shoved out of the way without an apology. Idiots walking along playing with their mobile phones will walk into each other in a way that is as rude as it is infantile and inconsiderate. If this last phenomenon doesn't convince outsiders that the Japanese are in no way intrinsically polite, then surely nothing will.

Japanese cyclists can be horrendous. There isn't much room for pedestrians and cyclists on the narrow roads in Japan. So back in 1981, some genius in the cabinet appears to have decided it would be a great idea to let cyclists use the pavements. There is a law that prioritizes pedestrians called "hokou yusen" or "pedestrian right of way". Try telling that to the cyclists. Most of them regard the sidewalk as their preserve treating anyone on foot as a moving obstacle course to weave and dodge around. Many can be observed riding at reckless speeds, ringing their bells, expecting anyone in their path to move. This isn't a reflection on the Japanese cyclist so much as a condemnation of the stupid rule that relegates people on foot to third class status. It does yet again demonstrate a lack of innate politeness where most cyclists in Japan are concerned. It was once estimated by someone in Osaka that there is an accident involving a collision between a cyclist and a pedestrian every six seconds.

In East Asia Japanese are distrusted by many people who still remember the atrocities committed by Imperial Japanese soldiers before and during the Second World War. Then how come Japanese are still regarded as being polite?

Is this is due to the custom of bowing? This is only the Japanese version of the handshake, but to a Western observer, it does come across as being very genteel. The Japanese tend not to speak their mind, which can either make them seem reserved or secretive, depending on the social situation. Japanese also tend to err on the side of politeness when meeting someone for the first time. They are unsure of where that person fits on the social scale relative to them. This is as much caution as politeness.

Then there are the linguistic barriers. No more than 20% of Japanese can speak English fluently and even many of those who do are very careful. They are afraid of making mistakes and have little practice in speaking outside of the classroom. Therefore when speaking with Westerners, they tend to stick to straight from the textbook frozen language as much as possible making them appear very formal and, of course, polite.

What about the English gentleman though?

What about him indeed? This is a similar myth that still persists in Japan and to some extent in the United States regarding the British. In particular, this applies to the English gentleman. Some argue that he was largely an invention of literature, of writers such as Thackery in the early 19th century and their ideals of how a middle class male should behave. We all know the old image, the gent in his bowler hat, umbrella in hand, always refined and polite to a fault. Some people perhaps think of Prince Charles when they hear about the English gentleman. How laughable considering that he was having an affair with Camilla, a married woman while he promised to love honour and cherish Diana in 1981. Their liaison endured throughout their star-crossed marriage.

Let's bring on the wrecking ball, shall we? John Steed of the Avengers TV series back in the 1960s wore a bowler hat. Even by then, that formal look had begun to disappear and by the 1980s was seen only rarely on the City streets. British people do tend to carry umbrellas though, nothing surprising about that, since the climate is wet and can be changeable. Take any rainy day in Tokyo, though and a far higher proportion of the population will be holding their umbrellas aloft. Japanese share with many Asian peoples a strong dislike of being rained on. In Britain, some people carry umbrellas, but a lot of men spurn their use. This might be some sort of macho pose; I don't pretend to understand the reason why.

The English gentleman exists, but he is representative of a very small segment of the population. Indeed, it is as much a value judgment as anything else. There are polite Englishmen of course, just as there are rude ones. Some people would regard the anachronistic "ladies first" attitude as a form of sexism. They would charge that the gentleman treats women in a condescending manner, as if they are poor weak creatures in need of his protection. Sexual equality means equality of treatment. Changing attitudes and advances in women's rights have helped make the "English gentleman" almost a thing of the past. Many men are afraid to appear chauvinistic any more.

Across the Channel in mainland Europe however, the British are often looked down on as being rude, pushy and above all else, stupid. The antics of football hooligans whenever England play on the continent have helped destroy any lingering images of cultured gentlemen. "It's disgusting," said one French woman being interviewed at the time of the 1998 World Cup while she was watching English fans hurl chairs and bottles. "They just seem to drink all day and sit on the beach and go red like lobsters."

Later on, after much damage to property and injury to random strangers and opposing fans alike the Deputy Prefect of Marseilles commented "All those in the police cells are so drunk that they cannot identify themselves in either French or English!"

This is not to say that all young Englishmen are football fans and more to the point, only a few of those fans are troublemakers. Surely far less than one in ten, but it is enough to establish the stereotype in the minds of many. It only takes yet another World Cup with the attendant carnage to reinforce it. It made me wonder what would happen in 2002 when the World Cup came to Japan for the first time. Would sake-crazed British football hooligans running riot through the streets of Tokyo finally put to rest the notion that the English are all gentlemen once and for all?   We shall see I thought.

In fact, there was not one recorded incident of trouble between a visiting English fan and the authorities, apart from a couple of ticket touts and one or two high jinks. The England footballer David Beckham became somewhat of an iconic figure, with kids sporting imitations of his "skunk Mohican" hairstyle. I concluded that the idea of the English as gentlemanly had survived. Ironically it was the working class lads and lasses with their tattoos and beer bellies, the antithesis of the traditional image of the gentleman or woman who had reinforced that image in the eyes of their Japanese hosts.

The so-called "yob culture" is much decried in Britain and Europe. English people are also infamous for behaving badly when abroad. This is especially true in Spain and France.

Much in the same way, young Japanese abroad rapidly gained a reputation for acting in ways regarded as rude, selfish or offensive by their hosts towards the end of the 20th century. These are typically in either Hawaii, or other East Asian countries. "Americans have been eclipsed by the Japanese as the world's most resented citizens." is a quote from the New China Morning Post from the late 1990s. This seems to have been short-lived for by 2014 the Japanese had fallen out of the top ten. The USA was first with the UK in second place. A similar poll in 2012 by Forbes Magazine ranked French, Russian and British as the three worse offending nations when it came to rude tourists.

Britons abroad typically behave much like the Japanese. They tend to seek out English pubs, food and fellow English people to hang out with. They make little or no serious effort to learn more than a very minimal smattering of their host country's mother tongue; even less when it comes to an appreciation of the culture.

Many foreigners make fun of the pampered Japanese on their package tours. They see it as laughable that they pay good money to be whisked around foreign countries in air-conditioned buses with bilingual guides. Also, they snigger at stories of Japanese who take bags of rice with them on their travels. To tell the truth, the British often have little to feel superior about.

When in Spain, for example, many British tourists neither want nor need any activities to be planned for them. They either lie on the beach "going red like lobsters" or find a pub and get drunk. Doing little more than changing pubs seems to be the attitude of far too many Britons on a foreign vacation.

There are plenty of Japanese and British people who are perfectly well behaved and orderly when abroad, but it doesn't take many bad apples to spoil the reputation of the rest.

Smoggy, Foggy Old London Town

The images of smog swirling around the coach and horses on a Victorian winters evening are surely known to anyone who has watched a Sherlock

Holmes film or TV programme. The carriages and horses clatter through streets barely visible due to the "pea souper" of foggy old London Town. This used to be true. In line with many industrial countries, Britain formerly relied on coal for much of its power. This resulted in smog (From "smoky" plus "fog") the filthy yellow stuff that choked up everyone's lungs and discoloured the buildings of London and other cities.

However, since the sixties, coal has declined as a source of fuel in Britain, especially in homes. Most houses now use gas or electric heating and the old smog has largely gone. Britain is not really much foggier than many other places. Some parts of the country have periods of drought, where water occasionally has to be brought in by truck or rationed with the use of standpipes. Climatic changes have also made Britain dryer than before and unlike Japan, there is anything but a surplus of water. People are urged to be moderate in their consumption.

As for smog, there is a new and even more unpleasant form, that resulting from emissions from cars. This smog is invisible, but none the less deleterious to health. It is found in Britain, Japan and of course anywhere where four wheeled vehicles are in profusion.   In 2002, major parts of the South of England were hit by smog as a result of a toxic stew of pollution from Europe, dust from Saharan desert and local emissions.

The picture below shows a modern-day smoggy London. St Paul's Cathedral can dimly be seen on the right.

Japanese still wear kimonos?

The Japanese and the kimono is another stereotype that still lingers. In contemporary Japan, Western fashions and especially Italian designs are in vogue. A kimono is a pricey commodity. (Some can cost over five thousand pounds or eight thousand dollars each!) Quite a lot of Japanese women no longer have a single kimono in their closet. Certainly, many cannot put one on without the assistance of a professional kimono dresser or "kitsuke." People who work in traditional Japanese restaurants, for example, wear them. Generally speaking, it is not much more common to see someone in a kimono in Japan as a morning suit in Britain. In both cases, it will usually be for a special reason.

On occasions where they are required to wear a kimono, women often rent one and have it wrapped around them and later removed by the professional dresser. Then they go off to their "Coming of Age Day" celebration for example. (This is held on January 10th in the year they turn twenty.) Formerly, parents would make a present of a kimono to a woman on her entering her adult year, but lately, many women elect to take the cash instead and use it for a foreign graduation trip to the States or Europe.

Japanese is too difficult for foreigners to learn, isn't it?

It is surprising just how many people in Japan and elsewhere still cling to this misconception. Granted, it is more of a challenge than the Romance languages for a Westerner whose mother tongue is English, but this simply is not true.

The structure of Japanese is really quite straightforward. There are far less illogical quirks in the grammar than exist in English. Once the student of Japanese gets used to the verb conjugation, he or she discovers that there are only two irregular verbs, as against well over two hundred in English and two basic conjugation patterns. Many people have assured me that Russian or German for example are at least as challenging.

One thing that can't be denied is the difficulty of mastering the writing system. There are over 2,000 "kanji" characters in daily use and Japanese students learn these over several years of schooling. Nonetheless, there are many foreigners fluent in Japanese. Some are close to native speaker levels. These include the American Dave Spector, whose sarcastic wit can be heard regularly on television along with British born Peter Barakan on the radio. Still, the myth that foreigners cannot learn to speak Japanese persists in some quarters.

In 1998, a television programme called "Strange Japanese Habits" appeared. This featured a panel of Japanese speaking foreigners and an equal number of native Japanese who debated various issued in front of a studio audience. Many of the non-Japanese were articulate and expressive. Surely if this show didn't finally convince everyone that the Japanese language is not impossible for foreigners to learn then nothing ever will. The only problem is that it probably made most Japanese think that all foreigners are as volatile and reactionary as some of the characters that appeared on "Strange Japanese Habits." Several of the more dominant panelists came across as just as racist, homophobic and narrow-minded as they furiously accused their Japanese hosts of being.

Monolingual, who moi?

On the subject of language ability, a poll around the turn of the 21st century found that 71% of Americans, 70% of Britons and 81% of Japanese could not speak a second language. Estimates vary, often hampered by innate Japanese modesty, but in 2013 it seemed about 12 to 15% were fluent in English while perhaps up to a quarter could at least manage basic communication.

In 2005 the BBC reported how "Earlier this year the former chief inspector of English schools, Mike Tomlinson, described Britons as "barbarians" when it came to learning foreign languages. Research published this week, which suggested fewer than one in 10 British workers could speak a foreign language, even to a basic level, appeared to show the accusation was well-founded." (From an article by Stephen Robb) In 2013 another poll by the British Council suggested only a quarter of Britons could speak a second language, most often being French.

In each case, it is clear why they are so linguistically inept. For most of the time, there is no motivation to learn a second language. When virtually everyone around you can speak your mother tongue, there is no pressing need to bother struggling to master another. In the United States, apart from areas with a large Hispanic population, this is also mostly true. This is not the case in much of Europe, Africa and India, for instance, where a second language is indispensable. Some Indians use English as a common language with people from different parts of the country, as theirs is one where scores of languages and mutually incomprehensible dialects are spoken.

The Japanese language is grammatically similar to Korean, Mongolian and to a far lesser extent to Turkish and Hungarian. The challenge facing Japanese learners of English is far greater than for a student whose native language is English learning a Romance language such as Spanish. To illustrate, the simple sentence "I go to Tokyo" when written in the word order of Japanese becomes "(I) Tokyo to-go." The personal pronoun "I" is usually omitted, when it is clear the speaker is referring to his or her own actions.

To take another more complicated sentence that many will recall from their childhoods: "This is the cow with the crumpled horn that tossed the dog that worried the cat that killed the rat that ate the malt that lay in the house that Jack built." In Japanese, it becomes something like "This is Jack- (subject particle) built-house in-laid was-malt (connecting particle) ate- it- rat that was by killed-cat was worried by dog that was tossed by-with crumpled horn- cow." This also shows why simultaneous interpretation between Japanese and English is impossible, as often the speaker of one language has to wait to the end of the sentence before knowing what will come at the beginning of the corresponding sentence in the other.

The English and Afternoon Tea

An amusing misconception that many Japanese and not a few people from other countries still persist in believing is that the English all sit down to "afternoon tea" every day. They have seen such English films as "Remains of the

Day" and "Room with a View" and seem to think this is standard. The afternoon tea is often said to have originated among middle-class English ladies in India who had several servants and nothing much to do. To help pass the time they took from the Indians the basic idea of drinking tea with milk and began holding extended tea parties in each other's homes.

The picture above shows afternoon tea in England circa 1907

There's an obvious parallel with the Japanese tea ceremony, which once again was a foreign idea, this time one that originated in China. Monks used to serve tea to keep each other awake in the small hours while they meditated, attended to their devotions, or whatever it is that monks do at such times.

Once again, we can see how an unrepresentative segment of society comes to be regarded as the norm. In fact, British people often have tea breaks while at work, but few people can afford the luxury of indulging in a traditional afternoon tea more than once in a while. Some of them probably wouldn't want to anyway!

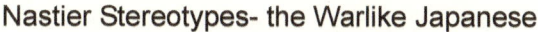

Nastier Stereotypes- the Warlike Japanese

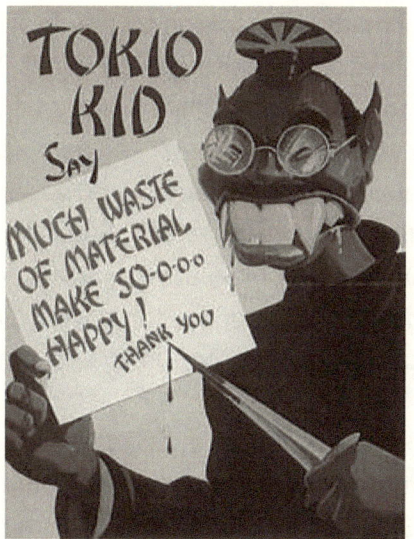

American anti-Japanese poster from WW2

We have all heard the story of the "Cruel and warlike Japanese, yellow skinned and buck-toothed, all looking exactly the same with thick glasses and black hair." While this is no consolation to the many that suffered atrocities at the hands of The Imperial Army up to and during the Second World War, it is a myth.

The cover of a 1998 edition of Time Magazine showed a young Japanese man wearing a headband embellished with the Rising Sun symbol yelling his head off at what seemed to be a martial rally. The article itself spoke of the threat of a resurgent militarism in Japan. In fact, the person featured on the cover was a university student and football fan cheering his country in the World Cup. Old prejudices die hard it seems.

The Japanese were not intrinsically expansionist as a race. Apart from the period from late Meiji (1867-1912) and up to the end of World War Two, they showed precious little inclination to make war on neighbouring countries. Granted the samurai were warlike and fought each other on and off for hundreds of years, but historical records show that attacks on mainland Asia by the Japanese were few and far between. For much of their history, the Japanese wanted nothing to do with the outside world.

Korea was attacked in ancient times, on several occasions in the first few centuries CE. Historically, the Korean peninsula was divided into three warring kingdoms and Japan was sometimes allied with one of them, fighting on the same side. By the tenth century, links with Korea had been significantly downgraded. It wasn't until 1592 that Japan again attacked Korea when Japan's ruler, Toyotomi Hideyoshi made the decision to invade. The attack was repulsed and Hideyoshi died. Negotiations with Korea had failed. The intention had been to pass through Korea and thus invade China which was the real target.

The eventual winner of the civil wars, Ieyasu Tokugawa founded the Shogunate or military government and from 1603, Japan was progressively sealed off from the outside world. First the Spanish and Portuguese were expelled; later only the Dutch and Chinese were permitted to engage in a limited amount of trade. The Chinese were confined to a walled off quarter of Nagasaki while the Dutch were obliged to live on Dejima, a small island in Nagasaki Harbour.

The Japanese had no further interest in military expansion until the late 19th century. Saigo Takamori was one of the leaders of the Meiji Restoration, the coup that restored the Emperor as the head of government and brought to an end over 250 years of military government. His proposal that redundant samurai be allowed to invade Korea in order to give them something to do was rejected by the government.

The Japanese were for the most part farmers. They cooperated in the planting, raising and harvesting of rice and other crops. It took a very determined effort by the government, backed by a sympathetic media to garner support for the military. Only after the defeat of China in 1895 and then Russia in 1905 did the tide of public opinion begin to turn toward favouring military expansion. Even by the Second World War, a sizeable minority, perhaps almost half of all Japanese were less than wholly supportive of their military aggression in Asia. They grudgingly accepted the need to obtain food and raw materials and to some extent supported the ideal of emulating the world powers of the time that controlled vast territories between them.

The Japanese are no more "yellow" than Africans are "black" or Caucasians are "white." This is just crude racial stereotyping. In fact, even among this relatively homogeneous race, there are a variety of skin types, ranging from the almost albino-pale to a swarthy nearly Mediterranean olive brown.

As for the Japanese all looking alike, they say precisely the same thing about Westerners! Younger Japanese are about the same height as people in the West these days.

But what about the buck teeth?

As for the "buck teeth" this is also a lie. There are no more people in Japan with protruding teeth than anywhere else. However, there are far more people with irregular or misshapen teeth than you might expect to find in an advanced industrial society. This is a sad reflection on the lamentable standard of dentistry in 21st century Japan more than anything else. Until quite recently, dentistry in Japan was far inferior to that of most Western countries. There are some skilled dentists in Japan, but plenty of others are almost laughably bad. Gold caps and fillings are still a common sight and orthodontics, or the idea of straightening children's teeth with retainers has only caught on since about the mid-1990s. Astounding when you consider this simple, yet effective method has existed in Britain and elsewhere since the middle of the 19th century.

A set of dental braces (or retainers) costs about £11 ($17) from a manufacturer in Britain and yet in Japan some dentists charge up to ¥1,000,000 over £5,000 or $9,000 US to fit one of their patients with a set. This is double what it costs in the United States. For anyone in the UK under eighteen years of age, thanks to the NHS, the procedure is free. It is my impression that a lot of Japanese dentists are little more than shameless con artists. They drag their compliant patients back over and over again for treatments that in Britain or America would take only one or at most two visits. I have heard stories that some dentists go from one patient to the next without changing their surgical gloves or even the instruments!   Even so, things are improving gradually.

Ironically, in Britain, under the Conservatives, National Health dentistry all but disappeared and what are termed "dental health professionals" started setting up shop. These were dental assistants empowered by new laws to open their own practices by taking advantage of loopholes in those laws, often with horrific results. They were only partially qualified at best. There were stories of people who sought out their services, who lost perfectly healthy teeth and even worse had permanent damage done to the nerves in their faces. Neither Prime Minister Brown and certainly nor his Tory successor honoured the Blair administration's broken pledge to resurrect National Health dentistry and put an end to these bungling amateurs. If not, for many people on lower incomes, the option will be to suffer at the hands of money hungry incompetents, just like in Japan.

But that still doesn't explain the atrocities of WW2

This is true enough. Let me state categorically that I am in no way attempting to excuse the Japanese military for their brutal deeds during the Second World War. However the Japanese are raised to obey those above them and to treat those below them with a certain amount of contempt. A soldier who surrendered was thought to have lost his dignity and to deserve no mercy. The Germans were similarly guilty of heinous crimes against humanity. Would any of us behave any better in this more enlightened age?

During the early 1960s, an American psychologist, Stanley Milgram carried out tests on a group of subjects recruited by newspaper advertisements. He got them to divide up into pairs comprising a "learner" and a "teacher." The learner was strapped into what appeared to be an electric chair and the teacher was told to administer increasing levels of shocks each time the learner got the answer to a question wrong. By putting his subjects on the "slippery slope" of obedience, as psychologists call it, he could get them to follow his orders little by little, starting with minor jolts then steadily building up the voltage.

In reality, the "learner" was always the same man, an actor, unknown to the "teacher" who didn't have any idea the pairings were rigged. No electric shock was delivered. The teacher was fooled into believing that he was hurting the learner. Incredibly, a full 65% of the teachers continued "shocking" the learner until he appeared have died from heart failure. Milgram concluded that his results went at least some of the way to explain how otherwise ordinary people will unquestioningly follow those they regard as being in authority.

Two thirds of a group of Americans, who pride themselves in being individuals and lovers of freedom, could be manipulated in this way. Thus it shouldn't be surprising that the Japanese could be persuaded to slaughter women and children in battle and torture prisoners in Burma and elsewhere. They had already received far more conditioning in the need to obey without question than

178

most people in the West.

A more contemporary example of this is in the attack by the cult Aum Shinrikyo on a Tokyo subway in 1995. Many of the perpetrators seemed pretty unexceptional, graduates from prestigious universities. So did some of Hitler's henchmen. Back at the end of the Second World War, Many people were amazed at how "ordinary" these men, reviled as monsters, seemed when appearing in court. Many stuck to the defense that they had just been obeying orders.

The English as a Nation of Animal-Lovers

Another stereotype is the English being renowned for their kindness to animals. We would perhaps rather forget Rex Harrison in his role as Doctor Doolittle talking to the animals. Australian Rolf Harris of "Tie Me Kangaroo Down, Sport" fame presented the highly popular "Animal Hospital" on British TV, showing there is still a market for this sort of thing.

In fact, the British attitude to animals is not so different to the Japanese (or for that matter of people in many other countries.) It is selective. The British and Japanese go for small, cute cats, dogs and such, while the animal pounds of both countries are full of ex-Christmas presents that outgrew their welcome.

In Britain, it is commonplace to have old and infirm pets painlessly destroyed once they are seen to be no longer able to live with dignity. Indeed, it is illegal to prolong the life of an animal that is clearly suffering. This is not so in Japan, where they will typically keep a dog or cat alive for as long as possible, no matter how feeble-minded or wretched it has grown.

A family of my acquaintance had a pet Chihuahua, a pampered, obnoxious creature that was barely housetrained. In its last couple of years of earthly existence, it was confined to a large cage in a corner of the living room. This was deemed necessary, as it had lost control over its bladder. It was about fifteen years old, increasingly senile and unable to walk far. It also appeared to be virtually blind and ate its own excrement if left to itself. I once suggested that it would be kinder to have it put down. They reacted with shock, telling me they could never do anything so cruel. After a few months, the dog's kidneys failed and its suffering came to an end.

So which is cruel? Was it my recommending the dog for euthanasia, or them keeping it alive in an increasingly pathetic state? It's a matter of opinion, really I suppose. Like in many countries, both the Japanese and British are selectively kind to animals. They will pet some, eat others and kill some purely for the enjoyment of it. People who hunted foxes in Britain did so knowing full well that they could see the fox torn to shreds by a pack of hungry dogs. Some Japanese hunters appear to kill bears for no other reason than it gives them some kind of perverted pleasure. In both cases, these are sick people who "love" living things only so they can abuse them. It is the cruelest irony that the head of the World Wildlife fund is Prince Phillip, a hunter who passionately defends blood sports. He no more appears to care about the pain he inflicts on living things than the bad feeling he routinely causes with his infamous and offensive remarks.

The Japanese are a Unique People.

You will not have to read much about the Japanese or Japan before you encounter the phrase above, in some permutation or other. Many Japanese regard this to be true, that they are unique in the world. There are also plenty of sycophantic Westerners who write similarly of how the Japanese are unlike any other people on the planet.

Once again, we are faced with the problem of language and how our use of particular words can trap us into all manner of stereotypical associations. In a sense, of course the Japanese are unique. So too are the Mongolians, the Germans, the British and the Americans. Or we could break it down and say that Texans are uniquely Texan, or there are some aspects of London life peculiar to London. Such trite observations are a waste of time.

However, there are Japanese writers who verge on the desperate when they try to prove that Japan is unique. They fail to see that they are both right and wrong. Every country in the world differs from every other one in some way. The Japanese "nihonjinron" are just too inward looking to see that.

The Japanese like to regard themselves as having a unique relationship with nature. This is offensive to say the least. Look at the environmental degradation, the concrete lined riverbanks and the mountains of garbage everywhere to see how nonsensical this is. American writer and long-term Japan resident Alex Kerr remarked in "Lost Japan" that "Environmental destruction ...has continued at an ever-increasing rate and now Japan has achieved a position as one of the world's ugliest countries. My friends from abroad who come to visit are almost universally disappointed.

It is said that of Japan's thirty thousand rivers and streams, only three remain un-dammed and even those have had their streambeds and banks encased in concrete. Concrete blocks now account for over thirty per cent of the several thousand kilometers of the country's coastline. The government manages the national forests with complete disregard for ecological balance (there are no forest rangers in Japan)...

And then the electric wires! Japan is the only advanced nation in the world which does not bury electric lines in towns and big cities and this is a prime factor in the squalid visual impression of its urban areas."

Mr. Kerr is not some whining foreigner fresh off the plane either. He wrote his book originally in Japanese after he had been living in the country for nearly seventeen years. He cares passionately about his adopted home, hence the title of the book that was originally "Last glimpse of Beautiful Japan."

The ancient Egyptians for example based their society upon a deep understanding of the cycles of the Nile River. Their gods were personifications of the animals and birds around them. The jackal seen scavenging around dead animals came to be associated with the messenger of the gods, Anubis who brought souls from the earth to be judged in front of Osiris, the god of the afterlife. Anubis was depicted with the head of a jackal. The Amazon Indians were able to live in harmony with nature until Westerners brought with them the devastation of the rain forests. Seen in context, the historical Japanese relationship with nature is nothing exceptional.

The samurai spirit is also seen as being uniquely Japanese. It closely resembles the code of the medieval knights of Britain and Europe. Indeed, after 1600, the samurai were increasingly remote from any kind of combat, more like sword-carrying bureaucrats who practiced martial arts in their spare time, even teaching them sometimes as a means of supplementing their incomes.

When it comes to the four seasons, it astounds me the number of Japanese who can hardly believe that other countries actually have them too. I have even met people who asserted that hay fever was unique to Japan! If this is true, I countered, then why do we have a word for it in the English language? Indeed, I endured worse hay fever in Britain as a child and teenager than since coming to live in Japan.

The manner in which Japan acquired ideas from other cultures and then adapted them is commonplace in other cultures; granted that Japan excels in this field though. As already described in earlier chapters, Britain took most of its early culture and indeed language from the invading Anglo-Saxons and

Normans, even from the Muslims that the Crusaders did battle with in the Holy Land.

Japan's borrowings were so different from what had gone before that they were more glaring and prominent. When the British copied printing techniques pioneered in Germany, nobody accused them of stealing. The Englishman Jonas Hanway (1712-1786) took the Chinese idea of the parasol and turned it into an umbrella. He was initially mocked, but eventually regarded as an innovator. He is believed to have been the first man who ventured to dare public ridicule by carrying an umbrella habitually in London. As he died in 1786 and was said to have carried one for thirty years, he must have started doing so around the year 1755.

A more contemporary example is in the development of popular music. The British took something from another culture, this being America, then re-invented it as something of their own.

Rock and Roll crossed the Atlantic in the mid-fifties. Bill Haley, Elvis, Chuck Berry in the first wave and later Buddy Holly and others quickly conquered the world, Britain included. At first, the homegrown rock and rollers were entirely derivative of their American role models. Billy Fury, Marty Wilde and others, everything from their hairstyles to their catchy names were carbon copies of US idols such as Fabian and Bobby Rydell. The "Teds" appeared shortly before rock and roll. They were named after their retro Edwardian (Ted) jackets with pearly waistcoats borrowed from the London Cockneys. They later adopted Presley hairstyles and blue suede shoes. One more example of how a style can be adapted to suit local sensibilities.

Less than a decade later the so-called British Invasion swept first across America and then the world. In February 1964, four lads from Liverpool, the Beatles had the top five places in the charts. Other bands and singers followed. Just about the only Americans to top the US charts that year were Roy Orbison and Del Shannon. Most of the rest were wiped out by the newcomers and swiftly consigned to the oldies concert circuit or Las Vegas dinner shows.

What had happened was that around 1960, a new generation of rock musicians had appeared. They still venerated the music they had grown up with, but wanted to take the basic forms and make their own sound. There you have it, taking something, reworking it to suit yourself and creating something new. Gerry Marsden of Gerry and the Pacemakers fame said in a TV interview in the 1980s that he reckoned the first to do that was Cliff Richard who around 1959 started making music in a softer, more pop-oriented style.

A couple of years passed and a trio of young Americans who weren't even related but called themselves the Walker Brothers came as unknowns to Britain. Their leader, Scott, brought with him knowledge of the production techniques of Phil Spector. Allied with British producers and arrangers together they created a series of songs unparalleled in their emotional intensity. They became famous first in Britain and then made it big back in their homeland.

A few years on and new-wave evolved in the USA, with such bands as The Patty Smith Group, the Ramones and the Talking Heads. It was underground music. Once again, these raw sounds crossed the ocean and not long after were to have some influence on the Punk Rock movement in Britain. The most notorious of these bands being the "Sex Pistols" who exploded on the scene in a whirlwind of raucous music and foul language; anarchy in the UK!

The Japanese make much of their homogeneity, but they originated from more than one race. The difference being that the migrations from China, Korea, Mongolia and probably the South Seas occurred at a much earlier time in their history which allowed the races to have already intermarried and blended by the dawn of recorded history. Since the 19th century, they also added a fair bit of Western blood as a result of numerous pairings with the steady flow of foreigners who arrived from the middle of the nineteenth century onwards.

A few Japanese have naturally auburn or even reddish streaks in their hair. Also, others have wavy hair. There was a ludicrous case a few years ago of a Japanese schoolgirl who was compelled to dye her hair the correct shade of black. Despite being pure Japanese, her hair was a shade lighter than is typical. So, in spite of there being a ban on students colouring their hair in that school, she ended up being forced to break one rule in order to uphold another!

Some Japanese men have thick beards, while others can barely muster the merest wisp of a goatee. Some Japanese have eyes of the deepest brown, while others are a shade of pale hazel.

Finally, are those so-called Asian values so unique? Charles Wolf Jr. writing in the Los Angeles Times discussed the results of his survey of Asian and Western values. "On only two of the nine dimensions of value did Asians significantly differ from those of Westerners. Asian respondents, on average place somewhat greater importance on relationships with family, while Westerners accord greater importance to leisure activity. Moreover, variance within the Asian and Western groups' responses was quite similar.... The conclusions that can be drawn are clear. First, Asian values are decidedly more similar to Western values that is usually presumed and second, for some dimensions of values, Asians diverge more from one another than they do from Americans and Western Europeans."

But the Japanese are totally unoriginal, right? All they do is copy stuff.

Around two thousand years ago, the Japanese were busy making little "dogu" statues. They are unique to Japan, as is Yayoi-period pottery with its patterns inlaid by pressing rope into the still damp clay. Later the Japanese developed the tea ceremony. Even though history books insist that it came from China, it was just the basic idea of serving tea as a drink. The entire ceremony is totally original in its conception.

It is true that the Japanese took many ideas and technologies from Korea and later the West and refined them to suit themselves. Any textbook on Japan will say as much. This is no different from the cultural borrowing that has been going on in Europe since the time of the Romans and before. Nobody said the British were copycats because they took the idea of serving tea with milk from the Indian subcontinent, or the printing press from Germany. Many people associate the rickshaw with India or China, but few realize that it was invented in Japan about 1868 and exported to neighbouring Asian countries. The name "rickshaw" is a corruption of "jin-riki sha" or "person-powered vehicle." During the period of isolation from the world, limited export of Japanese glassware continued. The West marveled at the beauty and, yes, the originality of these pieces. Many artists attempted in vain to copy them.

More recently, the world has been enslaved first by the "Tamagochi" virtual pets, later by "Play Station" computer games and recently the cartoon series "Pocket Monsters" which has captivated the hearts of children across the globe. Japanese animated movies, "anime" are highly regarded for their originality and striking imagery and yet, after all this there are still people who accuse the Japanese of being unoriginal.

Racism

Many critics find the Japanese and British both to be racist. There's the "little Englander," railing against the influx of coloured immigrants from former colonies such as the West Indies, Pakistan and India during the 1950s and 60s. In Britain, during the days of slavery London had a large population of Anglo-Africans, but by the turn of the 20th century, they had mostly disappeared. This was not due to migration, but absorption through intermarriage into the larger white community. This is a fact that the more conservative British like to forget; especially the unrepentant racists that might well be able to trace at least one ancestor back to the Anglo-Africans of the 17th to 19th centuries.

In Britain in the 1950s, it was common for non-white immigrants to be beaten up. Nowadays, some say racism is declining on the whole, even so members from the Indian and Asian communities seldom intermarry with Caucasians and stick to themselves. Anti-Islamic sentiments, often intertwined with racist feelings, have clearly increased. Politicians pandering to this intolerant and extreme religion have not helped and more English people than before admit to being Islamophobic. Racist attitudes are said to be rife in the police and army for example. It probably depends who you ask. Race has become an issue with the increase in immigrants and asylum seekers in Britain. The anti-immigration British National Party won seats in the northern city of Burnley in May 2002, which has seen race related riots and disorder. The BNP has since largely imploded but the United Kingdom Independence Party with its anti-EU and anti-immigration policies remains a potent third force in British politics.

In April 2000, the reactionary Governor of Tokyo, Shintaro Ishihara used an outdated, somewhat derogatory term when he mentioned foreigners in Japan while giving a speech. He was widely condemned inside and out of the country, but about seventy percent of the phone calls and faxes he received were supportive of his position.

I remember the 1980s when school kids would stare at me or yell things such as "Hey, America" or "Hello gaijin (foreigner)" at me. Nowadays they barely batted an eyelid. Foreigners have become a commonplace sight. Even so, just like in Britain, old attitudes die hard.

The Japanese Just Love Their Work, Don't They?

Not if a poll in the Daily Yomuri newspaper is to be believed. In this survey carried out in the summer of 1998, 63% of workers said they felt "A lot of stress" in their jobs. This had risen to nearly 70% in a fresh poll a few years after that. Many said they disliked their work, colleagues and working environment. A clear majority was deeply concerned over their futures and about half worried about their health. Another survey released by the Health and Welfare Ministry showed that one in three Japanese suffers from chronic fatigue, with roughly equal numbers for men and women alike.

Neither do they seem to enjoy all those company sponsored events and trips. Many Japanese I know simply loathe having to waste their time at hot springs on the company trip, but feel obliged to go. The number of companies that hold such events has declined in recent years from 76% in 1996, to about 60% four years later. "More companies have given up on trips because people are less loyal to their companies these days." A Sanro Research Institute official said. "These companies have probably realized that the trips do not bring them any benefits." Or put simply, they figured they were just wasting time and money.

One former English student once complained in class how the annual company trip was looming once again. He hated it, he told me. It was a complete waste of a weekend and he would rather spend the time with his girlfriend. The irony here was that he was the owner of the company and it was he who organized it in the first place! He told me that he was sure his workers wanted to go, that was the only reason he continued with the custom. As I have observed before, in such a restricted society, it is sometimes hard to tell the oppressors from the oppressed. Here is yet another example of "mutual victimization."

Individualism is selfish, collectivism is not.

I beg to differ. Many Japanese believe American society must be really selfish and that it's a case of dog eat dog. They forget that the volunteer spirit is often far stronger in America and other "individualistic" societies than in their own. Often in Japan, to "volunteer" tends to mean "to be volunteered" whether you like it or not. In any case I am firmly convinced that Japanese in a group will behave with total selfishness towards those who they regard as being outside their little band. Take the local residents association near me who let off their accursed booming fireworks first at 6.30 and then 7.00 on a Sunday morning to "remind" everyone that today's the day they are having a festival or some other event. Never mind that anyone who has plans to attend will be well aware of what date it is. How this is anything other than utterly selfish and inconsiderate behaviour employs a species of logic utterly alien to me.

Then there is the unholy racket that middle and high schools manage to make all through the day whenever they have a sports or cultural festival. Is all that deafening music and yelling through loudspeakers really so crucial to ensure that everyone has a good time? You tell me. During times of emergency or disaster, Americans are just as capable of coming together to work for the common good of their community. One good example was in the aftermath of the 1992 earthquake in San Francisco, where everyone pulled together admirably, just as the Japanese did when the city of Kobe was flattened by a similar quake disaster in the mid nineties.

The Japanese are shy.

This is more a case of reserved rather than shy. It is a fallacy to take one term and apply it to everyone within a society. Not all Americans are gun-toting God bothering rednecks. Only 39% of Americans carry guns, down from nearly 50% in the 1990s. Also, at least 75% are not born-again Christians.

Anyone who thinks the Japanese are shy should look at them when they sing karaoke and compare this with the English. The Japanese get up there one at a time and really give it all they've got. Karaoke arrived in Britain in the early nineties and has become a staple of "Karaoke Nights" in pubs and clubs since then. Typically, two or three British would-be singers huddle together trying to hide behind the screen in front of them and mumble their way through whichever song it is they have chosen for slaughter. So which is shy? The Japanese have no trouble getting into a communal bath with colleagues, friends, even family members. Most Britons are very uncomfortable with nudity and some even equate it with perversion or sexual deviancy.

Safe Japan?

One final stereotype concerns safety. The Japanese themselves no longer believe that their country is such a safe place. The foreign community still regards it as one of the real plusses of life here though. Crime rates in Japan have risen, though. Juvenile crimes especially have made the headlines, but Japan continues to be a relatively safe place to live.

The Sarin Incident early in 1995 changed everything. For many Japanese, it completely shattered their myth of a country where the crime, violence and lawlessness they considered to be endemic in other countries just didn't happen.

The Aum Shinrikyo (Aum Supreme Truth) cult released deadly sarin nerve gas into a Tokyo Subway one Monday in March 1995. Twelve people were killed and many more were hurt and traumatized. (At the time of this final edit, some fifteen years on, the ongoing trial of former cult members and their self-styled guru Asahara Shoko still makes headlines on occasion. Asahara was sentenced to death in 2004, but his appeals drag on.)

Meanwhile, cases of poisoning, such as one where the curry prepared for a local festival was laced with arsenic continue to make the news. The crime rate is certainly increasing and recently there was a wide-ranging scandal of corruption in the Kanagawa police force to the south of Tokyo with everything from hazing of new recruits to drug use and routine taking of kickbacks coming to light as the investigation unfolded.

Nevertheless, Japan still remains safer than many other countries, such as Britain where many categories of crime have risen. In a way, it might be a good thing that the Japanese may have lost the sense that they live in a uniquely safe place. It might make them more cautious when travelling abroad and less of a pushover for pickpockets and con artists who see them coming a mile off.

SOURCES AND NOTES

(1) Poll from Morton's " Japan- History and Culture" page 237

(2) The Avengers – 60s UK TV show starring Patrick McNee and Honor Blackman as a pair of suave secret agents.

(3) "Yob culture" an ironic term. "Yobs" are generally poorly educated usually young white males. They are often football (soccer) fans, prone to violence and heavy drinking.

(4) The Independent (newspaper)

(5) "The Ugly Japanese" by Friedman Bartu (Pub. Yen Books)

(6) Business Insider - "The 10 Countries With Notoriously Bad Tourists" May 18th 2013 article

(7) Daily Yomuri and BBC Internet

(8) Milgram – See "Basic Psychology" Pages 368-71 and 381 By Henry Gleitman (Pub. Norton)

(8) "Lost Japan" by Alex Kerr Page 50 (Pub. Lonely Planet)

(9) "The Myth of Japanese Uniqueness" by Peter N. Dale (Pub. Routledge)

(10) Gerry Marsden, in a TV interview in the early 90s.

(11) Los Angeles Times. Charles Wolf Jr. is senior economic advisor at Rand and a research fellow at the Hoover Institution.

(12) Statistics and quotes from Yomuri Newspaper articles

ENTERTAINMENT

In 1964, at the height of the British Invasion, yet another song crossed the ocean to become a huge hit in The United States. This time, it was from the opposite direction. The Japanese singer Kyu Sakamoto (below left) struck gold with "Ue o Muite Arukou" (Look Up as You Walk) better known in the West as "The Sukiyaki Song." (The record company felt that title was more understandable) It is a jaunty number, a song of a broken hearted man who holds his head up high as he walks to prevent his tears from falling. He proved only to be a one hit wonder in America and not the harbinger of a "Japanese Invasion." Sakamoto died in the 1985 JAL plane crash.

Indeed, ask a typical British music fan to name any Japanese artists and they

might remember the Yellow Magic Orchestra from the late seventies, who reached the top twenty once. If they are jazz fans they might have heard of saxophonist Sadao Watanabe and most will know Ruichi Sakamoto, from his film score for "The Last Emperor." They might perhaps recall his portrayal of a soldier in a WW2 prison camp in the movie "Merry Christmas Mr. Lawrence," with David Bowie. More recently there's Kyary Pamyu Pamyu but that's about it.

Surely everybody has heard of Akira Kurosawa, but only film buffs will be able to name many other Japanese movie directors. As for actors, the late Toshiro Mifune is about the only one that older movie goers will recall, along with Ken Watanabe, largely on the basis of his supporting roles in movies such as "The Last Samurai" (2003) and "Batman Begins" (2005).

In contrast, ask any typical Japanese film or music fan how many actors, singers or bands they know from Britain and the States and you will get a pretty long list that won't differ much from one composed by anyone in the West. They all know such artists as Celine Dion and Mariah Carey. The older Japanese and their thirst for nostalgia kept such 60s acts as the Brothers Four and the Ventures coming back year after year to make lucrative concert tours of Japan well into the present century.

Most Western singers and artists spend time touring the world, building up an international fan base. Most performers in Japan are content to settle for success in their homeland. One reason is the sheer effort required to crack the overseas market. It is hard for even the best Japanese vocalist to sound convincing singing in English. In the West, songs in foreign languages tend to be only irregular novelty hits. In Japan, music fans love to listen to Western artists such as Whitney Houston and Celine Dion, even though they cannot understand a fraction of the words. A few years ago when I was getting into one or two Japanese artists and went looking for some more of their CDs, the sales assistant in the CD shop tried to show me the way to the Foreign Music section. I daresay he couldn't imagine why I would want to buy CDs in Japanese. Never mind that I could understand a lot more of the lyrics than the usually monolingual fans of Mariah Carey who were humming along to her latest hit, without the faintest idea of its meaning

Japanese artists are typically a part of what is known as the "geinokai" which translates as the entertainer's society, "geinojin" being "entertainer." Members of this exclusive club generally hang out together, marry fellow entertainers and enjoy the backup and support of the management company who more often than not discovered them in the first place and groomed them for stardom. It is archetypically Japanese in the close-knit world it weaves around those within its borders.

It is standard practice in Japan for singers to also be actors both on TV and in the movies. This often has little to do with their real or imagined talent. One group of five young men, SMAP, whose name apparently stands for "Sports Music Action People," is not only a successful pop band steadily churning out pleasant but forgettable hits. They also have their own cooking programme and individually feature in numerous television dramas, talk shows and movies. I get the distinct impression that if the various members of SMAP were to suddenly disappear from the face of the earth the Japanese entertainment industry would go into severe recession. A couple of them are fairly decent actors though. Another example is the singer Shizuka Kudo, who not only maintains her music career, but also appears in talk shows, TV dramas and in 1999 held an exhibition of her oil paintings, adding yet another string to her bow.

In fact, it seems that most of the "genokai" are not only encouraged but expected to become the kind of all-round entertainer that is much less common in Britain. Their production company gives them all the necessary back up and away they go.

In comparison, British singers are usually only singers and relatively few cross over into acting or "all round entertaining" as in Japan. David Bowie has been trying to be taken seriously as an actor since his portrayal of an alien in "The Man Who Fell to Earth" in 1976 through his celebrated one-man Broadway performance as the Elephant Man in the 1980s down to his cameo as Nikolai Tesla in the 2008 mystery "The Prestige".

Often, musicians make the transition only after their musical career is over. Cilla Black was better known hosting the UK's version of "Blind Date" in the 1990s, but she was originally a singer who came out of Merseyside along with The Beatles. A couple of ex-Herman's Hermits moved into children's television in the early seventies. Martin Kemp, formerly a child actor became a pop star in the eighties with his brother Gary as part of Spandau Ballet. After the band's demise at the end of the decade, he returned to acting, eventually landing a leading role in "East Enders" a long running UK soap opera. The brothers played the London gangster Kray twins in a film. Once Adam Ant's stint as a pop star was over, he headed out to Hollywood. There he made a string of cameo appearances and took supporting roles chiefly in "b" movies such as "Slam Dance," and an episode of "Tales from the Crypt."

In America since the mid 1990s more artists than ever have been crossing over into movies. The singer Brandy appeared in the slasher flick "I Know What You Did Last Summer" Whitney Houston has starred in "Waiting to Exhale," and "The Preacher's Daughter" opposite Denzel Washington and "The Bodyguard" with Harrison Ford. Bette Midler is recently known more as an actress than a singer having starred in numerous movies such as "The Rose," and "For the Boys," and the Disney movie "Hocus-Pocus" playing a witch, where she manages to squeeze in her rendition of "You Put a Spell on Me."

This was far more commonplace in the forties and fifties in America. Bing Crosby and Frank Sinatra appeared regularly in movies and had their own television shows. Although both of them were talented, Crosby's movies were principally musicals. Sinatra was an accomplished actor and could handle anything from comedy to gangster drama. From the mid- 1950s to late 60s, Elvis appeared in a string of mostly forgettable films that many regarded as a waste of his talents.

Perhaps one reason for far fewer British singers making it as actors is the innately conservative nature of society. Until comparatively recently, people were expected to keep to one role, to take up the same profession as their father and stick to it. In America, there has always been the greater flexibility, the feeling that if you try hard enough, you can do whatever you want, the "American Dream"?

Rock and roll changed it all in the West. Suddenly, the Beatles and the Stones were writing their own songs and becoming increasingly independent. The Beatles made two movies early on in their career, but after "Help" in 1965, only a documentary and the narration for "Yellow Submarine." The music press castigated the Monkees when it was revealed that session musicians were used to help beef up their sound. This was something that ten years earlier wouldn't have raised any eyebrows. In order to have credibility, a band had to write its own material and a considerable say over its musical direction. They also had to focus more of their time and energies on music alone.

So the division between entertainers and musicians increased. In the 1970s, there were still singers who made movies of course. Rodger Daltry of the Who acted the title role in "Tommy." He also appeared in episodes of the US series "The Highlander" and in the late 90s as an evil vampire in the camp horror spoof "Vampirella." The Bee Gees made "Sergeant Pepper's Lonely Hearts Club Band" in 1978, critically panned for the lamentable acting of the Gibb brothers. Suffice to say, it wasn't exactly a runaway hit. David Essex was in "Stardust" along with Ringo Starr in the early seventies and the sequel. In 1980, he starred in "Silver Dream Racer" about a motorbike rider and his machine of the same name, which wasn't spectacularly successful. Over in America at about the same time, Michael Jackson and Diana Ross pranced their way through "The Wizz" a dismal remake of "The Wizard of Oz". Dorothy from the original Wizard of Oz, the late Judy Garland was a successful singer/actress, her daughter Liza Minelli too.

Once in a while actors turn to singing and from Richard Harris' "McArthur Park" in the sixties, Telly Savalis' spoken version of "If" and up to Bruce Willis' "Under the Boardwalk" in the late 1980s the results are often excruciating.

In America, there were always more singers who were also actors/actresses. One of the most notable is Barbara Streisand. She has starred in a string of hit movies and had a consistent musical career spanning four decades. More recently, there is Will Smith, the rapper who is also an actor, or is it the other way round? He performed the title track of the hit movie "Men in Black" (1998) in which he also starred, as well as "Wild Wild West" a year later. He also had a leading part in the blockbuster "Independence Day" in 1996. Other rap stars such as Ice T and LL Cool J have parallel acting careers.

In Japan, however, nothing like the revolution the Beatles engendered ever took place. Japan continued with business as usual, with the result that the all round entertainer carried on being the norm all the way through. Producers have a good deal of power over the bands they oversee and in many cases, they alone select new members for the group if one drops out. It is little changed from the situation in pre-Beatles Britain or America.

I recall in 1997 watching a documentary on TV where the Japanese pop Svengali, Tsunku was selecting members for a new band. As he looked over the gaggle of wannabe Lolitas in his studio clad in their skimpy dresses and caked on makeup, he toyed with random names for his new creation. He settled on "Morning Musume": "Morning Daughters." The eight girls he selected were all between thirteen and sixteen, with one rather atypically in her mid twenties. When one of them quit the band, he held auditions for her replacement and in the end signed up three more. The group eventually expanded to a regularly changing lineup of ten to twelve performers. More a dancing chorus group than anything else, Tsunku, also a singer, groomed them for stardom. Their music is the kind of empty-headed bubble gum pop that you can hear on any radio station in the world. The girls also appear regularly on various variety shows, giggling their way through whatever mindless nonsense has been devised for them to take part in. They even made a movie called "Pinch Runner", which was pretty dire according to most reports.

The whole "boy band" trend has existed in Japan since the 1950s. One group is "Arashi" (Storm) prancing around to their latest lip-synch hit. Then there is the gaggle of teenage lads who could easily be dates for Morning Musume, "Folder" who appropriately enough sang and danced to a Japanese version of the old Jackson Five number "I Want You Back."

From their beginnings around 2010, AKB48 is an even more blatant marketing ploy. It consists of three "teams" of ever-changing cute late teen to early twenty something girls who seem to have taken up from where Morning Musume left off.

But then is that really any different from what has been going on in the West for the past couple of decades? In the mid-1990s, the pop sensation The Spice girls were recruited by use of a newspaper advert. These five young women were put through the paces, taught to sing and dance passably well enough and went on to confound their critics. Nearly four years passed, Jerry Halliwell, one ex-member was a goodwill ambassador for the United Nations. Another, Victoria

"Posh Spice" had become a top model married to the hugely popular footballer David Beckham and the hits just kept coming. When they went into cold storage in 2000, nobody was laughing any more.

AKB48 (public domain)

The Spice Girls are not alone; there were also the girls in All Saints, another band assembled for stardom. In Japan, the band Max, four girls from Okinawa were quite similar in their style and presentation. The only difference was that the four members of Max were far better dancers than either the Spice Girls or All Saints would be in several lifetimes!

The Spice Girls and All Saints both made movies and neither was particularly successful. This was especially true of All Saint's effort that was pulled from the cinemas after a couple of weeks due to abysmal box-office takings. Seven years later, both Max and All Saints are pretty well forgotten and others have been assembled to fill their platform shoes.

Pop in the West has regressed to being dominated by producers and record companies who are interested only in sales figures. The Back street Boys in the USA for example were recruited and trained in much the same fashion as bands such as Morning Musume in Japan. They churned out a similar kind of pleasant but undemanding radio fodder guaranteed to keep their youthful fans coming back for more, at least until the next big thing comes along.

The same was true in Britain with "boy band" groups such as Take That, who were big in the 1990s, or Boyzone, who once again were aiming for the same teenage girls whose older sisters wept when Robbie Robertson left Take That.

Then there is Christina Aguilera from the USA who first hit the big time in 1999 with her massive hit "Genie in a Bottle" when she was just 18. The Observer newspaper reckoned that "Christina is like a flamingo-coloured blancmange, with turquoise eyes. She is as effervescent as champagne bubbles...She entered showbiz via Disney's show, The New Mickey Mouse Club....RCA Records spent $1 million on getting her 'ready.'" In many ways, she is no different from the Japanese "idol" singers such as Seiko Matsuda who were marketed for their cute appearance and meticulously groomed for stardom. Christina took the route to fame first appearing on the Mickey Mouse Show, similar to how such fifties starlets as Annette Funicello and many others got their big breaks.

Christina's approximate counterpart in Japan might be Ayumi Hamasaki, who although around thirty five at the time of writing, still targets the same teenage market. She is all tacky images, cute and sexy, with her flashy stick-on nails and mane of bleached blonde hair attachments. For a while, both Ayumi and Christina seemed to be trying to create the impression that they were about fourteen years old, the same as the majority of their fans.

By around 2005, Christina's image had matured into one of sensual sophistication in her duet with the singer Ricky Martin. Ayumi Hamasaki seemed to be trying for the same since she appeared in a provocative series of photos scantily clad with a male fashion model entitled "Ayumi Meets a Man."

It would be unfair to condemn all Japanese singers and bands as being just willing stooges who are controlled by their managers. Many of them write their own lyrics and have quite considerable control over their musical direction. Singer-songwriters have been common in Japan since the seventies, just as in the West.

As to why Japanese artists don't make it in the West, another reason is apparent. To devote time to touring and promoting themselves overseas would damage their careers in Japan. Many have a considerable following in Taiwan, Hong Kong and increasingly Korea and in some Chinese cities. That's a stable and fairly large market at home and in nearby Asian countries, so it isn't surprising that few are willing to risk throwing that away hoping to crack the notoriously tough American or European markets. One or two do try though and a handful makes it.

One such group is Mach Pelican, a punk-band who notched up some hits on the indie charts in Australia, where they had a large underground following. (They were virtual unknowns in Japan though.) Another band that made waves outside their native Japan is the oddly named "Thee Michelle Gun Elephant." Described as "kamikaze punks" in the foreign music press, they generated some interest in America and Europe. Their name was said to have come from the

founding member's mispronunciation of "Machine Gun Etiquette," the title of an album by UK punk band The Dammed back in 1979.

These two bands prove it can be done. And there are others such as Shonen Knife who had a hit with a punk thrash version of the Carpenter's "Top of the World" or the Frank Chickens who were the darlings of the NME for a while in 1981 or thereabouts.

Ironically, the most successful Japanese artist abroad in recent years is arguably the least talented. In 2013, the oddly named Kyary Pamyu Pamyu (left) whose real name is Kiriko Takemura first came on the scene. She has attracted worldwide attention with her bizarre fashion sense and super-cute image.

Videos of her dancing to her nonsensical songs went viral on YouTube and this helped make her a star worldwide. She markets herself as a sort of Japanese version of Lady Gaga. "Kyary" pretty well admits that she has no real musical ability. "My lyrics don't make any sense" she said in one interview. "Kyary is not supposed to be musically talented, she is about image," wrote London Sempai magazine in a review of her tour.

In film, much the same thing happens in Japan and Britain, not to mention most other countries of the world. This is the ongoing domination of the United States in the movie world with blockbusters such as "Avatar," "The Avengers" or "Armageddon." Everywhere you go local films are sidelined in favour of the latest Hollywood offering. And yet, Japanese and British movies have managed to hold their own from time to time, especially in the past few years.

In the mid 1990s, the unexpected success of "Trainspotting" made international stars of Robert Carlyle who played the role of drunken psycho Begbie and Ewan McGregor who starred as the heroin addicted Renton. It was followed by a spate of British movies, all huge hits. Carlyle appeared in "The Full Monty" a couple of years later, about a group of redundant steelworkers who stage a striptease show to make money with themselves as the performers! Then there was the anarchic "Twin Town" from Wales about the exploits of a couple of moronic twin brothers and their efforts to get even with a local gangster.

More recently, there was another hit from the UK, "Little Voice" about a stage struck performer who can faultlessly imitate any singer she has heard, but is too shy at first to sing in public. "Lock Stock and Two Smoking Barrels" came out at the end of the 1990s, Britain's brutal answer to "Pulp Fiction." One of the supporting roles was taken by Sting, another British singer who has been trying for years to make it as an actor with only limited success.

It is often assumed, erroneously that Japanese movies are just too difficult to understand and that they are based on kabuki plays, or some such nonsense. It is actually true that some of the first silent movies in Japan were simple films of kabuki plays, but the stylized acting of kabuki has about as much influence on contemporary Japanese film as classical ballet on hip-hop! Another reason for this misconception may be that when the movie era arrived, one or two former kabuki actors turned their hand successfully to a career on the silver screen.

One of the earliest hits from Japan was "Tokyo Story" directed by Yasujiro Ozu in the early 1950s. It was a straightforward tale of an elderly couple visiting their children in Tokyo and soon realizing that their presence was seen more as an inconvenience than anything else. It revealed the yawning chasm between the generations that the then emerging "salaryman" lifestyle and steady shift to nuclear families was engendering. Another hit was "Rashomon" made at about the same time and directed by Kurosawa. It featured the same story told from four different points of view and I feel it was among other things, a commentary on the inability of the human mind to remember objectively what had happened. It was also hugely entertaining.

Japanese movies have had some success as well.   In 1997, Unagi (The Eel) was a hit, winning the Cannes Film Festival award for best foreign film. It was a simple tale of an ex-con and his pet eel that sets up as a hairdresser and helps a young girl out by giving her a job. Takeshi Kitano (better known by his stage name Beat Takeshi) has had a number of international hits as both a director and an actor with such movies as "Hanabi" (Fireworks). He also starred alongside Keanu Reeves in "Johnny Mnemonic," and older readers will remember him as the shaven headed prison guard in "Merry Christmas Mr. Lawrence."

The animations of Studio Ghibli have been consistently successful overseas. Films ranging from 1997's "Mononoke Hime" (Princess Mononoke) "Spirited Away" (2001) and "The Wind Rises" which was released to some controversy in 2013. It told the story of the man who built the WW2 Zero fighter plane.

The problem facing many Japanese actors is identical to that of singers, namely how to sound convincing in English. Seiko Matsuda, the archetypal "idol singer," appeared in a few movies in her home country, but has yet to make much impact in the US, a market she has been trying to break into for about the last twenty odd years. Her movie roles to date were in a low budget dud "Surrogate Mother" and a "blink and you'd miss it" cameo role at the start of "Armageddon." The former only served to highlight her shortcomings in both English ability and acting talent, while the latter was obviously a joke. She appears briefly in the back of a taxi as a petulant Japanese tourist stuck in a New York traffic jam whining "I want to go shopping!" in purposely atrocious English. She has had no joy with her music either. Even a duet with Donny Wahlburg, ex of New Kids on the Block flopped. My one small claim to fame regarding Ms. Matsuda is that I was a good friend of one of her English teachers in the late 1980s. He reckoned she was nice enough but would never learn the language to any degree of fluency in this lifetime.

One of the most successful actors from Japan on the world stage more recently has been Ken Watanabe. He starred as the samurai leader Lord Katsumoto in "Last Samurai" (2003) and has appeared in a string of American movies since then.

Historically, both Britain and Japan had their troupes of wandering minstrels, going from village to village to entertain the people. The 12th century Sarashina Nikki mentions a trio of traveling singers "Their hair, which was extremely long, hung beautifully over their foreheads; they all had fair complexions and looked attractive enough to serve as waiting women. Our party was charmed by their appearance and even more impressed then they started to sing, for they had fine, clear voices that rose to the heavens."

The people of Britain and Japan both had their festivals and events on the religious calendar to entertain them. In Japan, the rule of the samurai also saw the development of the tea ceremony, of Noh drama and later of the bunraku puppet drama and of kabuki.

Noh is hard to understand, even by the Japanese. It has its followers, but is regarded by most as being too arcane and obscure to be of interest. There are usually only one or two mostly static performers on stage, while much of the action is suggested by stylized movements.

Kabuki is far more accessible. It first appeared in Japan around 1603, at the same time as William Shakespeare was busy writing his plays. Indeed, one of the most famous writers of plays for both the kabuki and bunraku, Chikamatsu

Monzaemon (1653-1724) later came to be known as "The Shakespeare of Japan." In actual fact, he wrote principally for the puppet theater rather than kabuki, which was still in its formative stages when he was alive. Later the plays were easily adapted for performance on the kabuki stage. The bunraku puppets (an example is shown here) were held aloft by their black-clad operators and

became immensely popular in Edo Period Japan.

Women were not permitted to appear on stage in either Britain or Japan at this time. Thus men were obliged to take both roles; in Japan this meant that a tradition of "onnagata" or "female-performers" has endured in kabuki until the present day.

In Elizabethan England, Shakespeare also took advantage of this restriction. The courtroom scene in "The Merchant of Venice" for example, had Portia (a woman played by a young man) who disguised "herself" as a man in order to defend Antonio in court against Shylock. Thus you have a man playing the part of a woman who is pretending to be a man! Regrettably little jokes such as this are mostly lost on modern audiences.

Kabuki has remained popular in Japan and the plays of Shakespeare have retained their appeal both at home and abroad. (Indeed, Kurosawa's film "Ran" was basically "King Lear" relocated to feudal Japan.) In the past decade, Shakespeare has become even more accessible due to film versions of several of his plays by the British actor/director Kenneth Brannagh. Purists may object, but nobody can doubt his screen adaptations have won the Bard many new fans.

Silent movies remained popular in Japan for several years after they had fallen from favour in the West. The reasons here were cultural rather than any technological shortcoming on the part of Japanese filmmakers. Many felt that silent movies were enough. They didn't need the addition of dialogue. This could be a continuation of the idea present in art and literature that the viewer has to impart something of his or her imagination to fill in the gap. Some directors didn't switch to making "talkies" until the end of the thirties.

Another reason was the strength of the "benshi" or movie narrators. They sat to one side of the theatre, explaining the action of the film especially foreign movies that it was felt the audience would be unable to understand. Sometimes their attention to detail was quite amusing, such as "The audience will now observe that there is smoke coming out of the chimneys." They had come to regard themselves as being of as equal importance as the movies and they had quite a following. The presence of a popular benshi at a screening would increase the number of people who came to see the movie.

The benshi resisted talkies for very obvious reasons; they were redundant. A few went on strike and a couple apparently committed suicide but eventually they could not stem the flow of progress. Some actually moved into movie acting, others found radio work and one or two started up the "kami shibai" or paper slide shows for the kids at festivals and other events. They would narrate stories that appeared on a series of paper slides, filling the same role as the "Punch and Judy" man in Britain at the seaside.

In the past few years, many people have voiced concerns that music has become just a commercial concern with little or no artistic merit. The Japanese songwriter Yu Aku summed it up as "we have music, we lack songs." He also reckoned that "adult society has lost attraction as a subject to be expressed in the form of songs in the last 20 years."

"When I attended college," he continued. "Rock 'n' roll and rockabilly music tried to break down barriers to the adult world. Everyone wanted to be a "grownup" back then and we tried to emulate them by trying to act and look older. Now adults have become children....In recent years, young people have grown up without role models, even for love." He seems to me at least to echo the misgivings about the "dumbing down" of society that many in Britain, the States and elsewhere share.

Many bands in Japan and Britain alike cater solely to the early teen market, since this is the segment with much more purchasing power than in previous generations. Also "the quickening pace of the music cycle has made it harder for consumers to appreciate a new release for more than a few weeks and has reduced the worth of a song to mere fad value." These are the comments of Sayaka Yakushiji writing in the Daily Yomuri. Much the same thing has happened elsewhere in the world and Britain is no exception. The charts are dominated by bands and performers who have almost no appeal to anyone over twenty-five. The bands themselves are as disposable as their music is forgettable.

The British satire magazine "Viz" amusingly parodied this trend with their

"Boys 'R' Us" comic strip in which three lads are whisked into a "hit factory."(A fourth is rejected because he is a real singer/songwriter!) First they are put on a conveyer belt where everything from their image to their songs is created for them, all they are required to do is smile and pose. At the end of the day, they are ejected from the building and dumped in a pile of manure to join the other has-beens that the music business has chewed up and spat out. Cynical, certainly, but is it really so far from the truth?

Japanese pop has made more impact in the West in the first decade of the 21st century. Female duo Puffy are well known across America thanks in part to the popularity of a cartoon in which they feature and their music sells well. Koda Kumi, the sultry singer known simply as Koda in the US is a big name, probably as much for her erotic videos as the music. Then there is Kyary Pamyu Pamyu for those fortunate souls who find some artistic merit in her performances.

Certainly it's ironic that in Britain, many people would sneer at the "conformist" Japanese in their identical suits and ties. They might be forgetting that take any typical teenager and they all seem to dress the same in their uniform of Nike shoes, sportswear and baseball caps (Nobody even plays baseball in Britain!). Or take their older brothers and sisters with their geometric tattoos and body piercings. There is nothing remotely original about any aspect of their appearance, nor the vacuous pap they listen to on their iPods. This is surely a case of the pot calling the kettle black.

SOURCES

(1)   The Observer (entertainment article)

(2)   Sarashina Nikki Pages 38-9

(3)   "The Japanese Film" by Anderson/Ritchie (Pub. Princetown)

(4)   Yu Aku, etc, quoted from Daily Yomuri Article

(5)   AKB48 photo used by permission of kndynt2099 (GNU)

(5)   Kyary Pamyu Pamyu photo used by permission of Georges Seguin (GNU)

(5)   Bunraku puppet image used by permission of Elly Waterman (GNU)

(6)   Viz Magazine – A vulgar and satirical UK magazine very popular in the 1990s

FUTURE

The obvious dilemma here is that whatever predictions made will probably be outdated or in need of revision by the time the book goes to press. I recall that at the end of 1998, the statement in my original thesis paper "The global economy has become a reality, while many of the countries within it are teetering on the brink of recession if not actual depression. At the time of writing, it seems that 1999 will see much of the world enter a period of economic downturn."

Along with numerous other harbingers of doom, I was wrong. By the end of the 20th century, the seeming inevitability of a global meltdown has not just receded, but the United States and much of Europe enjoyed continued prosperity. The best anyone can do is to make some general statements about where things in Britain and Japan seem to be headed and then withdraw gracefully.

This book draws attention to both similarity and contrast between the UK and Japan. Now in the second decade of the third millennium, in some ways, their relative positions could hardly be further apart. Yet in others, they are close and become closer day by day.

In Britain, the reformist Blair administration was a national disaster. It made several blunders, the worst of these in becoming a poodle for President Bush during his reign of error. Blair squandered the Labour government's chance of winning the contest for London's mayor on the May 6th 2000 election due to his authoritarian tendencies. Nevertheless, his party remained at close to 50% approval, 21 points clear of the hapless and hopeless Conservatives for most of that year. A leaked document from their central office more or less conceded that they would lose by the same landslide that swept them from power in 1997. William Hague ceased to be the leader of the opposition in 2001. Party membership had fallen to its lowest level for several decades and the Tories didn't appear to be recruiting significant numbers of new people.

A little more than a year after his historic third electoral victory, Blair was a lame duck. Opposition to the Iraq War and many of his reforms had compelled him to announce that by the summer of 2007, he would step down. Few were sorry to see him go.

Britain was able to avoid sinking into the quagmire that Japan has languished in for almost a decade. Prime Minister Mori held his coalition together for a while, even though his majority was slim. Sensing impending disaster, the LDP ditched him and in 2001 selected the flamboyant Junichiro Koizumi. He registered ludicrously high support rates above 80% for several months. With his Italian suits and "lion's mane" of flowing hair, he came across as a breath of fresh air. A series of blunders and the inevitable whiff of corruption surrounding his party saw his support slump to just below 40%. This suggested he would almost certainly be removed from power by early in 2003.

He not only survived, but carried through the promised restructuring of the bureaucracy and his desire to privatize the post office. Five years later, he retired in September 2006, having completed two terms, amongst the longest serving Japanese prime ministers of modern times.   Since the early part of this century, Japan seems to have been in recovery, albeit weakly.

However, in July of 2000, the EPA reported less robust growth and described Japan's recovery as being a little weaker than before. Stock prices have languished between 15,000 and 18,000 points for several years now, a far cry from the peak of 34,000 at the height of the "bubble economy." The EPA said "That there was no guarantee that the economy would automatically take a turn for the better and that things needed to be closely watched." One economist compared the pump-priming measures taken by the Japanese government to filling a punctured balloon. It would rise for a short time and then when the air escaped, start falling to earth once more. By no stretch of the imagination could the recovery in Japan be seen as either irreversible or particularly impressive. By 2006, it was finally safe to assert that fifteen years after the collapse, Japan was once again on a reasonably firm economic footing.

Britain saw lasting changes in the 1980s, ones that swept away the last vestiges of the relatively collectivist society that once existed. The ruthlessness of Thatcher brought about the destruction of the mining communities that were the backbone of whole towns. They were close knit in much the same way as traditional farming villages and small towns in Japan. They had intimate networks of self-help groups, even colliery brass bands and male voice choirs. These groups were less rigidly structured than in Japan, but functioned much in the same way. Thatcher relished the slaughter of these last bastions of working-class solidarity. As a result, many of them languished in poverty for years; some to this day have never truly recovered.

Others were reborn with the help of investment, both from within Europe and from Japan and Korea. The original closeness and sense of belonging has gone forever. In Japan too, the loss of a sense of community has been commented on. Neighbourhood groups still function, but those participating in them are often elderly. The young have less and less time or inclination to take part in such things any more.

In Britain as in Japan, neighbours are increasingly often strangers to each other. "Traditional close communities are under threat from a generation of Britons who are as likely to speak to friends in Australia as to their own neighbours" revealed a survey by Royal Mail's international division. It also showed that "The younger generation is communicating more and more by phone, the Internet and letter...the least neighbourly place to live was London, where one in three rarely, or never, speaks to the neighbours."

One telling sign of how rapidly Japanese society is becoming more private and less willing to participate in community activities showed in the result of the census. More precisely this was the difficulty in gathering information. The census is carried out periodically, just as in many Western countries. The 2000 census collected responses from up to 98% of citizens in many areas. Just five years later, the figure was expected to be far lower. Suspicion driven by rising crime and fear of crime has made many wary. One of my students, a local community activist told of how large numbers of people in his town had refused to answer the door when the volunteer collectors called round to pick up the census forms. He predicted that the whole concept might even be abandoned for the 2010 census if this trend persists.

The writer Masaaki Suzuki commenting in the Yomuri News came to similar conclusions regarding Japan. "Although the Japanese follow rules to maintain social order, human relations in urban areas are much more distant and icy than in the Middle East (where he had been living for six years) where there is far more killing (than in Japan.)" He lamented the fact that Japan "lacked friendly, warm human relations."

On periodic visits back to the UK I have noticed the same phenomenon. There seems to be pervasive boorishness, a lack of respect for the elderly or indeed for anyone or anything. It is a slack-jawed slouching "culture" of "chavs," drunken violent yobs making the town centres of many cities no-go areas after dark on a Friday or Saturday. There is more graffiti than ever and everyone seems to be dressed down in garish sportswear, or the "backwoods chic" of un-tucked flannel shirts. Britain has become the drug capital of the European Union. "More cannabis is smoked in England and Wales by both adults and teenagers than any other country in the European Union. The use of ecstasy, amphetamines and LSD in England and Wales is also higher than anywhere else in the EU."

The crass consumerism that Japan and Britain alike have willingly embraced might be some of the reason for this. Everything becomes a commodity to sell. The loss of any real sense of community and the promotion of greed and selfishness as virtues by the Conservative Party during its 18 years of misrule also played its part.

"Venture out into the towns and cities of this country this weekend and you'll find it hard to avoid the conclusion that young British men are in the midst of a crisis of time and role, of both maturity and masculinity. ... People who train all year round for Ibiza's party season, only to suck up legal highs they bought off strangers on the internet. Their heads are too small for their bodies, their shoulders are wider than a pub television and they have shit (singer) Robbie Williams tattoos. They look dreadful and bizarre; they are the modern British douchebag – pumped, primed, terrifyingly sexualized high-street gigolos. They have no concept of subtlety and they don't care." Thus wrote Clive Martin in an article that went on to describe the sense of hopelessness that pervades many young men in modern Britain. [27]

The "salaryman culture" in Japan is steadily eroding. Expensive hostess bars have gone out of business in the entertainment sectors of Tokyo. Many companies have tightened their belts and stopped or severely curtailed funding their executives' alcoholic excesses. Likewise, some golf courses have been on the brink of bankruptcy. One of its bastions, the seniority system, where workers were paid salary increases due to age and not ability is going the way of the dinosaur. No less than Toshiba introduced a voluntary performance-based salary system that more than half of those eligible for were expected to apply to join. The merit system is catching on rapidly. This will be yet another nail in the coffin of the post-war Japanese consensus. The Japanese have once again become frugal in their spending habits. They went on a binge in the eighties, felt the effects in a fourteen-year collective hangover and have sworn off it ever since.

In Britain, the traditional pub has declined. In rural areas, it is said that six pubs a week have been closing on average for the past few years. During the years 2003-4 when I worked in Local Government in the UK, I processed numerous applications for former pubs to be converted into dwellings. The smoking ban in the UK has been the death of many more. In cities, many pubs have been morphed into so called "theme pubs" and some of these garish places are little else than brightly painted family restaurants without a trace of atmosphere. Only the counter bar selling alcoholic drinks distinguishes them from fast food eateries. The most notorious of these are the chains "Yates' Wine Lodge." and "J.D. Weatherspoon."

A somewhat cynical journalist, Bill Murphy wrote a book detailing the cities he visited on an eight-month trip around England. "Of course the first pub I saw was Yates' wine Lodge. Who's bribing whom, I wondered, to make this the place that exists in the centre of every bloody English town and city?" and "Going the sanitized way...a monstrous J.D. Weatherspoons pub dominated the horizon approaching the main shopping centre, with all its new-age social bullshit and rules which eliminate any personality, individual freedom or imagination. 'Remember your table number at the bar, you cannot smoke in this section.' All very American.... redwood furnishings decorated in colourful plastic coated menus, which make the place resemble the start of a children's birthday party. " He concluded, "It's a tragedy to think these places are successful. Chains of this type have sterilised the centre of just about every town in England." After spending two years back in the UK from 2003 till early 2005, I could do little else but to admit that basically, he was right on a lot of fronts.   England had become a collection of ugly town centres each infested with contingents of violent thugs and drunken louts.

Murphy was harshly criticized for his comments on English towns and branded a reactionary, but he was like many others lamenting the loss of our heritage and the general ugliness of modern day Britain in general. "Much of the country has been physically destroyed by bogus homes erected in the past two decades. It seems a tragedy if all we can do is destroy the pleasanter legacies of the past and leave none for the future." His words echo those of many Japanese activists and Alex Kerr, the writer of "Lost Japan"

In Japan, something similar seems to be happening to the traditional drinking hole of Japan, the izakaya. It is so much like the English pub in its function and character. It has faced competition from izakaya "chains" such as "Shirokiya" and "Murasaki" which are homogeneous, bland, each precisely like the other branches wherever in the country you care to go. Just as in Yates or JD's, they are staffed mostly by young people who can't find a better job or college students making a little extra cash. I doubt anyone would want to make such places their "local." You will get the same politely indifferent service from the staff and forget the idea of actually having a "regular" landlord to talk with. The "manager" of these places seems to change regularly and of course nobody ever has the time not to mention the inclination to actually chat to customers for long in these joints.

Some family run pubs have gone under, unable to afford the increased rents and the landlord's desire to build a more lucrative apartment block or "put up a parking lot" as Joni Mitchell once sang. In my favourite drinking area of Ikebukuro, in northern Tokyo, several private or family run pubs and bars I used to frequent have closed down. The chains are steadily crowding them out. Is this is yet one more blow to the concept of community in both countries? Or does it simply herald a more standardized environment in which to get drunk?

From drink to food and in Japan junk food continues to inexorably tighten its greasy grip on Japan. McDonalds and its equally unhealthy local imitators are to be seen outside almost every Tokyo train station preying on the youth of Japan with slick advertising that would make the old Joe Camel ads look pretty tame. "Let's Healthy Menu" ran one of the most deplorable of the McDonalds posters a few years ago. If this trend towards an unhealthy fatty diet coupled with an increasingly sedentary lifestyle continues and there is little to suggest otherwise, then the world famous longevity of the Japanese will surely suffer. By 2006, obesity had risen to 30% of the adult population.

In Britain too, the malign influence of junk food is similarly pervasive and yet there is a conflicting trend. In the late 1990s, two environmental campaigners leafleting outside a McDonalds were eventually found guilty of defaming the corporation, although the judge sided with them on a number of points they had made. He conceded that the food sold was of poor quality and that the employees had basically dead-end jobs. One poll suggested that nearly half of British people wouldn't be seen dead in a McDonalds. Plenty of the remainder, however, frequents the "Golden Arches" with depressing regularity. The news that in March 2006, McDonalds announced the closure of 25 UK branches was certainly welcome.

In Britain, that conflicting trend is vegetarianism. It has firmly moved into the mainstream and now it is no longer uncommon to see up to a quarter of the choices on a typical restaurant menu marked with the "V" for vegetarian sign. It seems that while a substantial number of British people will be seen pigging out on junk, a smaller group will be across the street munching on their lentils in the vegetarian shop. Certainly, it is likely that some of those who continue to eat meat will consume less of it as this century progresses. This is true of Britain and of other countries of Europe and even the United States.

Other commentators have suggested that the improvements in British eating habits rarely extend far beyond the capital. Sue Dibb of the Food Commission stated: "This survey (of children's eating habits) shows a truly appalling picture of the nutritional health of our young people." Four out of five youngsters regularly ate snack foods and most young people were "inactive."

According to a review conducted by Dentsu Institute for Human Studies, a majority of Americans and Britons have strong confidence in the future of their nations. Japanese on the other hand are not nearly so optimistic. In the late 1990s, 63% of Americans and 56% of British people thought their countries would be better off in ten years' time, but only 34% of Japanese respondents felt this way. Worse, for the self-esteem of Japanese, they appear to have lost faith in the power of their economy, with only 29% still thinking it surpassed that of other countries.

Initially, Japan lagged behind other nations in the use of the Internet at the turn of the century, with only about 18% of Japanese hooked up, as against nearly 60% of Americans and almost half of Europeans. Nearly 45% of Britons had Internet access, although at the time, over a third said they had no interest in ever going online. This must be seen in context though, many Japanese use the Internet at the office and some of the "overtime" they put in is used for net surfing. Also, from the start, many Japanese cellular phones had e-mail functions, so this figure may be a little misleading. The explosion in the number of Internet cafes in Tokyo was also a factor. Nevertheless, it is certainly true that poor English skills and higher charges for Internet use were two factors initially holding the Japanese back.

Japan's middle class seems to be undergoing something of an identity crisis. Until the 1950s, incomes differed greatly and it was only with the onset of the lifetime employment system and seniority based wage structures that a great leveling off of the Japanese people took place. This was far greater that in some so-called Communist countries. Many workers began to think of themselves as "middle class" and about 90% of Japanese regard themselves as being in that strata of society at present. There has been a similar, but less pronounced trend towards this kind of mindset in Britain in recent years.

Professor Keishi Saeki of Kyoto University feels that "As the nation's economic system becomes obsolete and faces greater global competition, workers fear they will lose their jobs." This goes some way to explain the weakening of the LDP's electoral clout in the past few elections and the near wipeout they suffered in 2009 in the General Election.

Professor Saeki added "The middle class has long been mutually dependent and comprised a powerful force within companies, ensuring social stability and economic growth in postwar Japan. If this order collapses, the nation will be driven into economic and social confusion for some time." In 1998, the number of suicides rose from 24,000 the previous year, itself a 5% rise, to around 31,000. Japan currently has one of the highest rates of suicide in the world, with over 22 per hundred thousand taking their own lives, as against 12 per 100,000 in the USA and 7.5 in the UK. "In 1998, the male life expectancy figure fell slightly due to the surge in suicides" the Daily Yomuiri stated. In 2000, the figures showed a marginally higher total for 1999, giving Japan the dubious honor of being in the running for "suicide capital of the world." By 2012 the figures seemed to have leveled off, albeit at a worryingly high plateau.

Japanese also feel more stress at work than before. 62% said they feel "severe stress or anxiety." according to a survey the Labour Ministry released in 1998. In Britain, similar figures were recorded. Overall, 70% of Japanese felt stressed out some of the time.

British work practices have become more like those in America. One-year or even six- month contracts are now commonplace. Britons now work longer hours than most other Europeans. The new EC regulations on working hours, setting 48 hours a week as the legal minimum were only grudgingly accepted by the Blair administration. Blair's predecessor Major rejected them outright. In order to make itself capable of winning an election during the eighteen years spent in opposition, the Labour Party has moved so far to the right to render many policies almost indistinguishable from the SDP breakaway party of the early 80s, or even of pre-Thatcher Conservatives. Once, it was said of the late Edward Heath, the former Conservative Prime Minister that he now finds himself far to the left of his own party mainstream. It was also suggested that he was more radical than the then current Labour administration as well.

We could see this blurring of the UK political parties nowhere more clearly than in the May 2000 race for London Mayor. Here, the four or five main candidates sat at one debate after another and often were seen nodding in agreement as one of their number set out his or her blueprint for how to rejuvenate London. Only the issue of the London Underground (subway) system divided them significantly. Steven Norris, the Conservative candidate sounded more like a liberal with his calls to help for the homeless and support for gay rights, while Labour's Frank Dobson talked of making London a friendly place to do business and of partly privatizing the "Tube."

Along with his many failures, Blair has succeeded in reforming some aspects of anachronistic Britain. He has taken Britain firmly down the road into modern government. The House of Lords is evolving into something like a democratic second chamber, with all but 92 of the hereditary peers removed forever from their ancestral seats. The Scottish and Welsh Assemblies are slowly finding their feet and more crucially in Northern Ireland as well.

Family life has certainly suffered in Japan, but the same is true of Britain too. One reason has been the erosion of the traditional weekend. About half of men now work two jobs and often on Saturday or Sunday. Nearly 70% of married women continue to work after they have children. Families in Britain, as in Japan spend less and less time together and there is sometimes only the occasional day when everyone is off work. Traditions such as the "Sunday Lunch" seem to be becoming just a fading memory for far too many British people. Just as the Japanese seem to have accepted the idea of a five-day work week and to have begun to consider the possibility that having a life outside of the office is no longer a cardinal sin, the British seem to be giving up on the whole concept in increasing numbers!

According to an article on the BBC website, from September 2006 "Childhood creativity is being stifled by a combination of junk food, school targets and mass-marketing, a group of authors and academics has claimed. Dozens of teachers joined children's authors and psychologists to write a letter to the Daily Telegraph (newspaper). The signatories highlighted the escalating incidence of "childhood depression" and demanded action."

"Families are spending more than ever before on "convenience living" to cope with the demands of modern life" Three quarters of working parents pay someone else to do their housework and nearly half said they "were too busy to spend time with family or friends." These were the findings of a report in a UK newspaper, the Independent, one that mirrors the situation in Japan.

One couple I knew who returned to Britain after a decade of living in Tokyo complained that most of their old friends were a total washout when it came to getting together for a drink. Many of them had effectively given up on a social life once their children came and had much the same kind of lifestyle that my friends had regularly criticized the Japanese for. "The increasing pace of life has made it more difficult for nearly 70 percent of the population to manage their time." In both countries, that means having a social life is one of the first things to be sacrificed on the altar of "the grab and go society" that so many people have become a part of. Britain is said to have over a million workaholics who put in more than 60 hours a week. One couple in the UK I used to be on good terms with effectively cut off most of their old friends (myself included) after their second child was born in 2001. Both were once gregarious and outgoing, then for a time the husband became a henpecked workhorse, while his wife was a full-time homemaker who seemed to have largely shut the outside world out. Nobody was especially surprised to hear how that three years later he had walked out on her and initiated divorce proceedings.

A survey in the United States painted a similar picture: "nearly a quarter of people surveyed said they had "zero' close friends with whom to discuss personal matters. More than 50% named fewer than two confidants…people had a surprising drop in the number of close friends since 1985. Part of the cause could be that Americans are working more, marrying later, having fewer children and commuting longer distances." Much the same seems true in both Japan and the UK.

In Japan "There are several bleak scenarios on the horizon, including a further birthrate decline from its present record low of 1.29. As well, with a pension law revision that took effect in April 2007 that made full-time housewives entitled to up to half their husbands' pension, a divorce rush initiated by women is likely to further accelerate *jukunen rikon* (divorce among old couples). Government statistics showed that the number of divorces among couples married for 35 years or more surged from 300 in 1975 to 4,710 in 2004 -- slightly down from its peak of 4,963 in 2003.

At the end of the day, it was not love, but fear of insolvency that kept Japanese couples from going their separate ways, Ehara suggests. "A lot of women are holding their breath right now, waiting to get a divorce," she said. "The pension system is the number one reason why they have stayed away from divorces up to now.""

Technology may also be increasing the tendency for the more affluent to remain in their homes most of the time. A Los Angeles Times report in January 2000 described how we will soon have "smart houses" that will eliminate most of the need to actually leave home at all. What with groceries being delivered and the home entertainment offered by high definition television and cable movies, to name but two options some will find preferable to venturing out into the crime-laden streets. Combined with the ability to work from home, one employee at US market research firm "also worries that the fully automated home runs the risk of creating a society of "house potatoes" who will no longer be challenged to go out into the world for food, work, communication or entertainment"

Already in the USA and even in the UK of late, there are several communities of wealthy residents who are effectively sealed off by high walls safe from the outside world that they venture out into only when absolutely necessary. It seems like a modern day equivalent of the Heian Court living in splendid isolation from the world beyond its boundaries.

In Japan, cases of so-called "hikikomori," or social withdrawal are rising. The Japanese term literally translates as "the act of shutting oneself inside." Experts say that anything from 60,000 to almost a million suffer from the condition to some degree. Typically they are young males who live in a twilight world of online chatting, e-mail and computer games and venture out as little as possible while their parents slowly start to realize that something is wrong. Blame for this phenomena is once again put upon the "intense educational pressure and the changing structure of the Japanese family." It can also be seen as one side effect of a culture and of the technology that makes such a lifestyle possible.

In both Japan and Britain, the family certainly is under stress. In Britain, there are signs that the rate of divorce might have leveled off at about 47%. In Japan, divorce rates continue to rise inexorably. It is too easy just to blame this all on Japanese men. I have read plenty of times of selfish, lazy women who drive their husbands to despair. Some, for example, refuse to have anything to do with their in-laws while repeatedly inviting their family round to party at short notice.

I taught one woman, a Mrs. H, who lives alone in a huge apartment. Her elder daughter is married and the younger, a career woman has a house in Tokyo. She and her husband had lived separately for the past twelve years. When he came to stay, he used the guest-room. They only met up for the occasional get-together with his relatives, to maintain the illusion that they are actually still married in any sense of the word. She was a thoroughly idle, negative person, regularly moaning about her boring life and periodically complaining about what an awful man her husband was. Rather than divorce him, she seemed happy enough to fritter away vast amounts of his money on at least three foreign trips a year. The last time I saw her she whined on about how he virtually ignored her and sat at a table with his friends during her daughter's wedding. It's hard not to conclude that they are just as bad as each other. They were finally divorced a couple of years after that.

Another former student of mine, a Mr. S seems to have had much the same experience as Reiko, who you met in the chapters on marriage – in reverse. He is articulate, intelligent and seemingly quite normal. He went through a perfunctory o-miai and then married at 32, primarily to please his parents. He described his "hellish" marriage to a wife who was a tyrant that sought to control his every movement. Nothing was ever good enough for her. She even refused to have sex more than once every two to three weeks. After a couple of years, he left, telling her she could keep the apartment and everything in it (all of which he had paid for). She promptly divorced him. Once again, it seems to be a problem both of raised expectations and of a chronic lack of communication. The dutiful Japanese wife is starting to look like an endangered species, at least in the cities.

A recent survey by the Tokyo Metropolitan Government revealed that domestic violence is not nearly as rare as was once believed. One third of women said their husbands had physically abused them at least once. More than half of the women surveyed felt that their husbands either ignored, or patronized them on a regular basis. Fully five percent of wives are victims of life-threatening violence. Here we can see the tendency of the Japanese to avoid confrontation, traditionally by ignoring the problem. Since early 2002 there has been a domestic violence law in force where men can be arrested and tried for spouse abuse. The number of women complaining on hotlines has risen steadily as the realization that they can begin to do something about it sinks in.

Cases of domestic violence and the number of fatherless children due to suicide have also risen sharply in the past decade. Thirty children a day are estimated to lose a father to suicide in Japan. Child abuse by parents or guardians has also become more widespread. The police have been taking a harder line against this trend. "The increase in the number of cases in which parents are criminally charged may reflect a change in the public's attitude toward the need to combat child abuse" said one Japanese social worker.

Put simply, more and more young women see no advantage in getting married at all. "Japanese women have been disillusioned by their mothers. They devoted themselves to their children and husbands and what did they get for it?" One long time career woman said. (The same could be said of the men who devoted their lives to their companies only to find themselves made redundant in their mid-fifties in the past few years.) This is true both in Japan and Britain. Women opt to remain single, feeling that they can enjoy their freedom. Some of them think they may decide to marry at some time, but keep delaying it for as long as possible. Until recently, Japanese parents were able to pressure their children in to marriage. Overall this seems not to be the case anymore. Polls suggest that more and more young people are taking an independent and increasingly individual attitude towards marriage. To give an example, let's consider the case of an acquaintance of mine, Tazuko.

Tazuko was 40 at that time (2000), living with her parents who were both around 70 years old. She was a moderately successful career woman, who tried a few "o-miai" type introductions, but wasn't terribly impressed with any of the men she met. She saw no merit in marrying just to satisfy her parents or the dictates of society. Her parents and especially her father were forever nagging her to get hitched. Finally her father issued her with an ultimatum: get married or get out of this house! (This was blatantly illogical since whichever choice she made she would be leaving anyway!)

She was so angry that the next day she found herself an apartment. When she returned home to announce this to her parents, her father went down on his knees and almost touched his forehead to the ground. He begged her in the most pitiful manner not to leave, while in the background her mother sobbed uncontrollably.

After some moments, she agreed to stay with them on condition that they drop the subject of marriage for good. One year later Tazuko told me how she had got along with them just fine and if anything she reckoned that they showed her more respect than of old. The supreme irony of this story was how two years after that, Tazuko met and married a man of her own accord and promptly moved away to the other end of the country.

Here we can see once again the essential fragility of a social order that relies on coercion and of unquestioning obedience to function, as I have suggested before. Tazuko's parents behaved toward her in a manner no different from that of bullies and like most bullies, backed down in an instant the moment their "victim" fought back. This is the way I see much of what pass for "relationships" in Japan.

This is a subjective interpretation and many Japanese would not regard it in this way. They would say they are worried about their daughter's future and that she was likely to be lonely in her later years. A cynic would turn to them and reply that judging from a lot of their generation's marriages, being single would be more honest than being married to someone who they had absolutely no feeling for, but once again, it's all about points of view in the end.

Japanese society evolved rigid patterns of behaviour that seemed to serve them well enough in the past. Some Japanese complain that many people, especially career women have lost their sense of purpose: simply becoming obsessed with making money and then squandering much of it on brand-name goods.

In the late 1990s, I also read of increasing cases of mistreatment of in-laws who were being looked after by family members. This took the form of both verbal and physical abuse. For "family members" read "daughters-in-law" and the picture becomes much clearer. Some might dismiss this as tabloid nonsense, although it was widely reported in the mainstream press. As I see it, this is nothing but a case of giving back what you have been forced to endure. Many mothers-in-law are undeniably nasty to their precious little boy's bride and yet at the same time manage a spectacular feat of illogic in expecting all that spite to be repaid by being taken care of by them in old age. Who can seriously be surprised that a much put upon homemaker will be tempted to give back the years of unpleasantness that she was forced to suffer at the hands of her mother-in-law, in a similar fashion now that the boot is on the other foot? That it is now coming to light is probably more a result of increasing openness than some new phenomenon. This is cruelty breeding cruelty; or as Arnold Bennett dubbed it in his novel "Clayhanger," "the revenge of the generations." In the story, the hero built up a tremendous resentment of his tyrannical father and the son had sworn to "get his own back" when he was older. By the time he was finally in a position to do so it had become meaningless as the old man had become senile and absolutely pitiful.

The crime rate continues to rise to record levels. There were nearly a million crimes committed in Japan during the first half of 1999. The figure topped a million in the first half of 2000. Even though, it has a way to go before it approaches the levels seen in many Western countries. Crimes, often violent and those leading to deaths are increasingly committed by minors. By August of 2000, a government report concluded that violence in schools had reached record levels, especially in Middle Schools. Japanese children seem less and less able to cope with pressure than they were in the past. My friend Reiko commented that many parents were themselves immature and were consciously allowing their own children to control them. Something similar is apparent in Britain and other Western countries as well.

The chronic lack of discipline from parents, the pressures of "exam hell" the students were forced to endure until quite recently and the severity of the education system in general all play a part. Children who complain of being constantly tired and busy are increasingly likely to "snap" as the Japanese expression goes.

So are the Japanese getting more individualistic? More like the British, even as Britain moves closer to America, in a manner of speaking? My feeling is that this is so. The older generations complain that the younger generation is selfish. Clearly, from a collectivist viewpoint, individualist society must surely come across as very selfish. It will be interesting to see just how Japanese society evolves.

Nobody should be especially surprised. Since the end of the sixties, if not even earlier, the Japanese have essentially been living Western lifestyles. British diplomats in the mid-seventies concluded that Japan was outwardly almost entirely Western. The nuclear family is mostly the norm. They commute to offices, use computers, eat Western food and barely see their neighbours from day to day. Adopting the Western lifestyle meant the same problems endemic in the West automatically became prevalent in Japan as well. The pathetic attempts by Japanese corporations to foster a sense of company loyalty have been exposed as a con trick lasting fifty-something years. In some senses of the word, group-ism in Japan is largely dead. Some Japanese continue to play the game and delude themselves that they are one big happy family. Other, wiser souls step back for a moment to wonder why many aspects of their society seem in danger of falling apart.

During the mid-eighties when I first began my life in Japan, my impression was that here was a country largely living a fifties lifestyle. The conformity was like something out of the old TV show Happy Days, the odd rebel was most definitely without any definable cause. In the summer of 2002 as I prepared to complete the previous draft of this manuscript and planned my first return to the UK at the end of the year, I sensed that Japan has gone punk. It's Anarchy in the Land of the Rising Sun twenty-five years late.

I recall watching a TV programme around that time. It was the usual undemanding variety show, interviewing a group of young men around 19 or 20. They were all dressed in much the same mix of seventies retro, hip-hop styles and backwoods chic that seemed to be the fashion not just in Japan but just about everywhere else on the planet. Many had earrings, nose studs and a couple sported body piercing. Only one of them had hair that was its natural black and his was shaved up the sides, the top gelled into wavy spikes. The others mostly wore theirs in longish shaggy styles, like in the seventies, but cut better. They were red, brown, blonde and one even had silvered streaks. Graffiti was once a rarity in Japan, but no more, already some railway lines and underpasses are splattered with vile garish paint jobs and imitations of the same kind of inane designs that can be seen in many Western countries.

Take a walk down the crowded streets of Harajuku, the Kings Road of Tokyo and see for yourself. You might be mistaken for thinking you were back in the early seventies, or even the late sixties, what with the young people hugging and kissing openly while older and more conservative members of society look on disapprovingly. Until recently, tanning had been a fad, with many charring themselves as dark as possible, not long after there was a backlash against tanning and it became "in" to be pale again.

Young Japanese seem increasingly to be contemptuous of many aspects of their society. They don't want to work themselves into the ground. They want to have fun, to travel and in many ways they are much like modern teenagers in the West. They are certainly less group-oriented than their parents are or grandparents were. There are also those who say many young Japanese have become more inward looking. They are disinterested in working or travelling abroad and show little interest in the outside world apart from a fascination with Korean pop-culture.

For one thing, the Japanese are increasingly resorting to lawsuits to settle their differences. There have been more cases of Japanese widows successfully suing companies for huge sums of money. Their husbands have either died of "karoshi" or committed suicide and the women have refused to take it lying down. The courts are said to be becoming more open to work-related suicide suits. I also have read a few stories of men who have taken their employers to court to fight a "tenkin" or order by their company to transfer at short notice to the other end of the country, often without their family. Again, their numbers are as yet relatively small, but do seem to tentatively suggest that more Japanese are getting up off their knees and fighting against the injustices of their society.

Cases of sexual harassment are also increasing and laws against molesting women on trains have been taking effect. Some lines even have "women only" cars provided for rush-hour travel. Many Japanese are now beginning to accept that "sekuhara" as they have dubbed the practice is unacceptable. At the other extreme, some American women are said to complain that men will even avoid eye contact for fear of being accused of making sexual advances. Some would say that you can't have it both ways.

Britain's new diversity means "England is becoming more like the U.S. melting pot...we may find America's tougher, more callous attitudes to welfare come here too. A more porous England is one that is also unavoidably more open to drugs, crime and tensions between communities...It will be less stable." Once again, you can't have your cake and eat it. Ten years on, this has become the norm. The Cameron government has shown callous disregard for the poor and welfare is being steadily stripped away. One case of a suicide by a mentally ill woman forced back into work underlined the human cost of cost cutting.

Diversity also means the barbaric customs of other cultures are steadily working their way into British life. Reports of forced marriage, genital mutilation and even honour killings abound. Several cases have involved British Muslim men who have abused teenage and younger girls, typically in grooming gangs. Court cases have sometimes seen their solicitors use the defense that their religion sanctions child sex and mistreatment of women.

Nearly ten percent of people in the UK are from various ethnic minorities. The supine, almost servile attitude towards Islam adopted by many UK politicians is as disturbing as it is sickening. Many "liberals" are the worst, seemingly oblivious of the fact that the central tenets of Islam violently oppose things they hold dear such as women's rights, gay rights, the freedom of expression even freedom to leave the religion without fear of being killed (another tenet of Islam that its apologists are only too happy to overlook).

After an incident in 2013 when two African immigrants decapitated a soldier in broad daylight and did so in the name of Islam, leading politicians went out of their way to defend a faith that is increasingly despised by many in Britain and Europe. Many people consider it to be a nasty, misogynistic faith, one that is steeped in violence and extremism; a threat to the democratic and tolerant values of the British way of life.

The overwhelming influence of America economically as well as socially cannot be overstated. Here I am, in Japan using the software developed by one of two corporations that dominate the computer world. My spell-check is in American English. In the cinema, the United States undoubtedly rules supreme, with only the occasional challenge from Europe. American practices, be it in business or cultural have spread across the globe. Even so, for much of the world, the "global economy" is just a dream. In 2005, less than 5% of Africa was on the Internet.

But at the end of the day, is an individualistic society such as that epitomized by America really more democratic and open than a collectivist culture? Again, this depends on your definition of the term democracy. Why not ask the man who shot a rat in his backyard with a handgun who was then sued by his neighbour for causing him "mental anguish" at having to witness such a thing. (Thankfully, the judge threw the case out in an instant, but the fact that a lawyer was prepared to even consider it speaks volumes about the state of play in the USA today.) Try smoking in a public place in New York, joining the Boy Scouts if you are openly an atheist, any number of things and the "majority" will trample your "rights."

One British family stationed in the States that I read of was amazed at the petty nature of the rules in their condo. The pool could only be used when an attendant was present, due to paranoia about lawsuits in case of an accident; the front door must be painted white and the doormat could only be of a standard issue type. There were also endless regulations about what items could be left outside the door (no plants) and even what times they were permitted to use the laundry facilities in the basement. Then there is the regulated society where not only are seat belts obligatory, but now hardly anyone will dare ride a bicycle without one of those aerodynamic helmet things that have become the de facto law of the land. I wonder if this is so different from Japan's "stifling conformity" where those who stand out will be bullied and harried into line or ostracized as the last resort.

Are Americans simply forming larger, but less well-defined groups and excluding those who fail to fit in? Perhaps this is so. Provided you are a non-smoker and virtually teetotal, openly religious and supportive of gun-ownership and the death penalty, then you are accepted. In some parts of America, finding yourself on the wrong side of one or more of these issues could see you just as surely shunned as anyone in Japanese society who rocks the boat, or dares to be different.

Taking this one stage further, just how free is America anyway? The human rights organization Amnesty International reported among other things in 1999 that The USA was only one of two countries not to have ratified the Convention on the Rights of the Child. Also that it was one of just ten countries that had yet to ratify the UN Convention on the Elimination of All Forms of Discrimination against Women, lining it up with such paragons of progressive thought as Iran and Syria. Torture and abuse of prisoners were said to be common across the USA, as was the use of dangerous restraints on prisoners. Around 10,000 complaints of police brutality are received every year. "In a (police) training video, every criminal portrayed is black." Ron Hampton, a retired police officer admitted to Amnesty in 1998.

The religious right from one extreme and the politically correct "liberals" from the other have both helped to undermine freedom of speech and action, not just in America. In Europe, we now have several countries that have made it technically an offence for parents to physically punish their children, even at home. Britain thankfully has resisted this pathetic nonsense. The petty minded attack on the rights of smokers, even in bars continues. Now there are hints from the USA that once the cigarette companies are sued into bankruptcy, the fast food industry might be next. Would anyone be up for a class action lawsuit by morbidly obese ex-hamburger addicts? (I wrote that comment about six months before I read of just such a thing beginning in America.)

While admitting that the idea of watching a corporation such as McDonalds squirming in court trying to justify targeting children and poor neighbourhoods with their prettily packaged junk smugly appealing on one level, this is still worrying on another. It's as if nobody takes personal responsibility for anything anymore.

Nobody can just be disabled or handicapped these days. They have to have the suffix "challenged" tacked on in some way. We are in danger of being robbed of the language of Shakespeare, seeing it emasculated into vague ciphers, stripped of any real impact or meaning. The tendency for Japanese to flood their speech with meaningless "pseudo-English" words and phrases that even many of them don't really understand is just a parallel development to this trend towards imprecise, garbled discourse that makes genuine communication between individuals even harder than ever before. Perhaps it is akin to the "newspeak" that Orwell prophesized in his1984.

I was astounded by the spiel of a coach (long-distance bus) driver back in the UK the last time I visited. It was almost identical to the kind of preamble given prior to take off by an international airliner. We were warned to stow all baggage in the back, or under seats, there was no smoking on the bus, nobody must stand up while the bus is in motion unless they wish to visit the restrooms, etc. Once again, the fear of lawsuits originating from an injury is uppermost in the bus company's mind. Britain is increasingly becoming a society that resorts to litigation to solve disputes.

On a more positive note, the British are said to have better health than one hundred years ago and the life expectancy has risen to 79 for men and 81 for women. Around the turn of the century in Japan, the government took such steps as moving as many national holidays to Mondays as possible to create several three-day weekends. It was hoped this would be another way to encourage people to spend more on vacations and to actually enjoy themselves a little more. (And the Government hoped they would help to pull the country out of recession by spending more money on travel and consumer goods at the same time.)

The total marketing strategy was adopted by Japanese business in the post war years. Perhaps the greatest irony of all is that much of the so-called "Japanese business methods" that almost brought the West to its knees in the 80s were in fact the results of work by an American statistician, Dr W Edwards Deming (1900-93). During the 1950s, his ideas had few takers at home, but he brought his methods to Japan and found its business leaders much more receptive. His emphasis on quality control and efficient production was just what Japan needed, at the same time as the whole "salaryman" culture was appearing. Deming's efforts won him a medal from the Emperor for services to Japan.

In the past decade, however, Western firms have closed the gap. Ideas that American companies initially rejected have been adopted, with the result that Japan has lost much of the competitive advantage it once had. What is worse for Japan, many American and British firms now have greater productivity levels than Japanese companies. Even when it comes to commuting time, the average in Britain is only about 35 minutes, as against over an hour in Japan.

It is interesting that the same kind of "corporate culture" that the Japanese are now slowly turning away from seems to be thriving in the UK.   There is a whole cottage industry of "team building" away-days and "paintball" events in Britain. The risible notion that squandering resources on stupid, childish games helps build "team spirit" seems to have taken root in many companies and Local Authorities.   I remember how they organized one for the council where I worked for 18 months. It was a complete waste of time, half the people attending did so under surly duress and several of the members who were supposed to "bond" had left the authority within a year, either bullied out by their line manager, or off on long-term stress; so much for "bonding!"

Seismic changes have already come to Britain regarding the very nature of the country. The peace agreement reached in Northern Ireland seemed to be holding, even after the assembly was suspended early in 2000 over the question of the IRA and other paramilitary groups disarming. Supporters of the accord were victorious in the elections held for seats on the assembly. It could be argued that the North has less and less to fear from eventual reunion with the Republic of Ireland, which some observers still feel will come with time. The power of the Catholic Church, while still considerable, has declined in recent years. Scandals, some involving priests and little boys, have undermined the Church in many of its member's eyes. Divorce and contraception have both been legalized in the past couple of decades. (Abortion is illegal in North and the Republic of Ireland. Women who chose to terminate a pregnancy travel to Mainland Britain.) Perhaps North and South will ultimately enter into some kind of relationship falling just short of complete reunion, one where the North retains some control over domestic matters. Ten years on and the Assembly just overcame yet another hurdle, this time regarding policing.

Scotland and Wales now have their own assemblies. Many observers concurred that it was only a matter of time before the Scots voted to break away from England. Support for independence rose in Scotland from 40% in the late 90s to almost 50% by 2006. Then it fell again and is currently hovering just below half of the electorate. At the end of the day, perhaps the question of whether Scotland opts for total or partial independence from England is irrelevant. It already has many of the aspects of a separate country including its own currency, education system and laws. The Scottish Assembly voted to become the first part of the UK to abolish foxhunting early in 2002. With the increasing economic integration of Europe, will it really matter whether some issues are decided in the parliament of London or in that of the EU?

Scotland voted in September 2014 on a referendum to decide if it wished to remain part of the UK or become a separate country. The Scottish people voted "no", some would conclude, with their heads, not their hearts to keep the Union intact. However the surge in support and membership for the Scottish National Party and its popular new leader Nicola Sturgeon mean the issue is far from decided. Should Westminster renege on its promise of greater devolved powers for the Scottish Assembly, then we can expect a "yes" vote in the not too distant future. In the 2015 general election the SNP won 56 out of the 59 seats in Scotland.

In the other divided country, Korea, similar moves were afoot. The relationship between Korea and Japan has improved considerably in recent years. Korea announced in October 1998 that it would lift a long-standing ban on imports of Japanese cultural items such as movies, CDs and such. Five years later, Korean TV drams dubbed into Japanese are massive hits with middle-aged women and have made a matinee idol of their pretty-boy leading man, known in Japan as Yon Sama.   President Kim Dae Jung made a successful visit to Japan at that time, where both he and then Prime Minister Obuchi spoke of the need for reconciliation. In 2000, both Koreas have held meetings in the truce village of Panjaemun on the heavily fortified border between the two countries. Further meetings and a series of measures to lessen tensions were being discussed. However, recent events such as a gun battle between ships from the north and south make it unlikely that Korea will be reunited and at peace anytime soon. Former President Kim's "Sunshine Policy" towards the north seems to have set without much lasting success.

The issue of the Northern Territories seems unlikely to be resolved in the near future. Russia offered to return the two southernmost islands, but Japan remains adamant that it must regain all of them before concluding a formal peace treaty. Both sides made vague noises about working towards this end and hoped to sign the treaty by the year 2000.   President Putin was elected on his tough-guy image and it seems questionable how far he will be willing to compromise on the issue, given his ruthless stance over crushing the uprising in Chechnya. In spite of this, there was still a good deal of optimism that many outstanding issues between Russia and Japan could be settled within the next twelve months. Sadly that was not to be and at the time of writing (September 2006) it appeared that standoff would continue indefinitely. In 2015 there is nothing new to report.

The government has taken more power from the bureaucrats and many wonder whether most Japanese politicians will be able to cope with the novelty of actually writing their own speeches and formulating policy by themselves. Time will tell. In spite of promising to limit the practice, the bureaucracy was still seen widely practicing "amakudari" or "descent from Heaven" where retiring bureaucrats find jobs in industry, or as politicians. Fewer ex-bureaucrats were elected to the Diet in 2000, so that might be some modest cause for celebration.

The LDP finally lost its death-grip on politics in Japan in 2009. The 2005 election produced a landslide for Koizumi, although the Democratic Party held on to a passable 113 seats to just barely claim they were a government in waiting. It was fought on the issue of privatization of the Post Office, which ironically, saw a drastic reduction in the kind of "pork barrel" politics that helped the LDP retain its iron grip on power. Koizumi's real legacy was that a genuine two party system briefly emerged.

In any case, the policy differences between the LDP and the Democratic Party are so cosmetic as to be almost irrelevant. By the end of its long period of rule it depended heavily on Komeito as a vote-gathering machine to get out its supporters on Election Day. Ultimately, though, the link between LDP, business and bureaucrats is gone. Japan briefly evolved into a two party system with smaller parties capable of holding the balance of power. This might look like a recipe to emulate late 20th century Italy. This is not so in Japan since politics is usually more to do with personalities and support groups than any substantial policy differences, the Japan Communist Party excepted.

The governing Democratic Party of Japan was led from behind by Ichiro Ozawa, who was for many years an LDP hack. This only reinforces the sense that it is just two parties with few substantial differences vying for the votes of an increasingly cynical and indifferent public. This is not so different from the situation in the UK.

Britain's political crystal ball is a lot clearer. The future of the Conservatives as a party capable of forming a government by itself seemed fairly bleak until interest generated by the party's young and photogenic leader David Cameron revived its fortunes. In the eleven years since being forced from office the Conservatives made a cosmetic shift to the centre. In government they moved steadily rightwards.

The tragedy is that British politics has degenerated into debates over drinking limits and ever more social engineering. Having demonized smoking to the point where it is likened to heroin addiction, the politically correct turn now to obesity and drinking. "(The government's) main concern is that middle-aged people are too fat. It is also spending (or rather wasting) oodles of our money on an expensive advertising campaign suggesting that anyone ordering a third pint of beer had better book an undertaker to go with it." Simon Heffer lamented in a Telegraph article just prior to the spring 2010 General Election that as expected, saw the long serving Labour Government evicted from the corridors of power. Heffer's comment reflected on the modern-day obsession that throws the focus on irrelevant single issues and social engineering as a means to deflect from the government's inability to solve more intransigent problems that can't be simply wished away.

Just as Japan is becoming more like the West, the West has taken on many of the aspects of Japanese life that were once anathema. Americans work longer hours and for many, their society has become a tightly regulated, exhausting treadmill where they are too burned out to spend much time together as a family let alone for a social life. Just as the Japanese have struggled to get their people to take more holidays, the British have been working the longest hours in Europe, their workplaces increasingly mirroring the petty minded manual driven management styles that the Japanese were once past masters of.

The same enormous changes that Britain went through are now just beginning in Japan. If and when Japan undergoes the same shakeout of workers that the U.K. and other Western countries saw in the eighties, then the unemployment rate could rise to more than 10%. Even in May 2000, male unemployment had risen to 5.2%. At the close of the 20th century, there were huge numbers of surplus workers within Japanese companies ranging from elevator girls and store greeters to the so-called "madogiwazoku" or "window gazers." These were usually middle-aged men with little or no real work who the company was unable to lay off directly. Instead they gave them nothing to do, hoping they would quit out of sheer boredom. Some were quite literally gazing out of the window, if they were lucky enough to even have one to gaze out of. Some were relegated to the basement. Many of them did eventually resign, but others endured the injustice they were facing. They knew just as well as the company bosses who were treating them in such a callous manner that if they hung on, they would get their pension and substantial final bonus on retirement.

Homelessness in Britain has long been a problem, with thousands sleeping rough in the capital alone. What fewer people realize is that Japan now has its own army of men sleeping under the stars. Once regarded as lazy drunks and no-hopers that couldn't or wouldn't work, men who have been made redundant and fallen through the cracks have swelled their numbers in the past decade. One survey in Kawasaki, southern Tokyo showed that 90% of them wanted to work and about 70% had been homeless for over a year.

"We must be prepared to undergo a period of dynamic industrial transition which involves much pain in weeding out the waste" said one Kakuo Mizuno of Kokusai Securities Co. He was echoing the message of Thatcher and her ruthless cohorts when he spoke of the "redundant workforce of 5 million." Clearly there are people with ideas about what needs doing, but whether the government will be up to the task of grasping this economic nettle and virtually assuring its own defeat at the subsequent election is another matter. Ironically, at about the same time, an advisory panel to the government recommended the mandatory age of retirement should be raised from its current 60 to 65. This was intended to offset the shrinking workforce whose numbers began falling in 2007. That was the same year the Japanese population as a whole began to drop.

Several Japanese banks and other corporations are merging, something once considered unthinkable. "The mergers demonstrate a shift in emphasis toward profitability and away from the traditional ethic of group loyalty."

Britain now has one of the greatest disparities between rich and poor in the Western world, while Japan had one of the smallest until recently. The coming changes to the economy threaten this status quo just as in former Communist countries of Eastern Europe who have found with their embrace of markets and Western style democracy, a concurrent rise in the level of inequality. This is inevitable in Japan and be another factor in the undermining of the old consensus that has governed the land since the Second World War. By the end of 2005, regional disparities were said to be steadily increasing. There were signs this could even become an issue in future elections.

"The nation's treasured cultural homogeneity has largely been supported by homogeneity of wealth. Now, as innovative start-up firms sprout up and restructuring creates record high unemployment, the possibility of a chasm between the rich and poor is becoming a real threat."

Birth rates in both Japan and Britain have fallen steadily. This is the pattern across much of the industrialized Western world. There is only an average of 1.26 children in Spanish or Italian families. Japan has a rate of 1.29 while the figure for the UK is about 1.8. If not for massive levels of immigration, the populations of the UK and many other European countries would be falling. The average number of children born to Japanese women has fallen more sharply and faster in Japan than Britain, or many other countries. Commentators cite the enormous cost of raising a child and difficulties that confront working women as two of the reasons. The government is understandably concerned, given that if present trends were to continue, the population of Japan would drop from around 127 million in 2006 to about 70 million or less by the 2050s.

In Britain, it is increasingly condoned for fathers to be absent, working longer and longer hours, becoming more like their Japanese counterparts. "Society still takes a dim view of women who see their working life as anything but secondary." In Japan as in Britain, it is primarily the woman who is seen as the one to do the bulk of child rearing. In Japan, the murder of a 2 year-old-girl by a mentally disturbed 35 year-old neighbour resulted in over a thousand faxes and letters arriving at the offices of the Daily Yomuri newspaper. "Some of the responses were messages from mothers who said raising children puts a strain on their daily lives that their husbands and others simply do not understand....Many women have said their husbands have no interest in raising their children." A survey carried out by the same paper revealed that most respondents felt that the financial burden of having children, or another child deterred many would-be mothers.   Many mothers want more day care facilities to be provided.

The government's desire for women to have more children fails to take into account that this is a global trend throughout industrialized societies. This helps to illustrate one of the problems facing the leaders of Japan. It is their inability to see that Japan is behaving like any other industrial nation with a falling birth rate coinciding with a rapidly aging population.

Those both in Japan and the UK who argue that women are harming their children by working will be either relieved or disappointed by the results of research carried out in Britain. It showed that if anything, children of working mothers are more self-reliant and confident than those whose mothers remain at home. Although some may develop inferior reading skills very early on in life, the report reckoned that on balance, women should not feel guilty that working was harming their children.

In conclusion, is there any hope for Japan? The Nobel Prize winning author Kenzaburo Oe feels that "The fundamental Japanese malaise is a fatal combination of defective leadership and unthinking acquiescence. The Japanese are now left with having to face reality and pay for past neglect." Oe also believes that the "severest handicaps facing the Japanese are the absence of constructive debate in the media and in society in general and weak intellectual independence which prevents both self-knowledge and an understanding of the universal aspects of humanity."

Right-wing blowhards such as Shintaro Ishihara, the former governor of Tokyo, may make unpleasant remarks about foreigners living in Tokyo being likely to riot in an emergency and at the same time try to delude themselves that the atrocity of the Nankin Massacre never happened. With such closed-minded racist nonsense coming from someone who in Japan is widely regard as an intellectual, it is easy to understand Oe's fears for the future.

The writer Saul Bellow was of the opinion that he was lucky to have "Been spared the chief ambiguity that afflicts intellectuals and this is that civilized individuals hate and resent the civilization that makes their lives possible. What they love is an imaginary human situation invented by their own genius and which they believe is the only true and the only human reality." In such as Ishihara's case, who could argue with that?

All this might have given the impression that nobody in Japan has any idea of what to do to pull the country up out of its collective malaise. Several Japanese writers laid out their ideas of what steps must be taken to help their homeland. It is interesting to note that in the decade that followed at least some of these proposals seem to be taking root.

Shin-Ichi Terashima, a university teacher writing in the Japan Times reckoned that "Japan could use more logic, less poetry." he goes on to plea for tolerance and a change of the mindset of traditional thinking. "Individual creativity can hardly be expected to flourish in an environment where expressing one's views, particularly critical ones, is tantamount to antisocial behaviour." He feels the Japanese live too much in the present and need to break out of this thinking.

No less than the deputy business news editor of the Yomuri Shinbun wrote: "The country's economic system must be reformed to make the market mechanism work more efficiently. Such changes would also enable full use to be made of individuals' and companies' initiative and efforts toward progress. The fluidity of every economic resource, including money and the labour force must be increased.

To make these changes possible, the nation must break the spell of the wartime regime and be prepared for friction and confusion along the way." The "wartime regime," of course refers to the seniority system and lifetime employment, both of which are now largely discredited. Five years on and the "Iron Triangle" of bureaucrats, business and LDP is said to be rusting away steadily.

Japanese politics, like in the US and UK has tacked to the right and this trend seems set to continue. In 2006 many spoke of Japan's increasing assertiveness in the international forum. This is in part due to Koizumi's high profile compared with many previous prime ministers. His successor, Shinzo Abe, proved to be a major disappointment. The early signs, with one of his ministers resigning over a scandal where he let his mistress live in a government apartment and the ousting of several governors on corruption charges suggested "business as usual." One year later and he had resigned. Abe returned as Japan's prime minister in 2012 and critics regard him as being far more successful the second time around. Abe's replacement, Yasuo Fukuda, was a 71 year old "consensus" politician in the old model, precisely the kind of colourless "head-on-a-suit" who only reinforced the public image of the LDP as a dinosaur party incapable of real and lasting change. In the autumn of 2008, Japan had its third prime minister, Mr. Aso, in as many years and few had any real expectations of him. He was another clueless performer of what one commentator called "karaoke politics" where each has a brief turn on the stage.

Economist Yasuhiko Shibata went one stage further and effectively wrote off Japan as an economic superpower. He worried that the majority of the Japanese public is less interested in genuine reform and more in short-term fixes, much like the government in fact. "Japan is a heavily indebted nation - as the United States once was... Japanese companies and stocks, the values of which have decreased dramatically, are being snapped up cheaply by foreign investors. This is certainly not what is supposed to happen to an economic superpower." He stresses the need to accept this "harsh reality" of no longer being an industrial giant, while taking steps to resuscitate the economy.

Economics professor Ryuzo Sato basically echoes the sentiments of the above writers, also reminding us how "reform or building cannot be accomplished without discarding the old establishment. Scrapping the old-boy network (of the bureaucracy) is only one example...what needs to be scrapped most of all is the old mentality."

Japan has begun initiating banking reforms and the shedding of surplus workers. The results of this will be apparent over the next five to ten years. Even so, genuine restructuring has only just started, with excess capacity still widespread throughout industry.

An alternative view taken by Californian associate professor of political science, Steven K. Vogel is that "Japan has successfully modified and reinforced its own economic model – rather than surrendering to the American one – while fighting its way out of the prolonged stagnation it got mired in…during the early 1990s." He went on to point out that "more than 80% of Japanese companies still observe long-term or lifetime employment." (Source: Japan Times) By 2008, this had fallen to about 70%.

Since the election of Shinzo Abe in 2012, economic policies dubbed "Abenomics" have received mixed reviews. The IMF, for instance stated in a report issued in July 2013 "a unique opportunity to end decades-long deflation and sluggish growth and reverse the rise of public debt," but argued that "all three arrows need to be launched for the policies to succeed. Uncertainty about the ambition of fiscal and structural reforms is adding to underlying risks." The "three arrows" refer to fiscal policy, monetary policy and lastly strategy for economic growth. The first two of these were implemented shortly after Abe and the LDP returned to power. It remains to be seen how effective Abenomics will prove to be in seeing the third arrow reach its target. Broadly speaking, most commentators give the policies a fair to good chance of success.

Less certain is the path Abe's international policies will take Japan's relations with the rest of Asia. The BBC's Tokyo correspondent, Rupert Wingfield-Hayes described him as "far more right wing than most of his predecessors." Abe's efforts to reinterpret the Japanese constitution to allow for a standing army have sounded alarm bells both nationally and in countries such as Korea and China. Many observers, particularly from foreign countries regard Abe as being a right-wing nationalist. A March 2, 2014 New York Times editorial called Abe a "nationalist" who is a profound threat to US-Japan relations.

Anyone tempted to Japan off as a spent force need only look back to the end of World War 2. Tokyo was a pile of smoking rubble, the economy shattered, the country occupied by the Allies under General MacArthur. Yet less than twenty years later, Japan was regarded by Washington as a loyal ally. It was hosting the 1964 Olympic Games and well on the way to becoming an economic giant. Japan's economy may well be showing signs of modest recovery, but the resulting changes that will come to society are harder to predict.

Japan and Britain have indeed many aspects that are similar. Some will say that a good number of the points I have made about one or both and my "theory of cultural comparison" as I halfway tongue-in-cheek dubbed it could just as easily apply to any other culture. To them I would say, precisely. The underlying similarity of the human experience wherever we roam is soon apparent once we draw back the veil of culture.

Owari

SOURCES AND NOTES

(1)   Polls from Mori polling organization July 2000

(2)   Bill Murphy "Home Truths" (Mainstream- Publishing) Pages 167, 166, 193, 172, 12

(3)   Alex Kerr- ibid. (On Stereotypes pages 98-99)

(4)   Quotes from Daily Express on "Neighbours"

(5)   EPA – Economic Planning Agency

(6)   Sue Dibbs - BBC Internet health homepage Also BBC health homepage on "Drug Use"

(7)   Various quotes from Daily Yomuiri

(8)   Chav – violent, badly dressed UK youth (similar to a "yob")

(9)   Quote from Japan Times March 2006

(10) Quote from Yomuri article

(11) "The Tube" – the London Underground. (subway)

(12) Duke University study published in American Sociological Review

(13) Japan Times article by Robert J. Samuelson

(14) Nigella Lawson writing in The Daily Mail

(15) Amnesty International- quote and figures from BBC Internet, October 1999.

(16) First past the post – the party winning the largest share of the vote wins the parliamentary
       seat. With votes split between three major parties, the winner can be elected with
       little more than a third of the electorate. In 2005, Labour won just 36% of the vote but
       54% of the seats. In Scotland, there are usually four main parties contesting each seat,
       meaning the winner is sometimes backed by under thirty percent of the electorate.

(17) Daily Yomuri Newspaper quotes

(18) Kazuo Mizuno from Yomuri article

(19) Survey of working mothers- "Guardian" article

(20) Kenzaburo Oe, from Yomuri article

(21) Saul Bellow "Herzog" Page 311 (Pub. Penguin)

(22) "Happy Days" – US TV show set in the mid 50s to mid 60s centred around a small-town
       family and their friends.

(23) Joji Sakurai writing for the Associated Press

(24) Yasuhiko Shibata- from Daily Yomuri article

(25) Ryuzo Sato is Professor of Economics at New York University- from Daily Yomuri Editorial

(26) Simon Heffer in the Daily Telegraph 16th February 2010. "Can Anyone Explain What the
Conservative Party Stands For?"

(27) Clive Martin "How Sad Young Douchebags Took Over Modern Britain". – Vice.com

(28) In August 2014, the northern English city of Rotherham had an ongoing scandal involving

ethnic Pakistani Muslim rape gangs. As many as 1,400 victims had come forward at the time of publication.

(29) "Mr. Abe's Dangerous Revisionism" New York Times 2nd March 2014.

About the Author

I was born in a leafy London suburb in the spring of 1962. At the age of ten, my family moved to Bexhill on Sea, the first of two neighbouring south coast seaside towns. In the summer of 1978 when I was sixteen my family bought a house in Hastings.

Radicalized by the Thatcher years and their devastating effect on my family I became deeply engrossed in political activism. By the spring of 1985, disillusion with politics and profoundly dissatisfied with the direction of my life I was prompted to leave Britain for Japan. I'd been corresponding with a pen-friend in Nara since I was sixteen and curiosity drew me to experience the place for myself. An intended stay of six months to a year dragged out into almost eighteen. Working as an English teacher I got completely locked into the whole expatriate lifestyle of excessive drinking and serial womanizing. I began cohabiting with my future wife and her two daughters in 1997. The womanizing part ended there and then although the drinking endured. Then and now, my hobbies were learning new things, savouring fine cigars, drinking with a small circle of friends, hiking, learning to play the guitar and various writing projects.

My first book to be published on Amazon, "The Twain Shall Meet" detailed the histories of foreigners that impacted on Japanese history in one way or another. To date I have published five books, three under my own name. "The Chrysanthemum and the Rose" however, was the first one I began writing way back around 1999 or so.

I lived continually in Japan for just short of eighteen years. Exhausted by what had become nothing less than a relentless workaholic lifestyle, I increasingly longed to return to my roots. Thus, with my wife and elder daughter I relocated to the UK early in 2003, definitely not the most intelligent thing I ever did. I planned it poorly and struggled to reintegrate into English society after so long away. Working in an insultingly low-paid admin job for a local council I had an ongoing battle with clinical depression for several years.

Following two frustrating years, I quit the UK for the second time in January 2005 on being offered a job in Tokyo. Sadly, this turned out to be less than was anticipated. I have supported myself as a freelance teacher since then. We lived on the outskirts of Tokyo while my younger stepdaughter lived nearby. Our marriage lasted until 2013.

In July 2012, I moved back to the UK for the second time, although this proved only to be a brief ten-month sabbatical in my bifurcated life rather than any genuine removal from one to the other. Finally accepting that I am as much an outsider in what had been my homeland as in my adopted country, in June 2013, I once again returned to Japan to resume my ongoing meeting of the twain.

The original version of this book was the graduation thesis for my university degree in Asian Studies. It has undergone numerous incarnations, endless rewrites and updates. I can hardly claim to be the first to compare Britain with Japan; several writers have done just this, but only in passing. I set to go one stage further and write a whole book touching on the parallels, as well as the many differences between two island cultures that both developed on the edges of older civilizations separated by narrow straits of sea.

There are plenty of specialist books out there crammed with realms of facts and figures. My intention was to try and set ideas out in a clear and uncomplicated manner in order to reach as many people as possible. I am convinced that once we get past the differences of culture, it reinforces the simple fact that people really are much the same wherever we go.

It is my hope that this modest attempt will serve as a bridge of understanding between two peoples and help each to learn to respect and understand the other. Further, that the outline sketches I present will encourage interested readers to delve deeper. One of the largest sections of the book seeks to dispel stereotypes and myths that have grown up around Japan and Britain. In many cases, there are persistent mistruths that are not only wrong, but also perpetuate such foolish fable as insisting the Japanese are impossible understand, or that British men are all gentlemen.

I would like to thank Dr. Alexander Al-Jamie and David Bracey of the DLC Tokyo, who both helped and encouraged me greatly with my studies.

www.ingramcontent.com/pod-product-compliance
Lightning Source LLC
Chambersburg PA
CBHW030431290526
45786CB00001B/229